WORKBOOK

Linda Marks
Charlotte Addison

N English in Use

ESO 2

Burlington Books

New English in Use ESO 2 Workbook

by Linda Marks and Charlotte Addison

Burlington Books
P.O. Box 54411
3721 Limassol
Cyprus
Burlington Books is an imprint of the Burlington Group.

The publisher gratefully acknowledges the following for permission to reproduce copyright material:
© ASAP / Alamy: page 24 (tango dancers); © ASAP / TopFoto: page 21 (Asomov); © Celso Pupo / Shutterstock.com: page 56 (Leah and Adam); © Changing Places, MIT Media Lab / YouTube: page 51 (PEV); © Comstock.com: page 77 (easel); © Corel Corp.: page 5 (b); © dutourdumonde / Shutterstock.com: page 40 (8); © ETIENjones / Shutterstock.com: page 16 (demonstrators in Exercise 1); © Featureflash / Shutterstock.com: pages 20 (Spielberg), 21 (Mickey Mouse), 43 (Abagnale); © Ingram Publishing: page 77 (artist's body and pad); © Nando Machado / Shutterstock.com: page 51 (Thames Cable Car); © Photos.com / Jupiter Images: page 4 (picture frame in j); © Rex Features: pages 58 (Redgrave), 59 (Parry), 61 (*Pretty Little Liars*); © Shutterstock, Inc.: cover and pages 4 (all except for picture frame in j), 5 (all except b, d), 6, 7, 8, 9, 11, 12, 16 (all except for demonstrators in Exercise 1), 17 (newspaper), 18, 19, 20 (all except Spielberg), 21 (Victorian hospital), 24 (all except for tango dancers), 25, 26, 27, 28, 29, 32, 34, 35, 37, 40 (all except 8), 42 (train in Exercise 3), 43 (man with mask), 45, 48 (all except 6), 49, 50, 52 (all except grass and signs), 53, 56 (all except Leah and Adam), 57 (Norfolk Broads), 59 (compass and map), 60, 61 (channel surfing icon), 64, 65, 68, 69, 72, 73, 74, 75, 76, 77 (artist's head), 78

Material Curricular para la ESO, área de lenguas extranjeras: inglés, registrado en todas las Comunidades Autónomas que tienen competencias en materia educativa y que así lo requieren.

This series is compatible with the recommendations, guidelines and objectives of the Common European Framework of Reference for Languages.

ISBN 978-9963-51-665-0

10 09 08 07 06 05 04 03 02
25 24 23 22 21 20 19 18 17

Contents

Getting Started

Vocabulary

1 Find eight adjectives in the puzzle and write them next to their opposites.

s	w	x	y	z	l	a	z	y	f
s	t	r	o	n	g	x	v	c	t
m	f	h	u	v	h	z	l	u	w
a	d	j	n	q	p	k	i	r	r
l	f	b	g	r	p	u	g	l	y
l	k	n	i	t	l	d	h	y	f
p	m	d	s	h	o	r	t	j	g

1. old ....*young*........
2. straight ....
3. big ....
4. good-looking ....
5. tall ....
6. hard-working ....
7. weak ....
8. dark ....

2 Write the name of each room below. Then unscramble the letters of each word and write the word next to the correct picture.

kitchen • ~~bedroom~~ • living room • dining room

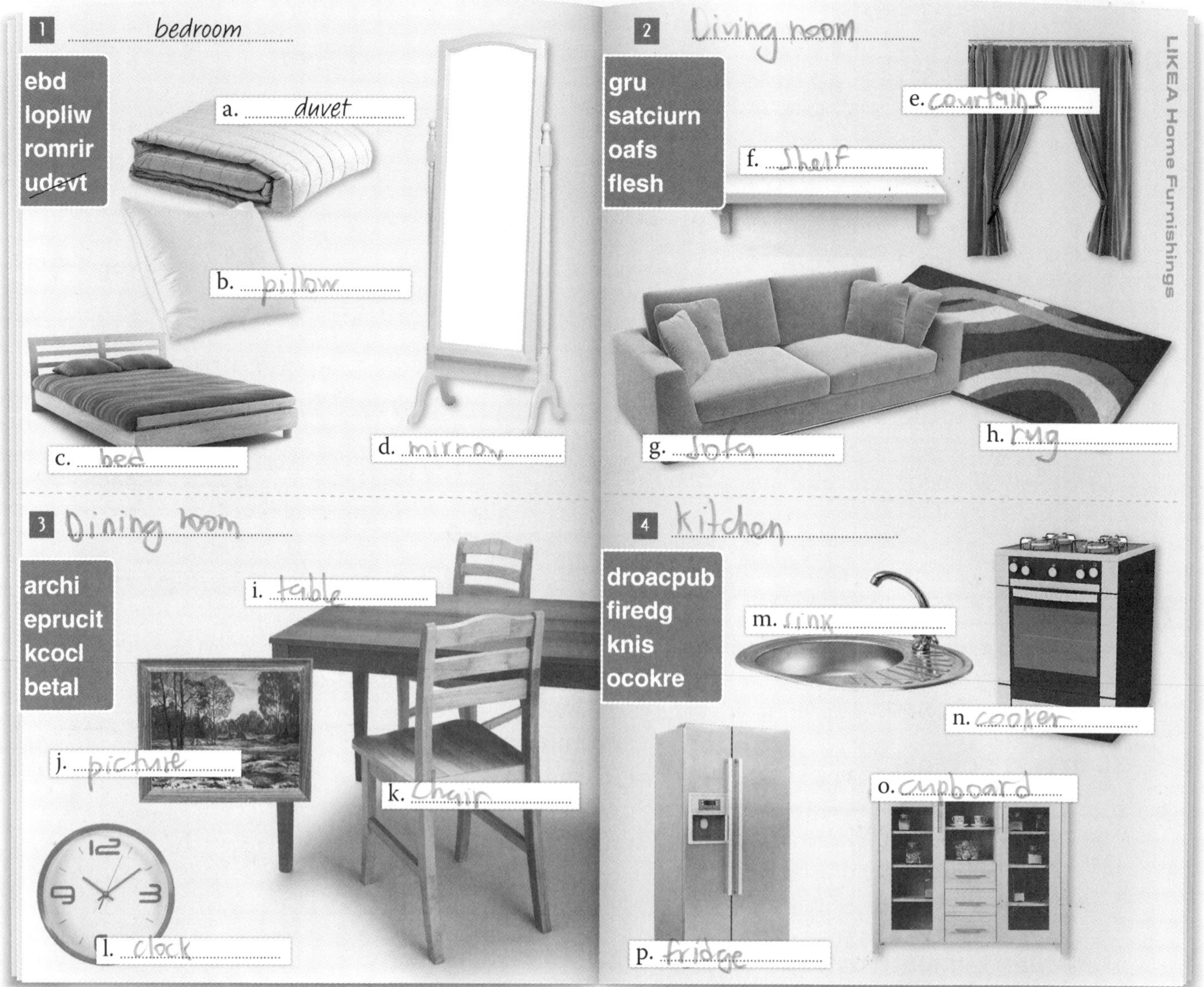

3 Write the words next to the pictures.

fly • giraffe • parrot • bat • dolphin • rabbit • tiger • iguana • turtle • wolf

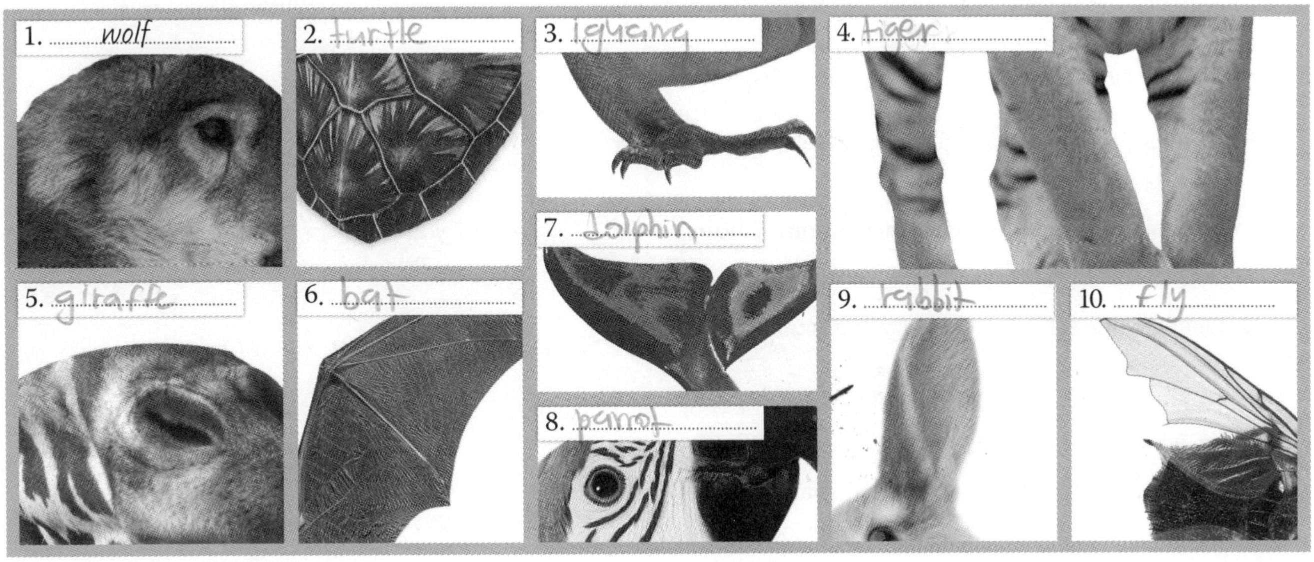

4 Circle the correct answer.

1. A **shark** / **crocodile** is a fish.
2. A **frog** / **mosquito** is an amphibian.
3. **A chicken** / **An ant** is an insect.
4. **An iguana** / **A parrot** is a reptile.
5. A **worm** / **sheep** is a mammal.
6. A **chimpanzee** / **cow** is a domesticated animal.

5 Match the places to the correct pictures.

1. amusement park
2. bank
3. chemist's
4. post office
5. police station
6. library

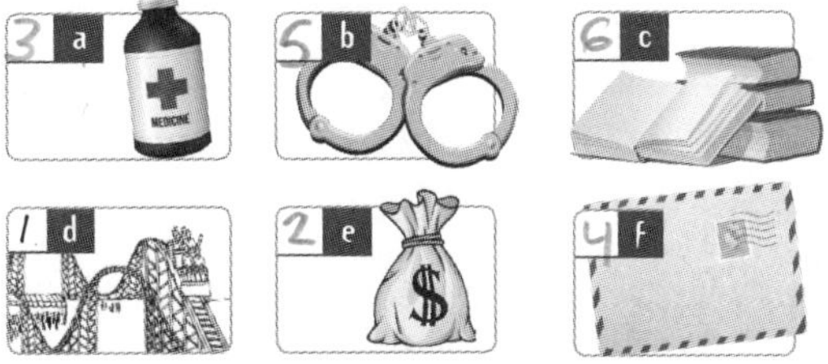

6 Where can you do the following? Circle two correct answers.

1. **buy clothes:**
   department store
   shopping centre
   church
2. **eat out:**
   hospital
   restaurant
   café
3. **play games:**
   sports centre
   arcade
   sweet shop
4. **relax:**
   cinema
   post office
   bar

7 Write the correct sport next to each description.

skiing • cycling • surfing • football • tennis swimming • dancing

1. Players kick a ball and score goals.
   football
2. Players use a racket to hit a ball over a net.
   ....
3. A winter sport. ....
4. You only do this sport in the sea. ....
5. You need a helmet to do this. ....
6. You do this sport to music. ....
7. You wear goggles when you do this.
   ....

Grammar

1 Complete the sentences with the words below.

its • yours • his • my • mine • theirs ours • her

1. I am a doctor. *My* name is Jenny.
2. Have you got a red pencil? Is this red pencil .... ?
3. Can you see those children? This ball is ....
4. My father bought a new car and gave me his old car. Now it's ....
5. Look at that girl. .... dress is beautiful.
6. Their car is new but our car isn't. .... is old.
7. Jim is in the basketball team. .... brother is, too.
8. Look at my rabbit. .... ears are long.

2 **Circle the correct answer.**

1. Owen and Alex are brothers. The **brother's** / **brothers'** / **brothers** eyes are blue.
2. **Jane's** / **Janes'** / **Janes** house is big.
3. The **student's** / **students'** / **students** bags are in the classroom, but the students aren't there.
4. There is a girl in the shop. The **girl's** / **girls'** / **girls** hair is long.
5. Look at those lions. The **lion's** / **lions'** / **lions** tails are long.

3 **Complete the e-mail with the correct form of *to be* or *have got*.**

Hi James,

We [1] .... in Edinburgh this week. It [2] .... the capital of Scotland, but it [3] .... (not) as big as Glasgow. The city [4] .... very beautiful and it [5] .... many shops, restaurants and museums. Our hotel [6] .... excellent, but it [7] .... (not) a swimming pool. The weather here [8] .... (not) great, but I [9] .... my hat and coat with me, so I [10] .... happy!

[11] .... you on holiday this week?

Liam

4 **Complete the sentences with the correct object pronouns.**

1. Look at that strange bird. Can you see .... ?
2. I can't do my homework. Please help ....
3. I have got a brother. I love ....
4. We are late. Please wait for ....
5. The students are thirsty. Have you got some water for .... ?
6. Where is Mia? I can't find ....
7. It's your birthday. I've got some flowers for ....

5 **Complete the sentences with the verbs below. Use the Present Simple.**

have • put • not live • play • look • not rain

1. We usually .... breakfast in the kitchen.
2. Whales .... on land.
3. Jill .... at her hair in the mirror many times a day.
4. I .... basketball at the sports centre twice a week.
5. Mike .... all his books on a shelf above his desk.
6. It .... here in the summer.

6 **Write questions with the words below. Use the Present Simple. Then answer the questions.**

1. cows / eat / smaller animals
....
....
2. a bar / sell / drinks
....
....
3. what / you / hit / in tennis
....
....
4. where / your best friend / live
....
....

7 **Write logical sentences with the words below. Use the Present Continuous affirmative or negative.**

1. the swimmers / wear / goggles
....
2. I / surf / on a mountain / right now
....
3. the bat / fly / near the apple tree
....
4. Tim / buy / a magazine / at the library
....
5. you / have / a shower / at the café / at the moment
....
6. Shelly / sit / on the rug / in her bedroom
....

8 **Complete the questions below. Use the Present Continuous. Then answer the questions. Make the answers true for you.**

1. .... you .... (write) in English now?
....
2. .... your best friend .... (run) right now?
....
3. What .... your father .... (do) at the moment?
....
4. .... it .... (rain)?
....
5. Where .... your classmates .... (sit) right now?
....

Getting ready for writing

1 Complete the paragraph with the sentences below.

It's an enjoyable holiday destination for all the family.
Buxton is a small town in England.
You can visit beautiful parks and gardens.

1. Buxton is a small town in England
There is something for everyone here.
2. You can visit beautiful parks and garden
There are many interesting shops and restaurants. You can swim, ride on a miniature train, watch plays and listen to music.
3. It's an enjoyable holiday destination for all the family

2 The sentences below are from different paragraphs. Decide if each sentence is an opening sentence (o), a closing sentence (c) or from the body (b) of the paragraph.

c 1. I'm really tired, but it was a lot of fun.
b 2. One of his most famous songs is *Imagine.*
o 3. Sean Penn is a great actor.
o 4. Paris is a beautiful city with many interesting places.
c 5. It was an exciting experience.
b 6. We hired bikes and rode to the beach.
o 7. Yellowstone is one of the most popular national parks in the United States.
b 8. Columbus called the island San Salvador.

3 Correct the mistakes in the sentences below. Check capital letters, punctuation and word order.

1. was liam born in february
Was Liam born in February?
2. you've got a dress pretty
You've got a pretty dress
3. have jim and bobby got green bikes
Have Jim and Bobby got green bikes?
4. our teacher has got hair long
Our teacher has got long hair
5. sammys bag is red and white
Sammy's bag is red and white
6. marie paul and denise are from france
Marie, Paul and Denis are from France
7. are you on holiday in london
Are you on holiday in London?
8. thats an amazing story
That's an amazing story

Speaking

4 Number each dialogue in the correct order.

1. 6 a. Thanks!
5 b. Welcome to our school.
1 c. Hi, James. I'm Mrs Keegan.
4 d. Yes, I'm from Glasgow.
3 e. Are you new here?
2 f. Nice to meet you, Mrs Keegan.

2. 3 a. This is Daisy's friend Lucy.
1 b. Is this 03-786293?
6 c. Sorry, she isn't here.
2 d. Yes, it is. Who's calling?
5 e. Oh, hello Lucy.
4 f. Can I please speak to Daisy?

5 Complete the questions with the words below. Then match them to the correct answers.

question • Where • spell • explain • ~~When~~ What • borrow

Questions

1. When is our school trip to the Science Museum?
2. Can I take a red pen, please?
3. What page are we on?
4. Where is your homework, Ben?
5. Can you spell this to me, please?
6. Who knows the answer to this question ?
7. Can you borrow this word?

Answers

5 a. Yes. It's m-a-m-m-a-l.
6 b. I do. It's 47.
7 c. Sure. Listen carefully.
3 d. We're on page 35.
1 e. It's on Friday morning.
4 f. Sorry, I forgot it.
2 g. Yes, you can. It's in my pencil case.

1 At School

Vocabulary School

★ 1 Match the subjects in A to the school items in B.

A		B
1. computer technology	5	a. glue
2. geography	6	b. microscope
3. French	4	c. calculator
4. maths	1	d. flash drive
5. art	3	e. dictionary
6. science	2	f. atlas

★★ 2 Unscramble the words. Then match them to the correct school items below.

1. psharubnit *paintbrush*
2. kettboxo textbook
3. corissss scissors
4. santip paints
5. repalts stapler
6. luge glue
7. actorculla calculator
8. belgo globe
9. lebtat tablet

★★ 3 Complete the sentences with the words below.

~~laptop~~ • ~~drama~~ • ~~English~~ • ~~literature~~ • ~~compass~~ • ~~music~~ • ~~history~~ • ~~sport~~

1. I want to be an actor. My favourite subject is drama .
2. Our music teacher has got a clarinet on his desk.
3. We learn about the past in history .
4. We learn the Present Simple in English .
5. I usually play football in Sport lessons.
6. We sometimes draw circles in our maths lessons with a compass .
7. We read poems by famous poets in Literature .
8. I don't need my laptop in sport, but I use it for many subjects.

★★★ 4 Which teacher asks the following questions? What school item does the student use to answer? There may be more than one correct answer.

	teacher	school item
1. Draw a circle. What is its radius?	*the maths teacher*	*compass*
2. Who was the King of England in 1066?	the history teacher	textbook
3. Has this mosquito got eyes?	the Scien teacher	microscope
4. How do you spell *children*?	the English teacher	dictionary
5. Can you show your partner how to copy homework onto a flash drive?	the technology teacher	computer

Grammar Present Simple / Present Continuous

*** 1 Complete the sentences with the verbs in brackets. Use the Present Simple or Present Continuous.**

1. They usually ~~talk~~ (talk) on the phone, but right now, they are chating (chat) online.
2. Colin usually cooks (cook) dinner, but today he is eating (eat) in a café.
3. We go (go) camping every summer. My mum love (love) camping!
4. I am studying (study) drama this year but I don't like (not like) it.
5. We aren't walking (not walk) to school this morning because we are riding (ride) our bikes.
6. Linda tries (try) to do the maths homework every day, but she doesn't always understand (not understand) it.

**** 2 Write questions with the words below. Use the Present Simple or Present Continuous. Then answer the questions. Use the words in brackets.**

1. where / Steve / work / every summer (at the swimming pool)
   Where does Steave work every summer?
   He works at the swimming pool
2. Susie / use / the new microscope / now (yes)
   Is Susie using the new microscope now?
   Yes, she is
3. you / hear / that noise (no)
   Are you hearing that noise?
   No, I'm not
4. what / they speak / at the moment (French)
   What are they speaking at the moment?
   They are speaking French
5. when / you / usually / bring / your atlas to school (on Mondays)
   When do you usually bring your atlas to school?
   I usually bring it on Monday.

***** 3 Complete the sentences so they are true for you. Use the Present Simple or Present Continuous.**

1. I sometimes draw .
2. Right now, I am checking my homework
3. My mum and dad usually talk so much .
4. My friend is in class at the moment.
5. I never travel to Asia .

***** 4 Complete the text with the verbs in brackets. Use the Present Simple or Present Continuous.**

SKI SCHOOL

The Vail Ski and Snowboard Academy is a special school in the USA. Students 1. come (come) from all over the USA to study at the Academy. What 2. do they study (study) there? In the autumn and spring, they 3. learn (learn) all the usual subjects, but in the winter, the timetable 4. changes (change). Students 5. take (take) skiing or snowboarding lessons all morning and they 6. don't go (not go) to classes until the afternoon. Right now, two students 7. are training (train) on the mountain. Zack 8. is skiining (ski). What 9. is Jill doing (do)? She 10. is practising (practise) on her snowboard. Every winter, some of the students 11. enter (enter) competitions all over the world. At the moment, some students 12. are flying (fly) to Europe. They 13. hope (hope) to come home with medals.

English in Use

Write at least three questions to ask a student at the Vail Ski and Snowboard Academy. Use the Present Simple and Present Continuous.

1. How much are the lessons this year?
2. How much time they usually do in Autumn
3. and in Spring lessons?
4. Do the students come to have fun every
5. lesson?

Grammar *There is / There are*; Articles and quantifiers; *How many / How much*

★ 1 Choose the correct answer.

1. We're learning about **a** / **an** / **the** sun.
2. I haven't got **any** / **a** / **many** glue.
3. We haven't got **a** / **a lot of** / **some** time.
4. I want to buy **much** / **some** / **an** umbrellas.
5. I'm phoning from the shop. Do you need **the** / **lots of** / **a** new calculator?
6. I haven't got **many** / **some** / **much** money.
7. There are **many** / **any** / **much** red notebooks.
8. I need **many** / **lots of** / **much** paper for my art project.

★★ 2 Use the chart to write sentences about the picture below.

		glue
	a	paper
There is	some	books
There are	any	paintbrushes
There isn't	many	stapler
There aren't	much	pens
	a lot of	water

1. There are a lot of paintbrushes
2. There isn't any paper
3. There aren't any book
4. There is a glue
5. There are many pens
6. There isn't a stapler

★★ 3 Circle the correct words to make questions. Which school lesson do you think each question is from?

1. **How many** / **How much** blue paint is there? art
2. **How many** / **How much** countries are there in Africa? geography
3. **How many** / **How much** does a blue whale weigh? science
4. **How many** / **How much** plays did Shakespeare write? literature
5. **How many** / **How much** is 20 times 3,000? maths
6. **How many** / **How much** hours does this type of battery work? technology

★★★ 4 Complete the paragraph with *a, an, the, some, any, much, many, a lot of, lots of, how many, how much* or the correct form of *There is / There are.* There may be more than one correct answer.

ROOKIEMAG

Tavi Gevinson is 1. an American teenager and she's the editor of 2. a teen website. 3. the website is called Rookiemag and it's very popular.

4. There are many articles about teen life on Tavi's website. 5. There is a page about films and TV, and articles like *How to plan a film marathon* or *How to make your room look like a film.*

So, 6. how many teenagers log on to Rookiemag every day? What do they say about it?

"I don't spend 7. much time reading but I really enjoy Rookiemag." (Lyn, age 15)

"I love magazines, but they cost 8. lots of money. You don't need 9. any money to log onto this website (it's free!) and there are 10. a lot of interesting stories on it!" (Jess, age 14)

11. How much time do you spend reading? 12. There are any interesting magazines or websites you can recommend? We're waiting to hear 13. some recommendations from you!

English in Use

Complete the questions with *How many* or *How much*. Then answer the questions. Make the answers true for you.

1. How many blue pens have you got ?
   I have got two blue pens
2. How much maths homework have you got?
   I haven't got maths homework
3. How much water do you usually drink?
   I don't know exactly
4. How much French do you know?
   I have no idea about French!

Reading

1 Read about a special school. Then tick (✓) the correct answers.

A Visit to Summerhill School

Do the students at your school receive a timetable with the subjects every year? Who chooses the subjects? At my school, the teachers don't choose the subjects on our timetables. The students do! I'm Hugh and I go to Summerhill School in England. Summerhill is a different type of school. Nobody tells the students what to study. They also don't tell them to go to lessons. Go to class or don't go to class – it's our choice. Why? Summerhill is a "free" school. It's democratic. Do you know what a democratic school is? Come and see.

So what's happening right now? At the moment, my favourite teacher is teaching maths to a group of students. They're drawing with compasses. Some other students are doing an art project with paints, scissors and glue. Do you see those students in the garden? They're reading textbooks. Two students don't want to study right now so they're playing a game. There are places in every classroom and all around the school for playing games because play is very important at Summerhill.

How many students are there at Summerhill? There are about 100 students here. We're all between the ages of five and 17. Students of different ages sometimes study together. We can study English, maths, history, geography and science. Some students study languages like German or Chinese. And everyone learns two important lessons here – responsibility and creativity. Teachers and students have special meetings and make decisions together about the school. There aren't any tests or marks at Summerhill School. We learn because we want to. We think it's a great school!

There are ... at Summerhill.

1. timetables ☑	3. textbooks ☑	5. tests ☐
2. teachers ☑	4. games ☐	6. marks ☑

2 Answer the questions.

1. Who chooses the students' subjects?
   The students too
2. What is Hugh's favourite teacher doing?
   She is teaching maths to a group of students
3. Where are there places to play?
   They are places in every classroom and all around the school
4. How old are the students?
   Between five and 17 year old
5. Why does the text mention responsibility and creativity?
   Because everyone learns this two importants lessons
6. Who makes decisions about the school?
   Theachers and students

Listening

5/01 3 Listen to Jasmine and Mike talking on Skype. Complete the sentences.

1. Jasmine isn't staying at a hotel .
2. Southbank Centre is near the River Thames
3. Jasmine's mum is wearing a red dress, green hat and gloves
4. Jasmine's dad has got an umbrella! .
5. Jasmine is excited about seeing Slava's Snow Show.

5/01 4 Listen again and answer the questions.

1. Where do Jasmine's grandparents live? in London
2. What is the Southbank Centre? An cultural centre
3. Who is sitting with Jasmine's mum?
   Her sister
4. What season is it? winter
5. What is Jasmine's dad doing?
   He is buying tickets

Vocabulary Activities

★ **1 Write the activities under the correct pictures.**

paint pictures • take a nap • play the piano • do judo • build models
go horse-riding • send text messages • learn competitive diving

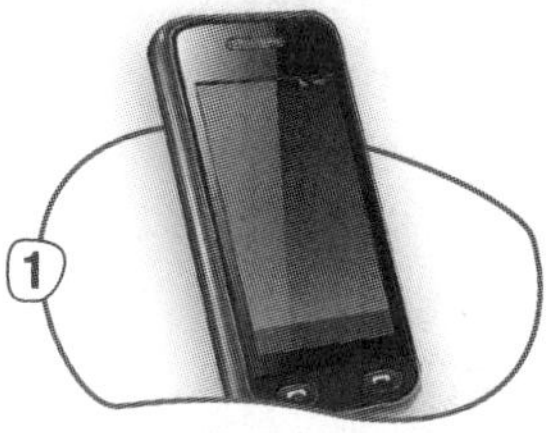

1 send text messages

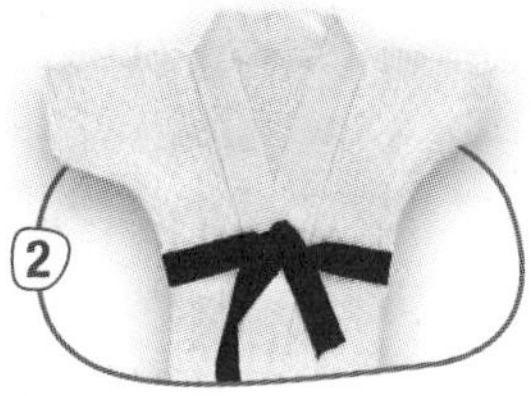

2 do judo

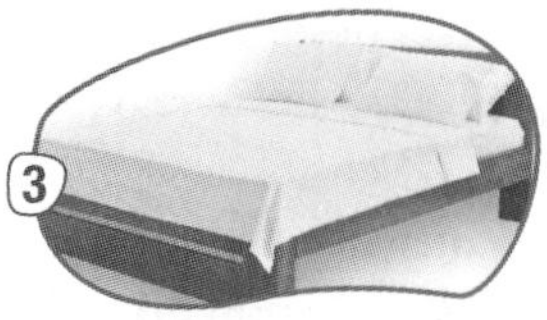

3 take a nap

4 do competitive diving

5 go horse riding

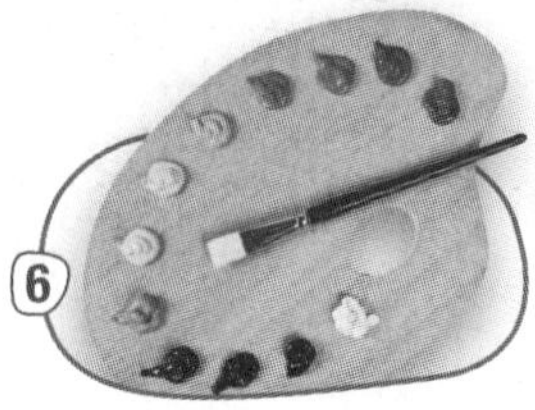

6 paint pictures

7 play the piano

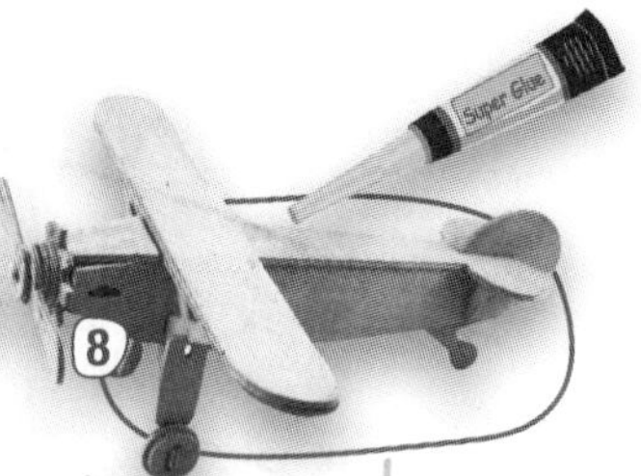

8 build models

★★ **2 Match A to B to make activities. Then complete the sentences below with the activities.**

A		B
1. do	4	a. a new language
2. perform	6	b. e-mails
3. repair	2	c. in a band
4. learn	5	d. photos
5. take	1	e. experiments
6. check	3	f. computers

1. Pam speaks French and Russian, and now she wants to learn a new language
2. We sometimes do experiments in our science lessons.
3. Jenna plays the guitar and she hopes to perform in a band one day.
4. Jim and Emma work at Technology 4 Today. They repair computers .
5. I listen to music, take photos , check e-mails and play games on my mobile phone.

★★★ **3 Which activities in Exercises 1 and 2 do you or a friend do? When / Where do you do them? Write five sentences.**

1. I send text messages every day at home
2. My friend do judo in Mosquitos twice a week
3. I sometimes do experiments
4. My mom rarely check e-mail
5. My best friend usually take photos from the streets

English in Use

Complete the dialogue according to the picture.

A: In the picture, the boy [1] 's doing experiments .
B: No way! He's [2] using a microscope .
A: There's a [3] textbook .
B: That's false.
A: I can see [4] a calculator .
B: That's true.
A: The girl looks [5] the calculator .
B: That's wrong! She's [6] writing in the notebook .

Writing A photo description

1 Complete the sentences with linking words.

1. Jason is wearing a scarf, ...but...... he isn't wearing a jacket.
2. It's raining today, ...and...... Helen isn't taking photographs outside.
3. My brother isn't swimming today ......because...... he doesn't feel well.
4. Barry is practising the piano ......and...... his mum is listening to him.
5. On Sundays, Dad cooks dinner ......or...... he orders pizza.

2 Read the description of the picture below and choose the correct linking words. Then tick (✓) the picture it describes.

Sunday at My House

Look at this picture of my family. We're at home. We always spend time together on Sunday afternoons. Dad is making tea 1. **and** / **or** / **because** maybe he's cleaning the kitchen. I can't remember. The good-looking boy sitting with my mum is my brother Adam. He's doing his maths homework 2. **and** / **but** / **or** my mum is helping him. The tall man near the cupboard is my dad's brother, Max. He often visits us on Sunday afternoons. He usually wears a baseball cap, 3. **so** / **and** / **but** he isn't wearing one in this picture. The young girl with curly hair is my sister Clara. She's only two years old, 4. **so** / **because** / **but** she usually takes a nap after lunch. I'm not in the picture 5. **so** / **and** / **because** I'm studying in my bedroom.

A ✓

B

3 Look at the picture you didn't tick in Exercise 2 and find information in the text to complete the chart below.

PERSON	DESCRIPTION	WHERE IN PICTURE	ACTIVITY
Mum	She has got blonde hair and wide lips	With Adam	Using the computer
Dad	He has got dark hair and a dark T-shirt	In the kitchen	Cooking
Adam	He is good-looking	In the desk	Using the computer
Clara	She's only 2 years old and she have got curly hair	Between the dog and the sofa	Playing with the dog
Max	He is tall and he has got a baseball cap	Near the kitchen	Eating a sandwich

4 Write a description of the picture you didn't tick. Use the information in the chart in Exercise 3 and the model in Exercise 2 to help you.

Check Your Progress

Vocabulary 20 points

1 What items do you need to do the activities? Match the activities in A to the items in B. (5 points)

A		B
1. paint a picture	......	a. laptop
2. build models	......	b. paintbrushes
3. check e-mails	......	c. microscope
4. learn a new language	......	d. dictionary
5. do experiments	......	e. glue

2 Complete the sentences with the words below. (5 points)

stapler • geography • scissors • calculator computer technology

1. You can use a .... to check your answers in maths.
2. The .... teacher has got a globe.
3. You need .... to cut paper.
4. We're learning about tablets in our .... classroom.
5. I use a .... to put pieces of paper together.

3 Intro 1 2 3 4 5 6 7 8 9 Circle the word that doesn't belong. (10 points)

1. bed • sofa • poster • chair
2. lamp • bat • lizard • pig
3. drama • art • music • science
4. arcade • toilet • café • bar
5. cycling • volleyball • goggles • bowling
6. scuba diving • surfing • swimming • golf
7. dark • shy • fat • small
8. atlas • flash drive • textbook • dictionary
9. lazy • funny • friendly • curly
10. snake • cow • horse • lion

Grammar 30 points

4 Write the words in the correct order to make sentences. Use the Present Simple or Present Continuous. (10 points)

1. sit / in the classroom / they / right now / .
....
2. your school / give / you / lunch / every day / ?
....
3. a photo / you / take / of me / ?
....
4. usually / you / walk / to school / ?
....
5. not build / Vicky / of a house / a model / .
....

5 Complete each sentence with one or two words. Use articles, quantifiers, the correct form of *There is / There are* or *How much / How many*. There may be more than one correct answer. (10 points)

1. There is .... orange stapler on the desk.
2. Are there .... paintbrushes in this classroom?
3. .... subjects are you studying this year?
4. We have .... maths homework, but not a lot.
5. .... a computer shop on Oak Lane. It's not far.
6. .... paint do you want?
7. I've got .... notebooks at home.
8. Where is .... art classroom?
9. Have you got .... new dictionary?
10. .... a globe in your classroom?

6 Intro 1 2 3 4 5 6 7 8 9 Choose the correct answer. (10 points)

1. **You are** / **Are you** / **Have you got** at school now?
2. **Sally's** / **Sally** / **Sallys'** sister is in my class.
3. **How many** / **How much** / **Is there** pens do you want?
4. There isn't **many** / **some** / **a lot of** time.
5. I **haven't got** / **has got** / **am** a dictionary.
6. Mandy **is buying** / **aren't buying** / **buys** meat for dinner tonight.
7. **Does Ann** / **Is Ann** / **Ann is** practise the piano every day?
8. What **do you do** / **are you doing** / **you are doing** right now?
9. The children need **they** / **their** / **theirs** shoes.
10. Does Tim **plays** / **play** / **playing** in a band?

Dictation 10 points

5 02

7 Listen and write the sentences.

1. ....
2. ....
3. ....
4. ....
5. ....

Speaking 10 points

8 Complete the dialogue with the words and phrases below.

~~There's a~~ • ~~looks like~~ • ~~I can see~~
~~In this picture~~ • That's wrong

A: Are those photographs from your holiday in Rome?

B: Yes, they are. 1. In this picture, we're getting off a bus near the Vatican.

A: 2. I can see a man with a camera. Who is he?

B: That's my dad. He's taking photographs. Mum's taking photographs, too, but you can't see her.

A: 3. There's a teenager in a black jacket near the bus. He 4. looks like Justin Bieber!

B: Oh, that's my brother. He isn't Justin Bieber.

A: Look! There's Mrs Shore, our maths teacher!

B: 5. That's wrong! It's not Mrs Shore. It's my mum's best friend.

Writing 10 points

9 Complete the sentences with a linking word.

1. Dad is tired, so he's taking a nap.
2. We aren't painting pictures today because we haven't got any paints.
3. You can bake a cake for the party but you can buy one.
4. Jim builds model trains and he gives them to his brother.
5. I sometimes send text messages, but I prefer talking to people.

Translation 20 points

10 Translate the sentences into English.

1. ¿Cuántos alumnos están haciendo judo en este momento?
How many students are doing judo at this moment?
2. Él está mirando el correo electrónico en su tableta.
He is checking e-mails in his tablet
3. ¿Usas un microscopio en tus clases de ciencias?
Do you use a microscope in science lessons?
4. Hay algunos pinceles, un atlas y un compás encima del escritorio.
There are some paintbrushes, an atlas and a compass on the desk
5. Ella aprende a hacer salto de natación en la piscina.
She is learning to make a swimming jump in the swimming pool

My Scores

Vocabulary __ / 20
Grammar __ / 30
Dictation __ / 10
Speaking __ / 10
Writing __ / 10
Translation __ / 20
My total score: __ / 100

Self-Evaluation

Do the following. Tick (✔) the box if you succeed.

1 Say ...

1. two school subjects and two school items. ☐
Literature, stapler
French, globe
2. four activities. ☐
play the piano, go horse-riding
do judo, do competitive diving
3. two sentences about things you usually do and two about things you are doing now. ☐
I usually play with the tablet
I usually watch movies in TV
I am checking homework at the moment
I am writing right now
4. one sentence with *There is* and one sentence with *How much*. ☐
There is a cake in the window
How much is it?

2 Answer the questions. ☐

1. Where are you?
I'm in English class
2. Who are you with?
I'm with my partners
3. What are you doing?
I'm checking homework
4. What are you wearing?
I'm wearing a T-shirt and leggings

3 Write sentences with the linking words *because*, *but* and *so*. ☐

1. She is hungry because she didn't eat last hour
2. I don't like cats, but I like dogs
3. I was boring, so I played cards with my sister

2 In the News

Vocabulary Verbs

* **1 Look at the pictures and complete the sentences with the verbs below.**

survive • light • demonstrate • fight • develop • bite • attach • freeze

Don't fight !

Let's light the candles now.

Let's go and demontrate , too.

Can he survives ?

These lakes sometimes freeze in winter.

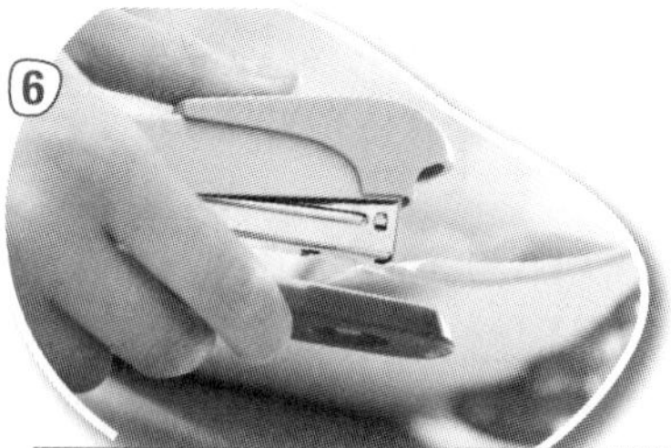

Use a stapler to attach the papers.

Don't worry. He doesn't bite .

They develops new medicines here.

** **2 The verbs in bold are in the wrong sentences. Write the verbs next to the correct sentences.**

1. Always look left and right before you **save** the street. cross
2. Do a lot of puzzles to **volunteer** your memory. improve
3. We **reach** at the animal clinic once a week. volunteer
4. The man took my money, but he didn't **improve** my phone. steal
5. Can I please **pull** a pen? I haven't got one. borrow
6. I don't think we will **cross** the top of the mountain today. reach
7. Did the bad weather **borrow** them from leaving? prevent
8. The doctors are trying to **prevent** his life. save
9. Babies sometimes **steal** their mothers' hair. pull

*** **3 Write a headline for each of the photos below. Use verbs from Exercises 1 and 2.**

A man stole an expensive necklace last week!

A group of persons tell people must save and improve the forest

A young climber reached the top of a high cold mountain

Grammar Past Simple

★ 1 Complete the sentences with the pairs of verbs below. Use the Past Simple affirmative.

volunteer / teach • fight / save • invent / send
sail / reach • survive / eat

1. Vasco da Gama, a Portuguese explorer, ... from Portugal in 1497. He .... India in 1498.
2. Ray Tomlinson .... e-mail in 1971. He .... an e-mail to his friends to tell them.
3. Peter Skyllberg .... for two months in his car after a snowstorm. He .... snow to stay alive!
4. In Australia, a family dog called River .... a snake and .... two young girls.
5. In 2000, Prince William .... in Chile. He .... English in schools.

★★ 2 Look at the pictures and guess what happened. Then complete the sentences with the verbs in brackets to see if you were right. Use the Past Simple.

1. On 26th April 2003, Aron Ralston .... (go) hiking in Bluejohn Canyon in the USA.
2. A 360-kilogram rock .... (fall) on his arm.
3. Ralston .... (wait) for many hours, but there .... (not be) any people around to help him.
4. He .... (be) hungry and thirsty because he .... (not have) much food or water.
5. His condition .... (not improve) and he .... (not know) how to escape.
6. After five days, he .... (use) his knife to cut off his own arm!
7. With only one arm, Ralston .... (climb) out of the canyon and .... (survive) his terrible accident!

★★ 3 Write questions with the words below. Use the Past Simple. Then guess the answers.

1. where / people / hear / the news / thousands of years ago
   .... ?
2. people / read / newspapers / before 59 BC
   .... ?
3. where / people / create / the first newspaper
   .... ?
4. people / buy / newspapers / in Rome / 2,000 years ago
   .... ?

★★★ 4 Complete the text with the verbs in brackets. Use the correct form of the Past Simple. Then check your answers to Exercise 3.

The First Newspaper

How [1] .... people .... (get) news before the invention of the newspaper? [2] .... they .... (hear) the news in other ways? Thousands of years ago, many people never [3] .... (go) to school, so they [4] .... (know) how to read or write. They [5] .... (meet) on the streets or in the centre of town and they [6] .... (tell) each other about the news. Then, in 59 BC, the Romans [7] .... (create) the first newspaper, but they [8] .... (sell) it to people. They [9] .... (put) it in different places around town. People [10] .... (read) the newspaper at those places and [11] .... (learn) about battles and other important news of the day.

English in Use

Write questions about Aron Ralston's accident in Exercise 2 according to the answers below.

1. ....
   No, Ralston didn't tell his family about his hiking plans.
2. ....
   No, he didn't have a mobile phone.
3. ....
   The Meijer family helped him by giving him food and water.
4. ....
   It took rescuers six hours to find Ralston after he cut off his arm.

Grammar *used to*

★ **1 Write sentences with the words below. Use the correct form of *used to*.**

1. my mum / volunteer / at a hospital
....
2. I / not cross / the street / alone
....
3. all my friends / live / close to me
....
4. our town / not have / a big shopping centre
....
5. my sister / borrow / clothes from me
....

★★ **2 Complete the sentences with the verbs in brackets. Use *used to*, affirmative or negative.**

1. I .... (watch) the news when I was younger, but now I watch the news every day.
2. My dad .... (read) the newspaper, but these days, he prefers reading everything on the Internet.
3. People .... (demonstrate) to prevent the building of new roads in town, but it didn't help much.
4. My school marks .... (be) good in primary school, but they improved a lot last year.
5. I .... (eat) a lot of hamburgers and steak, but now I don't eat much meat.

★★ **3 Ted is asking his grandmother about how things used to be when she was a child. Complete the questions with the correct form of *used to* and the verbs in brackets. Then match Ted's questions to his grandmother's answers.**

Ted's questions:

1. .... you and your friends .... (listen) to pop music?
2. .... your school .... (have) computers?
3. .... your mum .... (use) a cooker?
4. .... you .... (do) your homework at a desk?
5. .... you .... (see) cars on the streets?

Grandmother's answers:

..... a. No, it didn't. We found information in an encyclopedia, not on the Internet.
..... b. Yes, she did, and she made us hot meals every day.
..... c. Yes, we did, but they were expensive, so many people travelled by bus.
..... d. No, I didn't. I did my homework on the kitchen table.
..... e. Yes, we did. I loved Elvis Presley!

★★★ **4 Complete the dialogue. Add one or two words in each space.**

Seth: In the past, I didn't 1. .... to do anything special when I visited London, but last weekend, I 2. .... something amazing! 3. .... was a music festival in Hyde Park – the Wireless Festival. I enjoyed three days of great music! The weather 4. .... perfect, too – warm and sunny. There 5. .... a cloud in the sky.

Ali: 6. .... many people come to the festival?

Seth: Yes! On the third day, there 7. .... about 65,000 people in the park because Rihanna 8. .... a special concert. It 9. .... so crowded! People sang and 10. .... together.

Ali: When we lived in London, I 11. .... going to lots of concerts. It's great fun! So, 12. .... you see any other good bands?

Seth: Yes! I 13. .... to performances by my favourite singers – Drake and Jessie J. They 14. .... excellent!

English in Use

Complete the sentences with the phrases below and *used to* or *didn't use to*. Then tick the sentences that are true for you.

play football • eat salads • study much for tests wake up early

..... 1. I .... at all, but now I eat lots of vegetables every day.
..... 2. I .... at the weekend, but now I get up late every weekend.
..... 3. I .... with my friends, but now we usually play more basketball.
..... 4. I ...., but now I work hard before every test.

Reading

1 Read the news story. Then explain why the items below appear in the article.

THE NEWSIES

From the 1850s to the 1900s, before the Internet, TV or radio, people used to get all the news from newspapers. In the USA, they bought their newspapers from newsboys, or "newsies". These newsboys were usually young and very poor. They got up early every morning and bought newspapers from the newspaper companies. Then they spent the day selling their papers and they often worked until late at night. Newsies didn't make much money and their work conditions were terrible. Many of the boys came from poor families and some of them didn't have any families at all. For these boys, the streets were their homes and their lives were very difficult – especially in the winter, when it was very cold. It wasn't easy to survive on the streets!

By the end of the 1800s, there were many newspapers in New York City, but two of them were very popular and their owners, William Hearst and Joseph Pulitzer, were rich businessmen. They didn't care about the poor newsboys. They just wanted to sell a lot of newspapers. Finally, in 1899, more than 5,000 newsies decided to fight for better conditions.

The newsies stopped selling newspapers. They demonstrated on Brooklyn Bridge – a famous bridge in New York. They prevented cars from crossing the bridge and they talked to the drivers. Small newspaper companies wrote about the newsies' fight. The story reached the public and people stopped buying Hearst's and Pulitzer's newspapers. Newspaper sales went from 360,000 to 125,000!

In order to save their newspapers, Hearst and Pulitzer agreed to make changes. Finally, the newsboys' lives started to improve.

1. Internet, TV and radio ....
2. Poor families ....
3. William Hearst and Joseph Pulitzer ....
4. 5,000 ....
5. Brooklyn Bridge ....

2 Answer the questions.

1. When did the newsies start and finish work? ....
2. Where did newsies without families live? ....
3. How did the newsies fight for better conditions? ....
4. How did people find out about the newsies' fight? ....
5. What did the people do? ....

Listening

5 03 **3 Listen to two friends talking about a book. Match A to B.**

A		B
1. John Boot	.....	a. wanted to help a friend.
2. Mrs Stitch	.....	b. was the owner of a newspaper.
3. Lord Copper	.....	c. wrote about flowers and birds for a newspaper.
4. William Boot	.....	d. was a writer from London.

5 03 **4 Listen again and number the sentences in the correct order.**

..... a. Lord Copper sent William Boot to Africa.
..... b. John Boot wanted to find a new place to live.
..... c. Lord Copper gave John Boot a prize.
..... d. Mrs Stitch tried to help John Boot.
..... e. William Boot discovered a scoop.

Vocabulary Life events

★ **1 Match the sentences to the pictures below. Pay attention to the words in bold.**

1. He **graduated from** university last summer.
2. They met and **fell in love** in 1996.
3. We **moved to** Australia in 2012.
4. They **got divorced** last year.
5. They **belonged to** a sports club for many years.
6. My brother **had a child** last year.
7. I **received an award** for horse-riding.
8. She **joined** the army after school.

★★ **2 Number the sentences in the correct order. Pay attention to the words in bold.**

..... a. He wrote *The Adventures of Tom Sawyer* in 1876 but he didn't **receive an award** for it.
..... b. He **grew up** in Missouri in the USA with four brothers and two sisters.
..... c. He **died** in 1910.
..... d. Mark Twain left school at 15 to start work and didn't **go to university**.
..1.. e. Mark Twain **was born** in 1835.
..... f. He **got a job** at a local newspaper. It was his first job.
..... g. He **got married** to Olivia Langdon when he was 34 years old.

★★★ **3 Complete the biography of Steven Spielberg with words and phrases from Exercises 1 and 2. Make any necessary changes.**

Steven Spielberg

Steven Spielberg 1. .... in Ohio, USA on 18th December, 1946, but he 2. .... in New Jersey and then in Arizona. After his parents got divorced, Spielberg 3. .... California with his father. After high school, he 4. .... in Long Beach, California, but he didn't 5. .... university because he wanted to 6. .... and make some money. In 1985, he 7. .... to Amy Irving, but they 8. .... in 1989. Spielberg met actress Kate Capshaw when they made a film together and he 9. .... with her. They got married in 1991. In 2000, Spielberg went back to university and graduated in May, 2002. Spielberg won Oscars for his films *Schindler's List* and *Saving Private Ryan*. He also 10. .... from the Queen of England in 2000!

English in Use

Write questions about Whitney Houston according to the answers in bold.

Q: 1. ....

A: She was born **on 9th August, 1963**.

Q: 2. ....

A: She was **a singer and an actress.**

Q: 3. ....

A: She got married to Bobby Brown **in 1992**.

Q: 4. ....

A: **Yes**, they had a daughter – Bobbi Kristina.

Q: 5. ....

A: Whitney died **on 11th February, 2012**. She was 48 years old.

Writing A biography

1 Choose the correct connectors of sequence in the biographical paragraph about Isaac Asimov.

Isaac Asimov

1. **First / Then**, Isaac Asimov graduated from high school at the age of 15. 2. **First / Next**, he entered Columbia University. In 1938, he sold his first short story, *Marooned Off Vesta*. 3. **Then / Finally**, he received his Bachelor of Science degree in 1939. 4. **After that / First**, he went on studying at the same university. 5. **First / Finally**, he became a professor of biochemistry and continued writing stories, books and articles about science, science fiction and other topics.

2 Complete the biography of Walt Disney with connectors of sequence from Exercise 1. There may be more than one correct answer.

Walt Disney

Walt Disney was born in Chicago in 1901. He loved drawing pictures as a boy, but his career as a cartoonist really started in 1919. 1. ……………………, he moved to Kansas City and became a newspaper artist. 2. ……………………, he started working at the Kansas City Film Ad Company. 3. ……………………, he moved to Hollywood with his brother, Roy, in 1923 and they started their own animation company, the Disney Brothers' Studio. In 1928, Walt Disney became famous when he created Mickey Mouse. 4. ……………………, Disney created *Snow White and the Seven Dwarfs*, the first full-length animated musical feature film. That was in 1937. During the next five years, Walt Disney Studios completed other full-length animated classics such as *Pinocchio*, *Fantasia*, *Dumbo* and *Bambi*. 5. ……………………, in 1955, Disney made another one of his dreams come true – he opened a fantastic amusement park. Walt Disney died in 1966, but his wonderful creations live on.

3 Choose information from the timeline below to write a biography about Florence Nightingale. Use the model in Exercise 2 to help you.

- 1820 – born in Florence, Italy
- 1844 – decided to become a nurse
- 1851 – trained to be a nurse in Germany
- 1853 – worked in a hospital in London
- 1854 – worked in an army hospital in Turkey, helped soldiers in Crimean War
- 1856 – returned to England
- 1860 – opened school for nurses in London
- 1883 – received an award from Queen Victoria of England
- 1910 – died

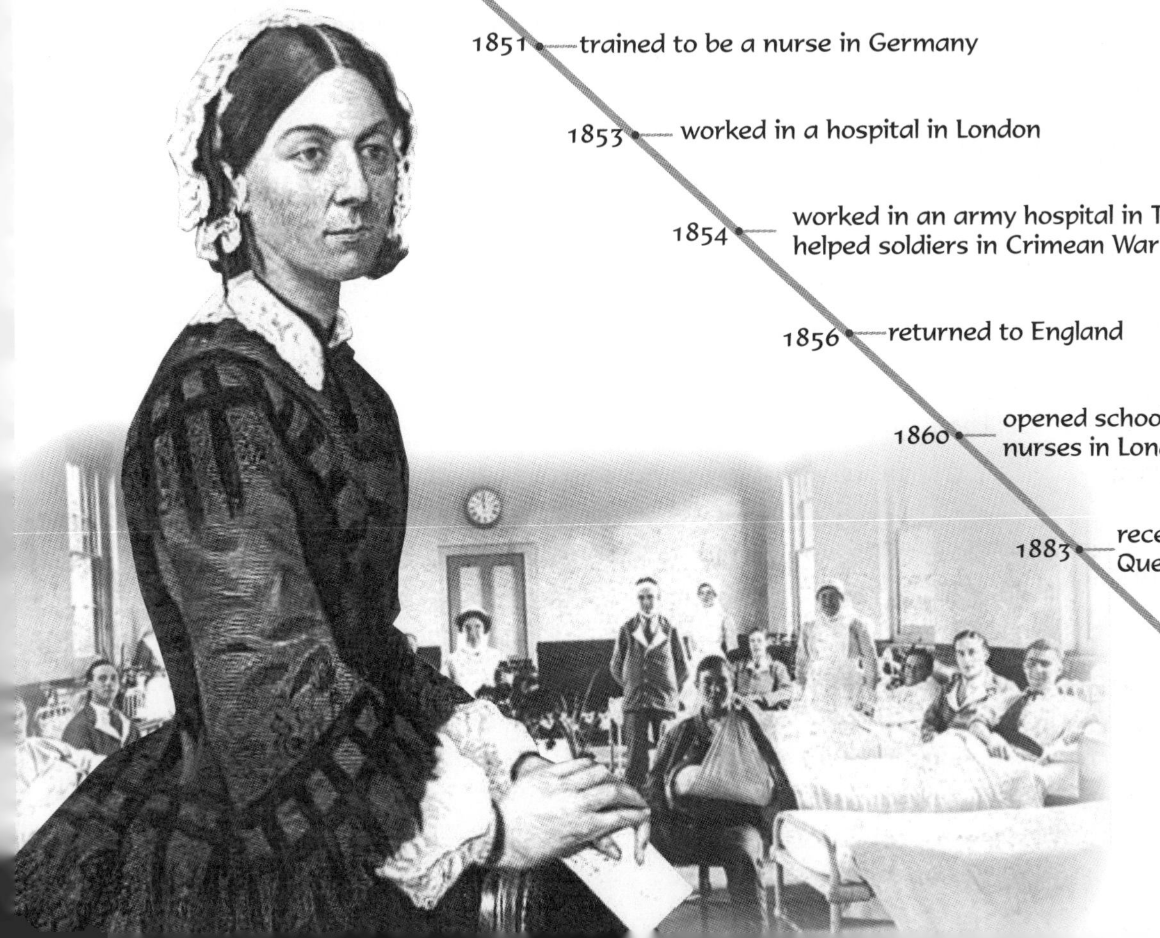

Check Your Progress

Vocabulary 20 points

1 Complete the sentences with the verbs below. (10 points)

belong to • reach • got divorced • volunteers moved to • died • is developing • light graduated from • survive

1. Camping is fun! We always .... a fire and cook hot dogs.
2. Jenna .... at the animal hospital.
3. Pablo Picasso .... at age 91.
4. Technology .... very fast.
5. Camels can .... without water for about two weeks.
6. I hope we .... the hotel soon.
7. Mr and Mrs Allen weren't happy together, so they ....
8. I lived in York. Then I .... Rome.
9. Do you .... any clubs at school?
10. After I .... university, I got a job.

2 Intro 1 2 3 4 5 6 7 8 9 Choose the correct answer. (10 points)

1. I live in Rome now, but I **joined** / **grew up** in London.
2. Angry dogs sometimes **cross** / **bite**.
3. It's very cold at the top of the mountain and people can **freeze** / **steal**.
4. Take your **compass** / **paintbrush** to the maths class.
5. We **do judo** / **take photos** in art class.
6. A **laptop** / **globe** is a mobile computer.
7. Many people fall in love and **take a nap** / **get married**.
8. Attach your **scissors** / **flash drive** to the computer.
9. Let's get chocolate at the **sweet shop** / **bar**.
10. A **bat** / **mosquito** is an insect.

Grammar 30 points

3 Complete the sentences with the correct form of the verbs in brackets. Use the Past Simple. (10 points)

1. Mark Zuckerberg .... (create) Facebook.
2. The Beatles .... (not record) any albums after 1970.
3. .... William Shakespeare .... (write) *Romeo and Juliet*?
4. John Lennon .... (invite) Paul McCartney to join his band.
5. When .... the Egyptians .... (build) the pyramids?

4 Complete the sentences with the verbs in brackets. Use the correct form of *used to*. (10 points)

1. Kate .... (volunteer) at a school.
2. Adam .... (not like) fish, but now he loves it.
3. .... you .... (have) long hair?
4. I .... (not speak) French, but I took many lessons.
5. We .... (live) near the beach.

5 Intro 1 2 3 4 5 6 7 8 9 Choose the correct answer. (10 points)

1. We **study** / **am studying** / **are studying** drama at the moment.
2. We haven't got **much** / **many** / **some** homework. Let's go to the cinema.
3. In 2009, Jordan Romero **climb** / **climbed** / **did he climb** Mount Everest.
4. **You used to** / **You didn't use to** / **Did you use to** read a lot of magazines?
5. **There was** / **There were** / **Were there** an interesting article about J. K. Rowling in the newspaper. Did you read it?
6. Your new dress **have got** / **is** / **does** beautiful.
7. I gave **he** / **his** / **him** a book about computers.
8. **How many** / **How much** / **Is there** dictionaries has the library got?
9. I can't find **a** / **an** / **any** orange markers.
10. Kim is **reading** / **read** / **reads** a lot of books every week.

Dictation 10 points

5 04 **6 Listen and write the sentences.**

1. ....
2. ....
3. ....
4. ....
5. ....

Speaking 10 points

7 Complete the dialogue with the questions below.

Did she go to university?
When did she die?
Where was your grandmother born?
When did she get married?
How many children did she have?

A: 1. ……………………

B: In England.

A: I didn't know that! 2. ……………………

B: No, she didn't. She got a job when she finished school.

A: 3. ……………………

B: In 1958. She met my grandfather in 1956.

A: 4. ……………………

B: Seven.

A: Wow, that's a lot! 5. ……………………

B: In 2010.

Writing 10 points

8 Put the sentences in the correct order.

….. a. **Then**, he fell in love with Mandy at university.
….. b. **After that**, Jim joined the army.
….. c. **Finally**, he received an award from the army.
….. d. **First**, Jim went to university.
….. e. **Next**, they graduated and got married.

Translation 20 points

9 Translate the sentences into English.

1. Abby nació en Madrid, pero se crio en Barcelona.
……………………
2. Él solía pertenecer a un club deportivo.
……………………
3. Ella recibió un premio porque fue voluntaria en un hospital.
……………………
4. Después de eso, no me uní a ningún grupo.
……………………
5. ¿Él solía robar cosas?
……………………

My Scores

Vocabulary __ / 20
Grammar __ / 30
Dictation __ / 10
Speaking __ / 10
Writing __ / 10
Translation __ / 20
My total score: __ / 100

Self-Evaluation

Do the following. Tick (✔) the box if you succeed.

1 Say ...

1. four verbs related to news stories. ☐
…………… ……………
…………… ……………
2. four life events. ☐
…………… ……………
…………… ……………
3. two sentences about events in the past. ☐
……………………
……………………
4. one thing you used to do but you don't do now, and one thing you didn't use to do but do now. ☐
……………………
……………………

2 Write questions about Kate Middleton for the answers below. ☐

1. ……………………
Kate Middleton was born on 9th January, 1982.
2. ……………………
She lived in Reading, England.
3. ……………………
She studied at the University of St Andrews.
4. ……………………
She got married to Prince William in 2011.

3 Write three sentences about someone's life events using connectors of sequence. ☐

1. ……………………
2. ……………………
3. ……………………

3 Seeing the World

Vocabulary Adjectives

* **1 Find the opposite of each adjective below in the word puzzle. Then write it under its opposite.**

1
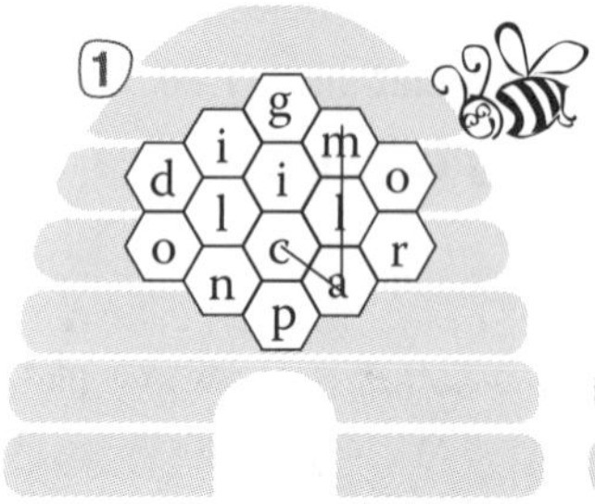

rough
calm
....

2
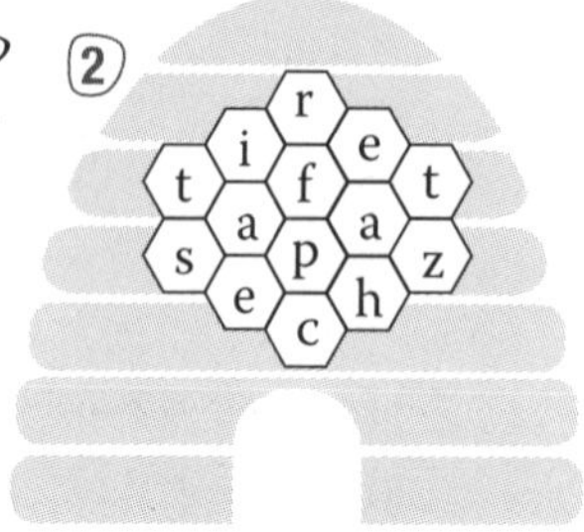

dangerous
....

3
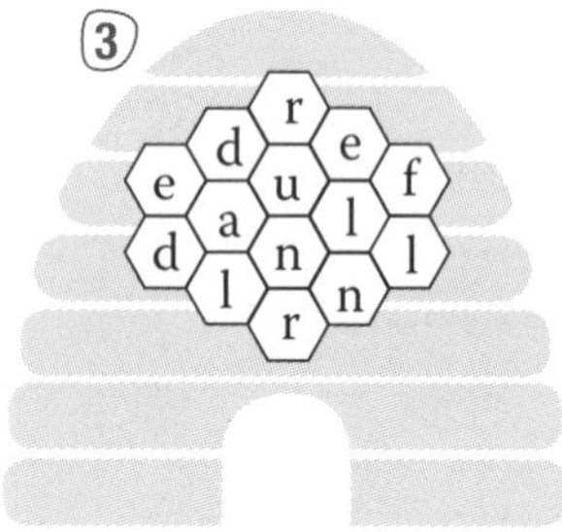

lively
....

4
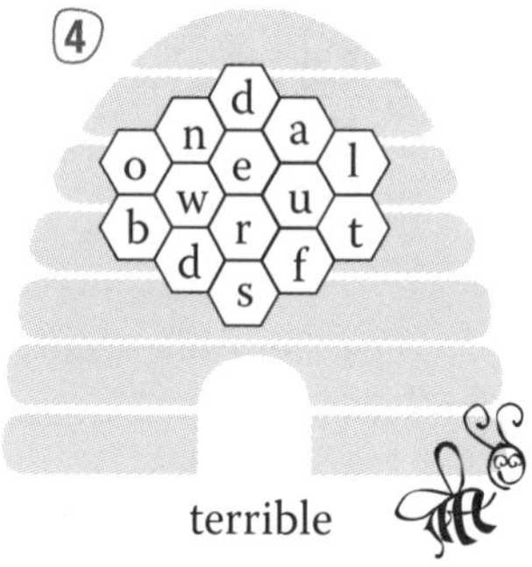

terrible
....

** **2 Choose the correct answer.**

1. This beach is too noisy. Let's go somewhere **peaceful** / **terrible** / **rough**.
2. She always wants to help people. She is an **elegant** / **extraordinary** / **isolated** person.
3. We sat on the beach and read all day. It was **lively** / **pleasant** / **extraordinary**.
4. I love sport and my **peaceful** / **relaxing** / **ideal** holiday is to go skiing.
5. My friend's dog tried to bite me. It was **frightening** / **dull** / **wonderful**!
6. The farm is the only building in the region. It's very **isolated** / **pleasant** / **lively**.
7. I love your new dress. It is nice and **ideal** / **elegant** / **terrible**.
8. I like taking a nap in the afternoon. It's **calm** / **relaxing** / **rough**.

*** **3 Describe each of the holiday destinations below with three adjectives from Exercises 1 and 2. Use as many different adjectives as you can. Then complete the sentence below.**

1

La Boca, Buenos Aires

....
....
....

2

Phuket, Thailand

....
....
....

3

Snowdonia, Wales

....
....
....

I think .... is the best holiday destination because ....

Grammar Comparison of adjectives

* **1 Complete the chart below.**

Adjective	Comparative	Superlative
1. calm	calmer than	
2.		the safest
3.	happier than	
4. isolated		
5. hot		
6.		the best
7.	worse than	
8. pleasant		

** **2 Complete the sentences with the affirmative form of *to be* and the comparative form of the adjectives in brackets. Tick (✓) the sentences that you agree with.**

..... 1. Spiders .... snakes. (frightening)

..... 2. Bread .... cake. (tasty)

..... 3. The food in Spain .... the food in England. (good)

..... 4. Dogs .... cats. (nice)

..... 5. Today, the weather .... yesterday. (bad)

** **3 Complete the questions with the superlative form of the adjectives in brackets. Then answer the questions with the places below.**

Russia • The Pacific • Vatican City
Cape York Peninsula • The Nile

1. What is .... (small) country in the world? ....
2. What is .... (big) country in the world? ....
3. What is .... (long) river in the world? ....
4. What is .... (large) ocean in the world? ....
5. What is .... (isolated) place in Australia? ....

Answers, see page 31

** **4 Write sentences with the words below. Use the comparative or superlative form.**

1. Mount Everest / high / mountain in the world

   ....

2. gymnastics / safe / judo

   ....

3. Mercury / close / planet to the sun

   ....

4. Spain / sunny / Norway

   ....

** **5 Complete the sentences with *less ... than* or *the least* and the adjective in brackets.**

1. Walking is one of .... types of sport. (difficult)
2. An adventure holiday is .... a beach holiday. (relaxing)
3. Female birds are .... male birds. (colourful)
4. I think history is .... subject in school. (interesting)

*** **6 Complete the text with the adjectives in brackets. Use the comparative or superlative form to make affirmative or negative comparisons.**

The Namib Desert

The Namib Desert in Africa is one of 1. .... (extraordinary) places on Earth. It is 2. .... (old) desert in the world and is 3. .... (dry) area in Southern Africa. The Namib Desert is also one of 4. .... (accessible) places on Earth. Very few people live in this isolated place.

The Namib Desert is famous for its high orange dunes. Some of them are 5. .... (high) the Eiffel Tower in Paris! The Namib Desert is also famous for its game reserve, Etosha National Park. It is one of 6. .... (big) game reserves in Africa. Maybe it is 7. .... (popular) other game reserves, but it is certainly worth a visit. It is home to many animals, including African Bush elephants. These elephants are 8. .... (large) Asian elephants and they are also much 9. .... (strong) them!

English in Use

Write sentences to compare the countries below. Use the comparative or superlative form of the adjectives in the wordbank. Make affirmative or negative comparisons.

England Spain Russia

big • small • cold • interesting • hot • pleasant

1. ....
2. ....
3. ....
4. ....
5. ....

Grammar *(not) as … as, too … , (not) … enough*

★ **1 Complete the sentences to compare three hotels. Use *(not) as … as* and the adjectives in brackets.**

1. The price at Jay's Hotel is .... (high) at Hope Hotel.
2. Blue Sky Hotel is .... (good) Hope Hotel.
3. Jay's Hotel is .... (old) Hope Hotel.
4. Hope Hotel is .... (new) Blue Sky Hotel.
5. Blue Sky Hotel is .... (big) Hope Hotel.
6. The price at Hope Hotel is .... (low) at Blue Sky Hotel.

★★ **2 Complete the sentences with *too …* or *(not) … enough* and the adjectives in brackets.**

1. Are the trousers long enough for John? No, they are .... (short).
2. I live near my school. It is .... (close) to walk.
3. I'm sorry, but I'm .... (busy) to meet you today.
4. Clare is 18 years old. She is .... (old) to drive a car.
5. We can't go to the USA on a short holiday because it's .... (far).
6. Don't walk around Central Park at night. It's .... (safe).

★★ **3 Complete the sentences with the adjectives below and *too …* or *(not) … enough*.**

rough • brave • hot • lively • big

1. These sandals are .... I need a larger size.
2. Are you .... to go scuba diving?
3. We can't swim in the sea today because it's ....
4. Let's sit under that tree. It's .... in the sun.
5. There wasn't any music or dancing at the party. It was ....

★★★ **4 Choose the correct answers.**

A Caravan Holiday

Camping can be fun, but for many people this kind of holiday isn't 1. **as comfortable as / comfortable enough / too comfortable**. Sleeping in a tent isn't 2. **too pleasant / as pleasant as / pleasant enough** sleeping in a hotel room and sometimes the weather isn't 3. **as good as / too good / good enough** to be outside. So what do many families do? They go on a caravan holiday. It is 4. **too exciting / exciting enough / as exciting as** a camping holiday and the prices for caravans aren't 5. **too high / higher than / high enough**.

English in Use

Complete the dialogue with the words below.

as comfortable as • too cold • too soft
close enough • big enough

Mel: How was your holiday?

Jane: Not great. It rained a lot and it was 1. .... to swim.

Mel: What was your hotel like?

Jane: It was OK, but it wasn't 2. .... to the centre of town.

Mel: What was your room like?

Jane: It was nice, but the bed wasn't 3. .... my bed at home. It was 4. .... and my pillow wasn't 5. ....

Reading

1 **Read about holidays for rich and famous people. Which questions can you answer according to the text? Answer those questions.**

Celebrities on Holiday

It isn't always easy for famous people to go on holiday and get away from the public. There are many wonderful places to go, but a lot of them aren't private enough.

So where do these famous people go? The TV presenter Oprah Winfrey loves travelling to Antigua, an island in the Caribbean. She loves sitting under huge palm trees next to the calm blue sea. Bill Gates, the creator of Microsoft and one of the richest men in the world, enjoys his holidays in colder weather. He enjoys visiting Greenland. It's a very peaceful country – ideal to get away from his busy life.

Many celebrities choose to travel to small islands. These islands are isolated enough to get away from the fans and the paparazzi, and they have usually got beautiful beaches and elegant beach houses. Some celebrities, like the singer Shakira and the actors Leonardo DiCaprio and Johnny Depp, have got their own islands. Johnny Depp's island in the Bahamas is about two kilometres long and 400 metres wide. There's a cottage and six beaches on the island.

Although many famous people try to stay away from the public during their holidays, the actress Scarlett Johansson prefers other destinations. She enjoys going to Disneyland because it's fun and there's a lot to do there. People at the amusement park are too busy to notice her. As she says, "At Disneyland, you are not the main attraction."

1. Why is it difficult for famous people to go on holiday? ....
2. How often does Oprah Winfrey go on holiday? ....
3. Why does Bill Gates prefer Greenland to Antigua? ....
4. Why are small islands good holiday destinations for famous people? ....
5. Where is Shakira's island? ....
6. How big is Johnny Depp's island? ....
7. Why does Scarlett Johansson enjoy Disneyland? ....

2 **Complete the sentences.**

1. The text mentions palm trees because ....
2. The text mentions Shakira, Leonardo DiCaprio and Johnny Depp in the same sentence because ....
3. Johhny Depp's island has got ....
4. Scarlett Johansson is a celebrity, but she can enjoy Disneyland because ....

Listening

5/05 **3** **Listen to Alex and his mother talking about a summer holiday for teenagers. Number the activities in the order you hear them.**

..... a. climb up a mountain
..... b. build schools
..... c. go rafting
..... d. volunteer in a children's centre

5/05 **4** **Listen again and complete the sentences.**

1. Costa Rica is in ....
2. The weather in Costa Rica is usually ....
3. The group isn't too big, so it will be easy for Alex to ....
4. San José is the .... city in Costa Rica.
5. At the children's centre, the volunteers help the children with ....
6. The highest mountain in Costa Rica is .... metres high.
7. On the last two days of the trip, the teenagers go ....

Vocabulary Geography

* **1 Complete the puzzle according to the pictures.**

Across → Down ↓

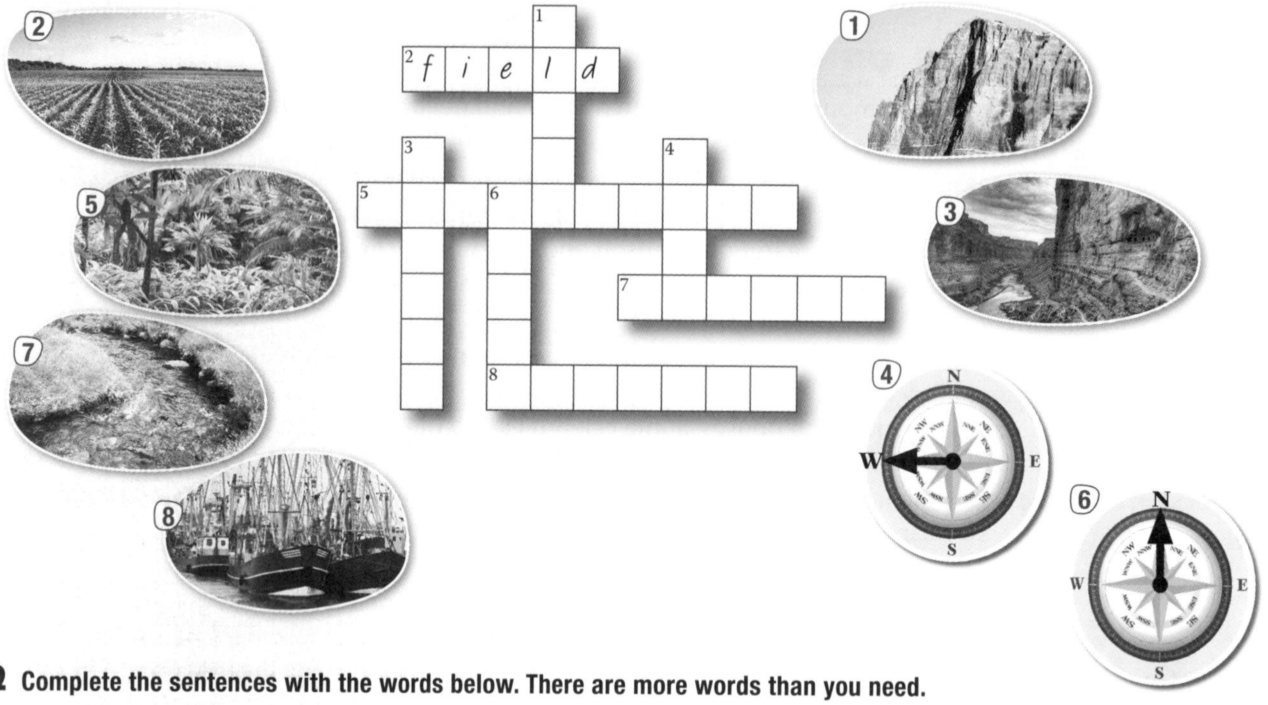

** **2 Complete the sentences with the words below. There are more words than you need.**

field • east • coast • ground • north • south • swamps • glaciers • scenery • coral reef

1. Spain is .... of France.
2. Crocodiles live in rivers, lakes and ....
3. We enjoyed the beautiful .... as we were hiking in the mountains.
4. You can only find .... in cold climates.
5. The .... is land next to the sea.
6. We saw many kinds of colourful fish near the ....
7. Valencia is on the .... coast of Spain.
8. My phone doesn't work because I dropped it on the ....

*** **3 Where do people go to do the following activities? Write appropriate geographical features from Exercises 1 and 2 above. There may be more than one answer.**

1. hiking ....
2. diving ....
3. fishing ....
4. climbing ....

English in Use

Put the words in the correct order to write questions. Then answer the questions to complete the interview. Make the answers true for you.

1. kind of holiday / what / you / want / do
   Q: ....
   A: ....
2. you / do / want / where / to / go
   Q: ....
   A: ....
3. want / you / go / when / do / to
   Q: ....
   A: ....
4. be away / long / do / how / you / want / to
   Q: ....
   A: ....
5. there / what / you / do / want / to / do
   Q: ....
   A: ....

Writing A report about a travel destination

1 The sentences below are from a description of the island Bonaire. Write where you think each sentence belongs – paragraph 1, 2 or 3.

a. I really recommend visiting this beautiful island. ....
b. Bonaire is a small island in the Caribbean. ....
c. Tourists can swim in the sea or relax near the pool. ....
d. The climate is pleasant all year round. ....
e. It's an ideal destination for a summer holiday. ....
f. You can also go diving and see the beautiful coral reefs. ....

2 The description of Lake Garda is in the wrong order. Read the description and number the paragraphs in the correct order.

Lake Garda

...... a. There are many things to do at Lake Garda. Visitors looking for an adventure holiday can enjoy windsurfing, cliff climbing, hiking and mountain biking. Tourists looking for a more relaxing holiday can enjoy eating the delicious local Italian food and exploring the beautiful old towns around the lake.

...... b. Lake Garda offers beautiful scenery and lots of fun activities. It is an ideal holiday destination for young and old people.

...... c. Lake Garda is one of the most popular tourist destinations in Italy. It's the largest lake in the country and there are some beautiful towns around it.

3 Complete the chart below about a place you like visiting.

Paragraph 1
Name of place: ....
Where it is: ....
General information: ....

Paragraph 2
Description of the place: ....
....
Things to see and do: ....
....

Paragraph 3
Opinion of the place: ....

4 Write a report of a place you like visiting. Use the chart in Exercise 3 and the model in Exercise 2 to help you.

Check Your Progress

Vocabulary 20 points

1 Circle the word that doesn't belong. (4 points)

1. west • north • cliff • east
2. field • swamp • stream • coral reef
3. calm • lively • relaxing • peaceful
4. safe • terrible • rough • frightening

2 Unscramble the words below and use them to complete the sentences. (6 points)

dognru • enatpsal • ynecsre • hutos aretndyoriaxr • fnetroiras

1. Look at the lake with the mountains behind it. The .... is beautiful here.
2. Antarctica is .... of Argentina.
3. There is a lot of snow on the trees, but there isn't much on the ....
4. The weather isn't too hot and it isn't too cold. It's very ....
5. The Ice Hotel is an unusual hotel, but it isn't as .... as the Salt Hotel.
6. It's always very wet in a ....

3 Intro 1 2 3 4 5 6 7 8 9 Write the correct word next to each sentence. There are more words than you need. (10 points)

desk • generous • weak • atlas • kitchen • bite canyon • save • microscope • survive

1. It's the opposite of *strong.* ....
2. You cook food here. ....
3. Students use this item in science lessons. ....
4. You do this with your teeth. ....
5. It's a book of maps. ....

Grammar 30 points

4 Write comparative and superlative sentences with the words below. Use the affirmative form of *to be.* (10 points)

1. bikes / slow / cars

   ....
2. the cheetah / fast / animal in the world

   ....
3. dolphins / frightening / sharks

   ....
4. an orange / round / a lemon

   ....
5. The *Mona Lisa* / famous / painting in history

   ....

5 Rewrite the sentences with the words in brackets. (10 points)

1. Jim and Peter are the same height. (as tall as)

   ....
2. It is too dangerous to dive off this cliff. (safe enough)

   ....
3. The sea isn't calm enough to go sailing. (too rough)

   ....
4. The field is too small to play football. (big enough)

   ....
5. A calculator is smaller than a laptop. (as large as)

   ....

6 Intro 1 2 3 4 5 6 7 8 9 Choose the correct answer. (10 points)

1. **Have you got** / **You are** / **Are you** in England?
2. Is this your phone? Yes, it's **me** / **my** / **mine**.
3. There is **a lot of** / **many** / **any** water on the rug.
4. Fish **is living** / **live** / **doesn't live** in coral reefs.
5. The baby **is sleeping** / **sleep** / **slept** now.
6. Sue **used to** / **didn't use to** / **did she use to** ride horses, but now she loves doing it.
7. **There is** / **There aren't** / **Is there** a big boat in the harbour?
8. **Was there** / **There weren't** / **There were** any crocodiles in the swamp.
9. We **didn't eat** / **don't eat** / **ate** in the hotel because we were late.
10. I don't want to go out. I'm **lazy enough** / **too lazy** / **not lazy enough**.

Dictation 10 points

5 06 **7 Listen and write the sentences.**

1. ....
2. ....
3. ....
4. ....
5. ....

Speaking 10 points

8 Complete the dialogue with the questions below.

How long do you want to be away?
What do you think of Jamaica?
What kind of holiday do you want?
Where do you want to go?
When do you want to go?

A: 1. ....
B: I want a relaxing holiday.
A: 2. ....
B: An island in the Caribbean.
A: 3. ....
B: In the summer.
A: 4. ....
B: About ten days.
A: 5. ....
B: Sounds perfect!

Writing 10 points

9 Write which paragraph (1, 2 or 3) each sentence belongs in.

a. Tourists can go for a walk along the lake. .....
b. It is an ideal holiday destination. .....
c. Montreux is a beautiful town in Switzerland. .....
d. I really recommend going there. .....
e. It is on the east shore of Lake Geneva. .....

Translation 20 points

10 Translate the sentences into English.

1. Es demasiado aterrador andar por ese acantilado.
....
2. La costa este está más aislada que la costa oeste.
....
3. No es suficientemente seguro entrar en el cañón.
....
4. Estos son los arrecifes de coral más extraordinarios del mundo.
....
5. El puerto no es tan bullicioso como la playa.
....

My Scores

Vocabulary __ / 20
Grammar __ / 30
Dictation __ / 10
Speaking __ / 10
Writing __ / 10
Translation __ / 20
My total score: __ / 100

Self-Evaluation

Do the following. Tick (✔) the box if you succeed.

1 Say ...

1. four adjectives. ☐
....
....
2. four words related to geography. ☐
....
....
3. two sentences comparing holiday destinations using comparison of adjectives. ☐
....
....
4. two sentences describing geographical features using *too* ... and *(not)* ... *enough.* ☐
....
....

2 Write questions for the answers below. ☐

1. ....
An adventurous holiday.
2. ....
In the summer.
3. ....
Two weeks.
4. ....
I want to go on a trek.

3 Write three sentences describing a place. ☐

1. ....
2. ....
3. ....

Answers Page 25, Exercise 3
1. Vatican City
2. Russia
3. The Nile
4. The Pacific
5. Cape York Peninsula

4 Everyday Life

Vocabulary The weather

* **1 Write the words below in the correct places.**

cold • warm • cloudy • stormy • rain • hot • sunny • cool

** **2 Complete the puzzle according to the clues.**

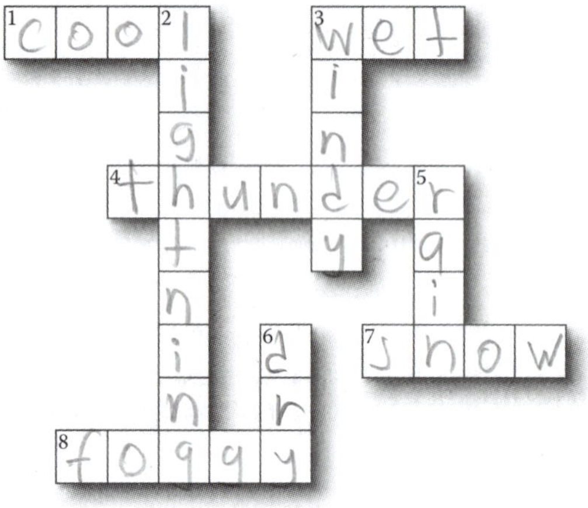

Across →

1. The opposite of *warm* is ..... .
3. This storm is terrible. My trousers and shoes are ..... .
4. I hate ..... ! It's noisy and scary.
7. The garden is white. There's ..... everywhere!
8. I can't see the street. It's very ..... outside.

Down ↓

2. I don't like going out in a storm because I'm afraid of ..... .
3. It's great to go windsurfing on ..... days.
5. Look at the ..... outside! You should take an umbrella.
6. It's hot and ..... in the Sahara Desert.

*** **3 Write sentences about the weather according to the photographs. Use words from Exercises 1 and 2.**

① 

It's *cold and there is snow everywhere.*

② 

It's hot and sunny at the beach

③ 

It's warm and cloudy

④ 

It's cool and is a rainy day

Grammar Subject / Object questions

* **1 Write the words in the correct order to make questions. Then test your knowledge and circle the correct answers.**

Trivia Quiz

1. built / the tallest snowman / who /
   ....
   a. people in Hamar, Norway
   b. people in Omsk, Siberia
   c. people in Bethel, Maine, USA
2. the least sun / in the world / what place / gets
   ....
   a. The South Pole c. Britain
   b. The North Pole
3. lightning / how often / the ocean / does / hit
   ....
   a. 20% of the time c. 90% of the time
   b. 50% of the time
4. 92 people / what / in Bangladesh / killed / on 14th April, 1986
   ....
   a. a typhoon b. ice balls c. a tornado
5. the Mississippi River / did / freeze / when
   ....
   a. in 2014 b. in 1902 c. in 1899
6. how often / thunderstorms / start / on Earth / do
   ....
   a. all the time c. about once a week
   b. about once a day

Answers, see page 39

** **2 Write questions for the answers in bold.**

1. ....
   All my friends take the bus to school on rainy days.
2. ....
   We learn English **three times a week**.
3. ....
   I wear **a jacket** on cool mornings.
4. ....
   Thunder is making that sound.
5. ....
   I'm reading about **life in the desert**.
6. ....
   Lisa is calling you from the garden.

*** **3 Complete the dialogue. Pay attention to the words in bold.**

Brian: 1. .... ?
Anders: I live **in Swedish Lapland**.
Brian: 2. .... ?
Anders: I live with **my parents and my sister, Nina**.
Brian: 3. .... everyday life in Lapland special?
Anders: **The eight seasons** make everyday life in Lapland special!
Brian: *Eight* seasons? *We* only have four seasons.
Anders: Yes, but you see, there's a big difference between summer and winter in Lapland. There can be a difference of 70°C between these two seasons, so we see lots of other changes in nature and the weather during the year.
Brian: 4. .... ?
Anders: **Spring-winter** is my favourite season.
Brian: 5. .... ?
Anders: It falls **during March and April**. In spring-winter, it's finally sunny after many difficult months of winter weather. You hear the birds sing. Everyone loves it!
Brian: 6. .... in spring-winter?
Anders: After school, I **ride my snowmobile over the sea ice**.
Brian: 7. .... with you?
Anders: **My sister Nina and my friend Lars**. Come and visit us and you can join us, too!

English in Use

Complete the questions about Lapland in A with *What*, *Who*, *Where* and *How often*. Then match each question to an answer in B.

A

1. .... lives in Swedish Lapland?
2. .... does it snow in Lapland?
3. .... do many people go to see the Northern Lights?
4. .... prevents mosquitoes from biting you in Lapland?

B

.... a. Very often – there's snow between 175 to 225 days a year.
.... b. The Sami people live there.
.... c. Smoke from large fires helps to keep mosquitoes away.
.... d. They go to the Aurora Sky Station in Abisko.

Grammar Adverbs of manner

* **1 Choose the correct answer.**

1. The baby is sleeping ..... in his bed.
   a. quietly
   b. more quietly than
   c. less quietly than
2. Kate did the project ..... her friends and got the best mark in the class.
   a. successfully
   b. more successfully than
   c. as successfully as
3. My father isn't careful enough. He drives ..... my mother!
   a. carefully
   b. less carefully than
   c. as carefully as
4. I don't understand what you're saying. Please speak ..... !
   a. clearly
   b. more clearly than
   c. less clearly than
5. Pam finished reading the book yesterday, but I'm still reading it. I don't read ..... Pam.
   a. quickly
   b. less quickly than
   c. as quickly as

** **2 The words and phrases in bold are in the wrong sentences. Write the correct word or phrase next to each sentence.**

1. My parents are talking **less bravely than** in the kitchen. noisily
2. Alice is lying **faster than** on the sofa. lazily
3. Charlotte is dancing **as seriously as** her partner because her feet hurt. less happily than
4. In slalom skiing, athletes move **lazily** in snowboarding. faster than
5. I was driving the snowmobile **noisily** you were because it was very frightening! less bravely than
6. Ron is an excellent student like his brothers and he studies **less happily than** them. as seriously as

*** **3 Complete the text with the correct adverb form of the adjectives in brackets.**

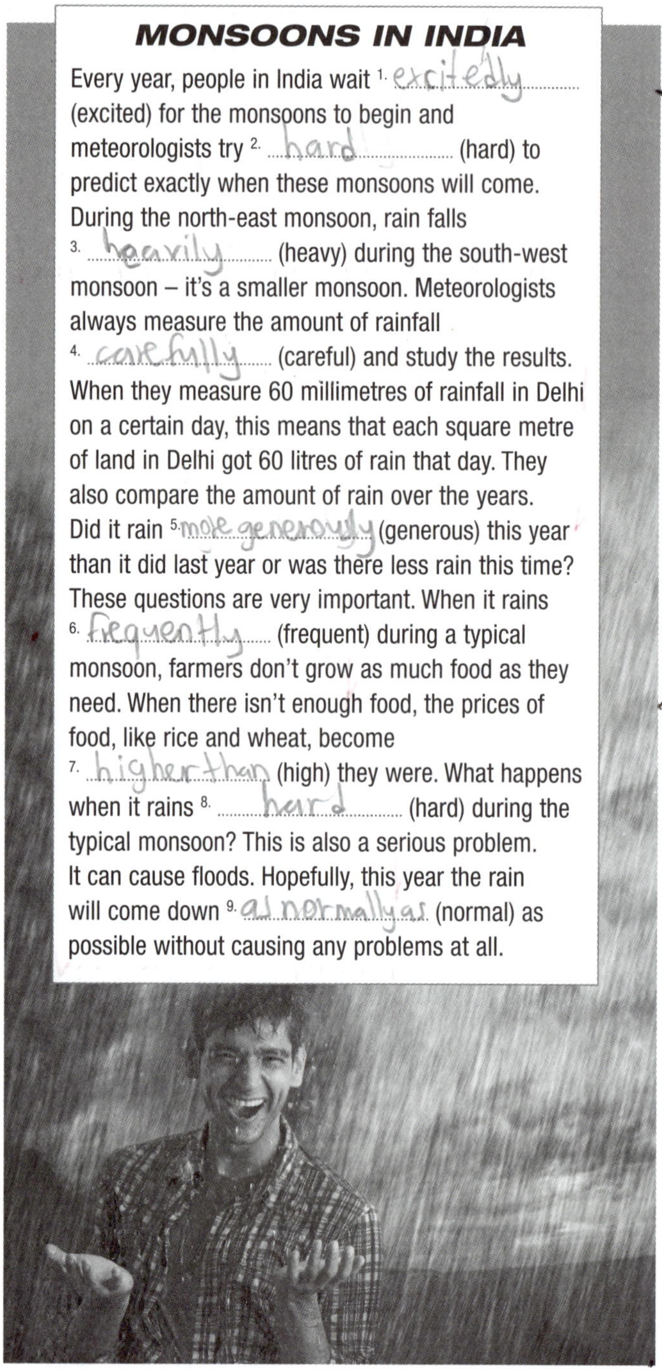

MONSOONS IN INDIA

Every year, people in India wait 1. excitedly (excited) for the monsoons to begin and meteorologists try 2. hard (hard) to predict exactly when these monsoons will come. During the north-east monsoon, rain falls 3. heavily (heavy) during the south-west monsoon – it's a smaller monsoon. Meteorologists always measure the amount of rainfall 4. carefully (careful) and study the results. When they measure 60 millimetres of rainfall in Delhi on a certain day, this means that each square metre of land in Delhi got 60 litres of rain that day. They also compare the amount of rain over the years. Did it rain 5. more generously (generous) this year than it did last year or was there less rain this time? These questions are very important. When it rains 6. frequently (frequent) during a typical monsoon, farmers don't grow as much food as they need. When there isn't enough food, the prices of food, like rice and wheat, become 7. higher than (high) they were. What happens when it rains 8. hard (hard) during the typical monsoon? This is also a serious problem. It can cause floods. Hopefully, this year the rain will come down 9. as normally as (normal) as possible without causing any problems at all.

English in Use

Complete the sentences to make them true for you. Change the adjectives in brackets to adverbs.

1. My dad plays basketball more badly than (bad) me.
2. My mum writes more clearly than (clear) my dad does.
3. I dance less beautifully than (beautiful) my sister .
4. I speak French less well than (good) my mum .
5. I run more quickly than (quick) my best friend.

Reading

1 Read Kevin's blog about his town. Then complete the sentences with words from the text.

Kevin's Blog

My name is Kevin. I live in Canada in a small town called Churchill. It's near the sea on the Hudson Bay. Churchill is very cold and snowy in the winter. Snow falls frequently. In fact, it can fall all year and it usually rains between June and September. My favourite season is autumn. Why do I love it? I love autumn because that's when the polar bears come to town.

Polar bears live in very cold places around the North Pole. In the winter, sea water freezes completely and becomes ice. The polar bears live happily on this ice and they hunt fish and other animals. In the summer, some of the ice becomes water and the bears can't hunt. They wait for the sea to freeze again, but this takes a long time. They look for food in other places, but it isn't easy to find. Polar bears usually stay away from people, but in the autumn the bears are very hungry, so they come to our town to look for food.

When we see polar bears in town, we don't run. We call the Bear Patrol. The Bear Patrol takes them to a special zoo. The polar bears stay there until the sea freezes again. Then helicopters carefully carry them back to the sea ice. You can visit Churchill in the autumn and see the polar bears. But bring a warm coat because it's very windy!

1. Churchill is a town in Canada.
2. The weather is rainy in the summer.
3. In warm weather, it's hard for polar bears to find food.
4. Polar bears don't usually go near people.
5. When Kevin sees a polar bear in town, he calls to the Bear Patrol

2 Answer the questions.

1. Why is autumn Kevin's favourite season? Because he can see polar bears
2. What do polar bears eat in winter? Because sea water becomes ice and they can hunt fish
3. Why do polar bears go into Churchill? ......
4. What does the Bear Patrol do? It takes polar bears to a special zoo when people see them in town
5. How do the polar bears return to the sea ice? The helicopters carry them back to the sea ice
6. Why does Kevin mention a warm coat? Because in Churchill is very windy.

Listening

5/07 **3 Listen to part of a radio interview with Vineeta, a girl from India. Which of the following does she mention? Tick (✓) the correct answers.**

.... 1. when she went to sleep last night
.... 2. the weather today
.... 3. her mum's cooking
.... 4. her typical breakfast
.... 5. her sister's timetable
.... 6. the last lesson in her day

5/07 **4 Listen again and complete the sentences.**

1. It's almost ...... o'clock in New Delhi at the moment.
2. Today, it's more than ...... °C in New Delhi.
3. Every morning, Vineeta is on the bus to school at ....
4. Vineeta's yoga teacher speaks ....
5. There are ...... students in her class.

Vocabulary The family

* **1 Match A to B to make female-male pairs.**

A	B
1. aunt	..... a. son
2. niece	..... b. grandson
3. daughter	..... c. husband
4. wife	..... d. nephew
5. grandmother	..l.. e. uncle
6. granddaughter	..... f. grandfather

** **2 Complete the puzzle according to the clues below and find the hidden word.**

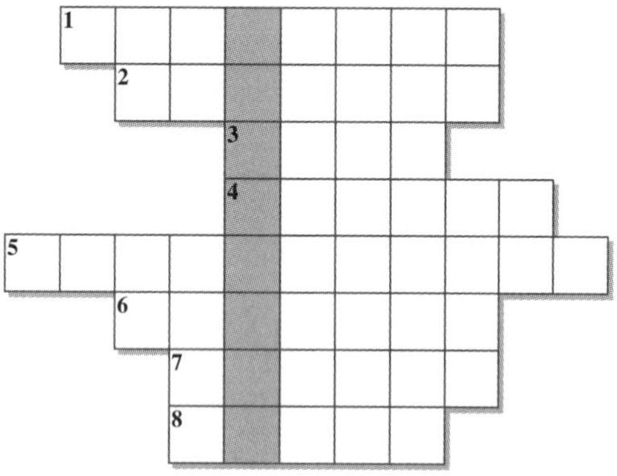

1. I've got two children – a son and a ..... .
2. Robert is our son. We're his ..... .
3. I'm a woman and you're my niece. I'm your ..... .
4. My sister has got a son. He's my ..... .
5. I'm Sally's mother's mother. I'm Sally's ..... .
6. I'm Mrs Adams. Mr Adams is my ..... .
7. My dad's sister has got a son. He's my ..... .
8. You're my dad's brother. You're my ..... .

The hidden word is ....

*** **3 Draw your family tree. Then write sentences about the people. Use the words in Exercises 1 and 2 to help you.**

1. ....
2. ....
3. ....
4. ....
5. ....
6. ....

English in Use

Write the words in the correct order to make questions. Then answer them to complete the interview. Make the answers true for you.

1. are / what / school subjects / your / favourite

   Q: ....

   A: ....
2. after-school activities / what / do / do / you

   Q: ....

   A: ....
3. do / you / watch TV / how often

   Q: ....

   A: ....
4. brothers and sisters / how many / got / have / you

   Q: ....

   A: ....
5. where you live / the weather / what's / like

   Q: ....

   A: ....

Writing A personal profile

1 Rewrite the sentences using the adverbs of frequency and time expressions in brackets.

1. It snows in Los Angeles. (rarely / in the winter)
   It rarely snows in Los Angeles in the winter.
2. I don't do my homework. (always / at the weekend)
   ....
3. Robbie gets up early. (never / in the morning)
   ....
4. We go on holiday. (in the winter / sometimes)
   ....
5. The girls play volleyball. (usually / three times a week)
   ....
6. Jenna goes swimming. (in the summer / often)
   ....

2 Read Jenny's description of her grandfather in the school magazine. Are the words in bold in the correct order? Find two mistakes and correct them below the text.

My Grandfather

My grandfather's name is Leon. He is 74 years old and **he lives in Brighton**, England, with my uncle, Mark. My grandfather has got three children and five grandchildren.

In the summer, he often takes my cousins and me to the beach in the afternoons. We enjoy swimming in the sea together. In the winter, **it usually is cold** in England. My grandfather goes on holiday in December or January because he doesn't like the cold weather. **He travels often** to Tenerife. **It's never cold there** in the winter.

My grandfather enjoys living in Brighton and spending time with his family. He's happy as long as he's near the beach.

1. ....
2. ....

3 Complete the information about a member of your family.

Paragraph 1
Personal details: ....
....
Family members: ....

Paragraph 2
Summer activities: ....
....
Winter activities: ....
....

Paragraph 3
Feelings: ....

4 Write a personal profile of your family member. Use the chart in Exercise 3 and the model in Exercise 2 to help you.

Check Your Progress

Vocabulary 20 points

1 Complete the sentences with the words below. (10 points)

grandsons • husband • snow • uncle • wet parents • foggy • hot • cousin • thunder

1. My .... aren't at home. Dad's at the library and Mum's at work.
2. We can't have our picnic today. The ground is very ....
3. My dad's brother is my ....
4. It's 37°C today. That's very .... !
5. My grandfather has got two .... – my brother, Tom, and me.
6. There's .... on Mount Fuji all year.
7. Jim and Helen are .... and wife.
8. I can't drive because it's very .... I can't see the street!
9. You see lightning before you hear ....
10. Your father's niece is your ....

2 Intro 1 2 3 4 5 6 7 8 9 Circle the word that doesn't belong. Then add a word from below to each group. (10 points)

stapler • granddaughter • rainy • get married clever

1. lazy • dark • creative • ....
2. steal • die • grow up • ....
3. sunny • cloudy • friendly • ....
4. compass • sink • globe • ....
5. nephew • aunt • chemist's • ....

Grammar 30 points

3 Write questions for the answers. Pay attention to the words in bold. (10 points)

1. ....

   Australians speak **English**.
2. ....

   Dad washes the car.
3. ....

   It snows here **two or three times a year**.
4. ....

   Birds are making those sounds.
5. ....

   I described **my nephew**.

4 Complete the sentences with the correct adverb form of the adjectives in brackets. (10 points)

1. North Africa doesn't get much rain. It rains .... (heavily) in North Africa than it does in Europe.
2. The snow is falling .... (quiet).
3. Please drive .... (slow) you did yesterday. Be careful!
4. Kate and Kim are two wonderful dancers. Kate dances .... (good) Kim.
5. I'm a terrible singer. I sing .... (bad)!

5 Intro 1 2 3 4 5 6 7 8 9 Choose the correct answer. (10 points)

1. This is my helmet, not **you** / **your** / **yours**.
2. Mel and Bob never **watch** / **is watching** / **watches** TV before school.
3. John completed the exam **quickly** / **more quickly than** / **less quickly than** Lily, so he waited for her outside the classroom.
4. **Have you got** / **You are** / **Are you** in Year 9?
5. There is **some** / **an** / **any** English homework.
6. **You went** / **Did you go** / **You didn't go** to the cinema alone?
7. **Laura used to** / **Laura didn't use to** / **Did Laura use to** live in Leeds, but she lives in York now.
8. Today was **calm** / **calmer than** / **the calmest** day of the week.
9. I don't want it. It's **not nice enough** / **too nice** / **nice enough**.
10. How many children **was there** / **were there** / **there are** at the party?

Dictation 10 points

5 08 **6 Listen and write the sentences.**

1. ....
2. ....
3. ....
4. ....
5. ....

Speaking 10 points

7 Match the questions in A to the answers in B.

A

1. How many cousins have you got?
2. How often do you play basketball?
3. What sport do you do in the summer?
4. What's the weather like in the autumn?
5. Where do you go surfing?

B

..... a. It's usually cool.
..... b. I go sailing on warm days.
..... c. Five.
..... d. Every day.
..... e. At Fistral Beach.

Writing 10 points

8 Write the words in the correct order to make sentences.

1. in July / often / our cousins / to Paris / fly
....
2. in the morning / have / I / breakfast / rarely
....
3. never / we / in August / umbrellas / use
....
4. drives / always / at 8.30 / Aunt Sally / to work
....
5. Harry / goes / twice a year / usually / on holiday
....

Translation 20 points

9 Translate the sentences into English.

1. ¿Quién llamó a tu mujer?
....
2. ¿Quién está corriendo sobre el suelo mojado?
....
3. Mis padres están bailando alegremente bajo la lluvia.
....
4. Mi tía corre más deprisa que mi tío.
....
5. No nado tan bien como mi primo.
....

My Scores

Vocabulary __ / 20
Grammar __ / 30
Dictation __ / 10
Speaking __ / 10
Writing __ / 10
Translation __ / 20
My total score: __ / 100

Self-Evaluation

Do the following. Tick (✓) the box if you succeed.

1 Say ...

1. four words to describe the weather. ☐
....
....
2. four family members. ☐
....
....
3. one subject question and one object question about your friend. ☐
....
....
4. two sentences comparing your friends' actions with comparative adverbs. ☐
....
....

2 Answer the questions. ☐

1. What's the weather like today?
....
2. What do you do on Saturdays?
....
3. How many cousins have you got?
....
4. What is your favourite sport?
....

3 Write a sentence with an adverb of frequency and a time expression. ☐

....
....

Answers Page 33, Exercise 1

1. c	4. b
2. a	5. b
3. c	6. a

5 It's a Crime

Vocabulary Crime

★ 1 Write the words under the correct pictures.

police officer • fingerprints • court • ~~gun~~ • ~~knife~~ • ~~murder~~ • prison • ~~criminal~~

1. criminal

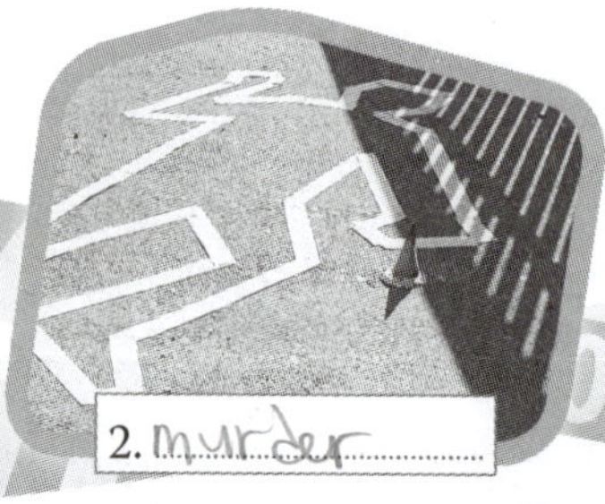

2. murder

3. gun

4. knife

5. prison

6. court

7. fingerprints

8. police officer

★★ 2 Choose the correct answer.

1. Did the police **investigate** / **murder** / **arrest** anyone for stealing the money?
2. A **police officer** / **criminal** / **weapon** stopped that man for driving too fast.
3. There were no **knives** / **guns** / **fingerprints** on the cup.
4. Five terrorists **arrested** / **hijacked** / **investigated** a bus last night.
5. There was a **robbery** / **court** / **prison** at the First National Bank yesterday.
6. It's not a real **fingerprint** / **gun** / **criminal**. It's just a toy.

★★ 3 Complete the headlines with the words below.

investigate • arrest • robbery • weapon • hijack • evidence

1 **Terrorists** hijack **aeroplane – pilot saves passengers**

2 **Bank** robbery **– two men steal £500,000**

3 **Murder in hotel room – police officers** investigate **crime but don't find a** weapon

4 **Fingerprints on window end murder investigation – police discover new** evidence **in murder investigation and** arrest **two men**

★★★ 4 Use the words in Exercises 1, 2 and 3 to write four newspaper headlines of your own.

1. A man hijacked a car driver two days ago
2. A police officer arrested a murderer last day
3. They found fingerprints in the suspect's gun
4. The suspect murdered to the victim with a knife

Grammar Past Continuous

* **1 Read the descriptions. What were the people doing? Complete the sentences with the verbs below. Use the Past Continuous affirmative.**

sleep • take • investigate • steal • hijack • paint

1. A police photographer was in the bank.
   She was taking photos.
2. The police officers found some fingerprints.
   They were investigating a crime.
3. The men pointed their guns at the passengers and told them to sit down.
   They were hijacking a bus.
4. The police officer was tired.
   He was sleeping in his car.
5. The girls had paints.
   They were painting graffiti on the walls.
6. Ned put the expensive rings and necklaces in his bag.
   He was stealing some jewellery.

** **2 A police officer is questioning five men about a robbery. Complete the conversation below with the verbs in brackets. Use the Past Continuous.**

Officer: Good morning, Pete. What 1. were you doing (do) at 7.00 yesterday?

Pete: I 2. was making (make) dinner with my daughter.

Officer: Bill, 3. were you having (have) dinner at 7.00 last night?

Bill: No, I 4. wasn't. I 5. was drinking (drink) coffee with my friends in a café. We 6. were chatting (chat) until 10.00.

John: And I was at home all evening. My wife and I 7. were relaxing (relax) in the living room at 7.00.

Kevin: I 8. wasn't eating (not eat) at 7.00. I 9. was talking (talk) to my son and we 10. were downloading (download) music on the computer.

Officer: What about you, Mick?

Mick: My wife and I were at the museum. We 11. were looking (look) at paintings until 8.00.

*** **3 Look at the picture. Write questions with the words below and answer them. Use the Past Continuous.**

1. Jim / cry
   Was Jim crying?
   No, he wasn't.
2. what / Jim / hold
   What was Jim holding?
   He was holding a rat.
3. what / Rob / eat
   What was Rob eating?
   He was eating an apple.
4. what / Alex and Hank / play
   What were Alex and Hank playing?
   They were playing basketball.
5. Rob / read / a book
   Was Rob reading a book?
   No, he wasn't. He was reading a newspaper.
6. Alex and Hank / wear / sandals
   Were Alex and Hank wearing sandals?
   No, they weren't. They were wearing shoes.

English in Use

Complete the questions with the time expressions below. Then answer the questions. Make the answers true for you.

five minutes ago • yesterday afternoon
last Saturday • before school

1. What were you wearing last Saturday?
   I was wearing a coat and gloves.
2. Who were you chatting to yesterday afternoon?
   I was chatting to my friend.
3. What were you thinking about five minutes ago?
   I wasn't thinking anything.
4. What was your best friend doing before school?
   She was having breakfast.

Grammar Past Continuous / Past Simple

★ 1 Choose the correct answer.

1. We **watched** / **were watching** TV when we **were hearing** / **heard** the noise.
2. While we **were sitting** / **sat** in court, a police officer **was coming** / **came** in.
3. Some police officers **were examining** / **examined** the flat while others **talked** / **were talking** to the neighbours.
4. Daniel **was driving** / **drove** home when his car suddenly **was stopping** / **stopped**.
5. The robbers **stole** / **were stealing** the money and **ran** / **were running** out of the shop.
6. Tess **was flying** / **flew** to London when two men **were hijacking** / **hijacked** the aeroplane.

★★ 2 Complete the sentences with the correct form of the verbs in brackets. Use the Past Simple or Past Continuous.

1. While the police officer .... to the students, they .... in their notebooks. (write / talk)
2. The criminal .... his money when the police officer .... him. (count / catch)
3. While the woman .... the aeroplane, the police officer .... her. (arrest / get on)
4. The criminal .... from prison while the prison guards .... (sleep / escape)
5. I .... in the cupboard when I .... the weapon. (find / look)

★★ 3 Complete the text with the correct form of the verbs in brackets. Use the Past Simple or Past Continuous.

The Great Train Robbery

On 8th August, 1963, a train 1. .... (travel) from Glasgow to London. There were money bags on the train. The train 2. .... (stop) at a red light. While the train driver 3. .... (look) at the light, a robber suddenly 4. .... (appear). The robber 5. .... (hit) the driver on the head. A train worker 6. .... (hear) a noise. He 7. .... (call) for help when some of the robbers 8. .... (attack) him. While some of the robbers 9. .... (take) the money bags, the other workers on the train 10. .... (wait) for the train to move. They 11. .... (not realise) what 12. .... (happen). The Great Train Robbery was one of the biggest robberies in England. The robbers 13. .... (steal) £2.6 million!

★★★ 4 Complete the sentences. Use the Past Simple or the Past Continuous.

1. I .... on my computer when suddenly ....
2. While the students ...., their teacher ....
3. I .... on my mobile phone while ....
4. He .... on the train when ....
5. We .... in a restaurant when we ....

English in Use

Write sentences about the people in the picture. Use the Past Continuous.

Yesterday...

1. one robber ....
2. the train driver ....
3. the man ....
4. the woman ....
5. the other robbers ....

Reading

1 **Read about Frank Abagnale. Then complete the sentences according to the text.**

A MAN OF MANY FACES

Frank Abagnale was born in the USA in 1948 and he grew up in New York. He was a happy child until his father and mother got divorced. After that, he started to steal from shops, but he soon got bored and wanted to make more money. He stole money from banks, but he didn't plan robberies with guns or knives. He found ways to get money from the banks illegally and the banks never saw the money again.

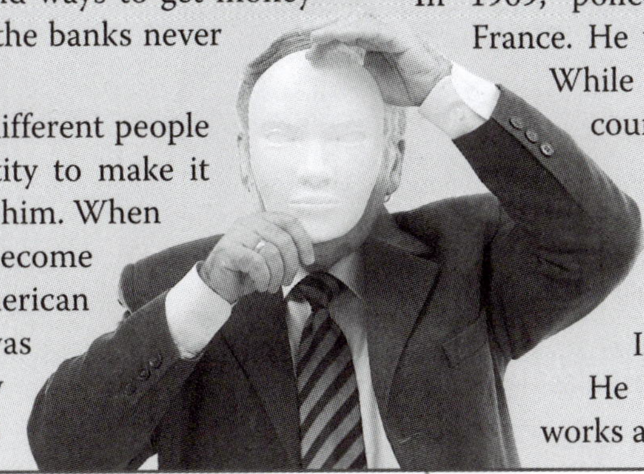

Abagnale enjoyed imitating different people and often changed his identity to make it harder for the police to catch him. When he was 16, he decided to become a pilot. He phoned Pan American Airlines and told them he was a pilot and needed a new uniform. He collected his new uniform, created a false pilot's licence and flew to 26 different countries! While he was "working" as a pilot, he stayed in hotels around the world for free. Later, he worked as a doctor at a hospital in Atlanta, Georgia for 11 months. He never learned medicine, of course! Abagnale also taught at a university without a teacher's certificate and became a lawyer without going to law school.

In 1969, police officers arrested Abagnale in France. He went to court and then to prison. While Abagnale was in prison, 12 other countries were investigating his crimes and collecting evidence. After six months in a French prison, he went to prison in Sweden and then in the USA.

In 1974, Abagnale got out of prison. He isn't a criminal anymore and he works as a fraud prevention consultant!

1. Abagnale was unhappy after ~~his~~ until his parents got divorced.
2. Abagnale stole money from banks without guns or knives.
3. Abagnale became a pilot after he created a false pilot's licence.
4. Abagnale worked at different jobs without going to a university.
5. Abagnale was in prison between the years 1969 and 1974.

2 **Find the following information in the text.**

1. two weapons: guns, knives
2. five jobs: pilot, doctor, teacher, fraud prevention consultant, lawyer
3. two cities: Atlanta, New York
4. three countries: USA, Sweden, France

Listening

3 **Listen to the conversation and tick (✓) the correct person in the chart.**

Who …	Holly	Jake	Jake's dad
1. is playing on a tablet?			
2. got the game *Cluedo* as a gift?			
3. likes the character Professor Plum?			
4. thinks the library is a good place for a murder?			
5. wants to play *Cluedo* on a board?			

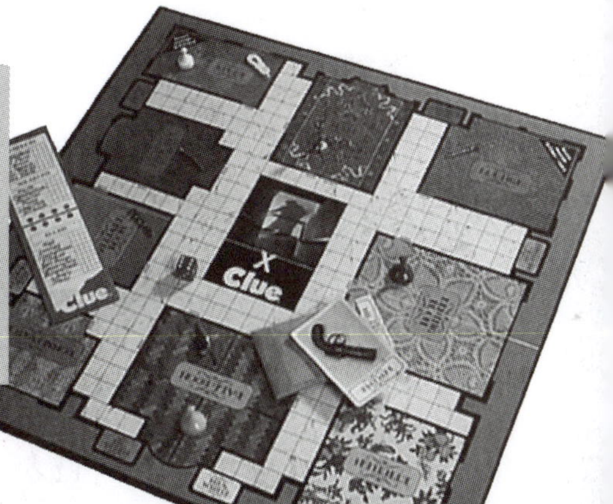

4 **Listen again and complete the sentences.**

1. The game *Clue* investigates a ....
2. You can play *Clue* on a .... and *Cluedo* on a ....
3. Each character in the board game is a different ....
4. In the board game, there are six characters and six ....
5. The board is a house with .... rooms.

Vocabulary People and crime

* **1 Label the people in the picture below.**

~~judge • lawyer • jury • suspect • witness • security guard • thief~~

** **2 Write the correct words next to each sentence.**

~~forensic scientist~~ • ~~victim~~ • ~~detective~~ • ~~burglar~~ • ~~expert~~ • ~~forger~~ • ~~prisoner~~

1. I usually work at night and steal items from shops and houses. burglar
2. I collect evidence from crimes and examine it in my crime laboratory. forensic scientist
3. I'm in prison because I murdered a man. prisoner
4. I copy documents and make them look authentic. forger
5. I investigate crimes and often interview suspects. detective
6. I know a lot about different types of weapons. expert
7. Someone stole my car. victim

*** **3 Look at the picture in Exercise 1 again and write five sentences about what was happening in court.**

1. Jury was boring at the court
2. The witness was explanning what he saw.
3. The judge was listening to the suspect's lawyer
4. The lawyer was trying to defensed to the suspect
5. A thief tried to stole the security guard's money

English in Use

Write questions to complete the dialogue.

Detective: 1. Where were you when the robbery happened?
Witness: I was standing at the bus stop when the robbery happened.
Detective: 2. What did you see?
Witness: Two men ran out of the shop, got in a car and drove away.
Detective: 3. What they looked like?
Witness: One man had blond hair. I think the other man had brown hair, but I'm not really sure.
Detective: 4. What they wore?
Witness: Jeans and black jackets.
Detective: 5. Did you remember the type of the car?
Witness: Yes, I'm quite sure their car was a black Volvo.

Writing A narrative

1 Choose the correct narrative linkers.

1. I saw children painting graffiti **while / a few minutes later** I was walking home.
2. **While / When** I arrived at court, the judge wasn't sitting in his chair.
3. I was doing my homework. **Suddenly / The next day**, I heard a loud noise.
4. We looked around. **A few minutes later, / When** we found the weapon.
5. A lot of people were shopping at the supermarket **this morning / suddenly**.

2 Read the narrative and complete it with the narrative linkers below.

while • on Saturday night • a few minutes later
the next day • suddenly • when

Robbery at South Cliff School

1. .... , while I was coming home from a friend's, there was a robbery at South Cliff School. I was walking next to the gym 2. .... I saw two men in the school field. They were holding laptops and running across the field. I called the police and hid behind a tree. 3. .... , a car appeared and the men got in. I took some photos of the car with my mobile phone 4. .... I was waiting for the police to arrive. 5. .... , three police officers arrived and I showed them my photos.
6. .... , everyone was talking about the incident. The police officers caught the burglars, thanks to my photos!

3 Complete the chart below about a hijack with ideas of your own.

Paragraph 1
The incident: *a hijack*
When: ....
Where: ....

Paragraph 2
The sequence of events:
First, *two men got up and pointed their guns at us.*
Next, ...
After that, ...

Paragraph 3
What happened in the end: *Soldiers ran onto the aeroplane and saved us.*

4 Write a narrative about the hijack. Use the chart in Exercise 3 and the model in Exercise 2 to help you.

Check Your Progress

Vocabulary 20 points

1 Match the words in A to their meanings in B. (10 points)

A

1. fingerprints
2. prisoner
3. investigate
4. gun
5. expert
6. burglar
7. hijack
8. knife
9. witness
10. suspect

B

..... a. This is a criminal in prison.
..... b. This person steals.
..... c. You cut things with this.
..... d. This is a type of weapon.
..... e. People leave these marks when they touch things.
..... f. This person knows a lot about a subject.
..... g. The police think this person is a criminal.
..... h. Detectives do this to solve a crime.
..... i. Pirates do this to boats.
..... j. This person sees a crime.

2 Intro 1 2 3 4 5 6 7 8 9 Complete the sentences with the words below. (10 points)

department store • robbery • move to • cloudy rainforest • do experiments • aunt • honest terrible • borrow

1. There was a .... at the jewellery shop last night.
2. It's a .... day today, but it isn't raining.
3. It's hot and wet in a ....
4. I haven't got anything to wear for the party. Can I .... your blue T-shirt, please?
5. When I grow up, I want to .... the USA.
6. My .... and uncle live in Scotland.
7. Scientists .... in their laboratories.
8. She told the truth. She was ....
9. We had a .... holiday. I don't want to go to that place again!
10. You can buy almost everything you need at the .... on Rose Street.

Grammar 30 points

3 Complete the sentences with the verbs below. Use the Past Continuous. (10 points)

look • not walk • repair • work • stand

1. I .... my dog at 3.00.
2. .... the lawyers .... late last night?
3. At midnight, thieves .... at a jewellery shop window.
4. .... Dad .... the car when you arrived?
5. A detective .... at the corner.

4 Complete the text with the verbs in brackets. Use the Past Simple or Past Continuous. (10 points)

At 9.00, a robber [1] .... (run) out of the bank. He [2] .... (look) around, but a car [3] .... (not wait) for him. A few minutes later, he [4] .... (cross) the road and [5] .... (stand) at the bus stop. While he [6] .... (wait) for a bus, a police officer [7] .... (walk) past the bus stop. The robber [8] .... (wear) a mask and he [9] .... (hold) some money. The police officer [10] .... (arrest) him!

5 Intro 1 2 3 4 5 6 7 8 9 Choose the correct answer. (10 points)

1. **Did / Were / Was** the lawyer talking to you?
2. We **hike / are hiking / hikes** every weekend.
3. **There are / There was / There were** a lot of people in court yesterday.
4. Who **stole / did steal / steal** the money?
5. There weren't **some / any / much** witnesses.
6. You don't ride your bike **quick / quickly / more quickly than** me.
7. Kelly **take / is taking / takes** a nap right now.
8. There isn't **many / some / much** snow on the ground.
9. The forger wasn't **as clever as / clever enough / too clever** the detective.
10. The film was **better than / the best / too good** the book.

Dictation 10 points

5/10 6 Listen and write the sentences.

1. ....
2. ....
3. ....
4. ....
5. ....

Speaking 10 points

7 Complete the dialogue with the questions below.

Can you tell me any more information?
What were you doing in the museum?
What did you do? • What happened?
Can you describe the woman?

A: 1. ....

B: I was looking at a painting by Monet.

A: 2. ....

B: A woman took a painting and ran out of the room.

A: 3. ....

B: I think she was wearing black, but I didn't see her face.

A: 4. ....

B: I called the police on my mobile phone.

A: 5. ....

B: Not really. There were a lot of people and it was difficult to see what was happening.

Writing 10 points

8 Complete the sentences with narrative linkers.

1. ...., I read about the robbery on the Internet.
2. We were eating at a café .... we heard a loud noise.
3. ...., a man ran out of the bank.
4. .... Mike was taking fingerprints, Bob was questioning the witness.
5. All the students were in the classroom ....

Translation 20 points

9 Translate the sentences into English.

1. El jurado estuvo sentado en el tribunal durante tres horas.
   ....
2. El investigador forense no estuvo trabajando en su laboratorio ayer.
   ....
3. El falsificador estaba pintando un cuadro cuando el policía lo arrestó.
   ....
4. El guarda jurado estaba durmiendo a las 10:00.
   ....
5. El detective estuvo mirando huellas dactilares toda la mañana.
   ....

My Scores

Vocabulary __ / 20
Grammar __ / 30
Dictation __ / 10
Speaking __ / 10
Writing __ / 10
Translation __ / 20
My total score: __ / 100

Self-Evaluation

Do the following. Tick (✔) the box if you succeed.

1 Say ...

1. four words related to crime. ☐
   ....
   ....
2. four words to refer to criminals and jobs connected to crime. ☐
   ....
   ....
3. two sentences about what you were doing at 9.00 yesterday morning. ☐
   ....
   ....
4. one sentence with *while* and one with *when* using the Past Continuous and the Past Simple. ☐
   ....
   ....

2 Write questions for the answers below. ☐

1. ....
   I was walking home from school at 2.00.
2. ....
   I called my parents.
3. ....
   I think a red shirt and a black skirt.
4. ....
   Yes, she was quite short, about 1.50 metres.

3 Write three sentences from a narrative using narrative linkers. ☐

1. ....
2. ....
3. ....

6 Going Green

Vocabulary Transport

* **1 Circle seven types of transport in the wordsearch. Then write them under the correct pictures.**

1

....

2

....

3

....

a	b	e	m	s	a	e	r	o	p	l	a	n	e	g
f	o	c	o	k	y	d	e	c	a	s	f	i	j	a
e	k	a	t	c	h	e	l	i	c	o	p	t	e	r
r	r	j	o	x	o	r	c	l	a	t	e	z	e	b
r	e	e	r	m	l	q	u	e	d	u	m	u	p	h
y	b	t	b	i	f	u	g	o	t	r	a	m	t	o
s	a	p	i	n	r	h	l	r	v	i	n	u	a	p
w	i	x	k	v	o	w	j	s	i	n	a	s	m	i
u	n	d	e	r	g	r	o	u	n	d	p	u	y	z

7

....

4

....

6

....

5

....

** **2 Complete the chart with the names of types of transport.**

Sea	Air	Land
1. ...ch...	4. he...o...r	6. ...i...iv...
2. m.......rb...a...	5. ...r...p...a...	7. ...rr...
3. c...ui... s...i...		8. ...oo...r

*** **3 Complete the sentences with words from Exercises 1 and 2.**

1. You can travel below the city on the ....
2. We drove our car onto the .... and crossed the river.
3. There are too many people in my family for a car, so we've got a ....
4. My mum usually takes the .... to work because it stops right outside her office.
5. Every morning, a huge .... brings fresh food to the supermarket next to our house.

Grammar Future tenses

★ 1 Complete the sentences with the verbs in brackets. Use *will* or *won't*. Then match the sentences in A and B.

A

1. Maybe we will take (take) a train to the cinema.
2. Mum won't be (not be) happy to see her kitchen like this.
3. Don't worry. We won't miss (not miss) the bus.
4. I'm sure Nick will come (come) to the party tonight.

B

2 a. Let's clean it quickly so she won't know (not know).
1 b. We will leave (leave) our car at home.
4 c. He won't stay (not stay) at home.
3 d. We will arrive (arrive) at school on time.

★★ 2 Write questions for the answers below. Use *will*.

1. Will be it cold tomorrow ?
No, I don't think it will be cold tomorrow.
2. Who will win the match ?
Our team will win the match!
3. What will you probably buy ?
I'll probably buy **a dress**.
4. Will he finish the marathon ?
Yes, I think he'll finish the marathon.
5. Where will the judge send the criminal ?
I'm sure the judge will send the criminal **to prison**.

★★ 3 Complete the e-mail. Use *be going to*.

Hi Beth,

Guess what! My parents [1] are going to take (take) me on a fantastic holiday this summer. We usually travel to Brighton on the south coast of England but this year we [2] aren't going to go (not go) there. We [3] are going to sail (sail) on a cruise ship around the Mediterranean. We [4] are going to stay (stay) on the ship for seven days, and the ship [5] is going to stop (stop) at three places – Naples in Italy, Piraeus in Greece and Chania in Crete. My mum wants to relax on the ship so she [6] is going to take (take) some books. I [7] am not going to read (not read) any books but I'll have my laptop. [8] Are you going to do (do) anything special this summer?

★★ 4 Write questions about the Hiltons' plans for Saturday. Use *be going to* and the words below. Then answer the questions according to the diary.

8.00:	Dad: wash jeep
10.00:	Mum and Zoe: go shopping
5.00:	Tom: have guitar lesson
9.00:	Mum and Dad: meet friends

1. when / Dad / wash / the jeep
When is Dad going to wash the jeep ?
He is going to wash the jeep at eight o'clock
2. Tom / play / football / at 5.00
Is Tom going to play football at 5.00 ?
No, he isn't. He is going to have guitar lesson
3. what / Mum and Dad / do / at 9.00
What is Mum and Dad going to do at 9.00 ?
They are going to meet friends

★★ 5 Look at the Hiltons' diary in Exercise 4 again. Write sentences about their plans using the Present Continuous with future meaning.

1. Mum and Zoe are going shopping at ten o'clock
2. Tom is having guitar lesson at five o'clock
3. Dad isn't washing jeep at half past eight
4. Mum and Dad aren't meeting friend at ten o'clock

★★★ 6 Write two sentences about your plans for the summer. Use *be going to*. Then write predictions about these plans. Use *will*.

This summer I will go to Italy
I will swim at the swimming pool in June
I am going to eat out this summer
I am going to read this summer

English in Use

Write questions about future plans with the words below. Then write answers that are true for you. Add predictions about your plans.

1. you / sleep / at your friend's house / this weekend
Will you sleep at your friend's house this weekend ?
No, I won't
2. you / do / sport / this afternoon
Will you do sport this afternoon ?
No, I won't
3. you / go / to the shopping centre / tomorrow
Will you go to the shopping centre tomorrow ?
Yes, I will
4. what / you / have / for dinner / tonight
What will you have for dinner tonight ?
I will have fish for dinner tonight

Grammar First Conditional and Second Conditional

★ **1 Choose the correct answer.**

1. If I **will use** / **use** this plastic bag again, I **will help** / **help** the environment.
2. Unless you **will drink** / **drink** water, you **won't feel** / **don't feel** better.
3. My mum **will be** / **is** angry if I **will spend** / **spend** a lot of money.
4. If the population **will grow** / **grows**, there **will be** / **are** more cars on the road.
5. Glaciers **will melt** / **melt** if the weather **will get** / **gets** warmer.
6. Unless you **will water** / **water** the flowers, they **won't grow** / **don't grow**.

★★ **2 Choose a phrase from each group to make sentences. Use the First Conditional. Use each phrase once.**

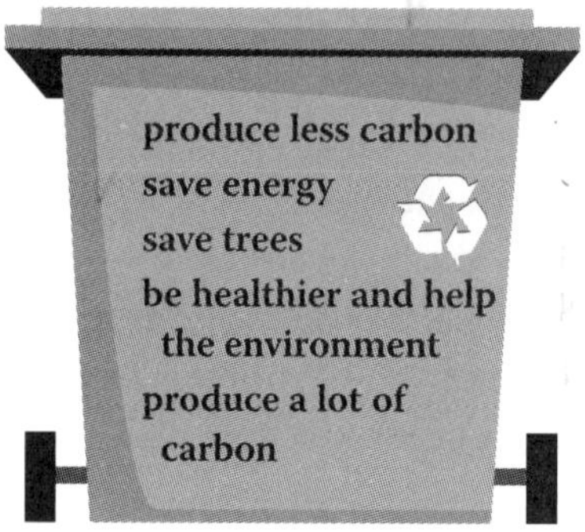

1. ....
2. ....
3. ....
4. ....
5. ....

★★ **3 Complete the sentences with the verbs in brackets. Use the Second Conditional.**

1. If you .... (take) care of the environment, the world would be a better place.
2. We .... (save) electricity if we used solar energy in our home.
3. If Mum .... (not print) all her material, she would use less paper.
4. If it were my decision, I .... (choose) to live in the forest.
5. I would clean up the forests and the beaches if I .... (be) a politician.

★★★ **4 Complete the dialogue with the correct verbs in brackets. Use the Second Conditional.**

Jim: There's a lot of traffic in the mornings. I'm always late for school.

Debbie: If I 1. .... (**be** / **take**) you, I 2. .... (**walk** / **jump**) to school.

Jim: That will take me 40 minutes!

Debbie: That's not a lot. If you 3. .... (**sleep** / **get up**) 20 minutes earlier, you 4. .... (**have** / **be**) time to walk. Also, you 5. .... (**get** / **play**) some exercise if you 6. .... (**make** / **choose**) to do this.

Jim: If I 7. .... (**hate** / **want**) to do sport, I 8. .... (**play** / **do**) basketball with my friends.

Debbie: Well, you can do that, too. If I 9. .... (**not live** / **not study**) opposite the school, I 10. .... (**have** / **be**) happy to walk with you. It's a good time to talk to friends.

Jim: I guess you're right, Debbie. Maybe I'll walk to school tomorrow.

English in Use

Complete the sentences.

First Conditional

1. If I study hard, I ....
2. I'll be happy if ....

Second Conditional

3. If my family moved to China, ...
4. I would be happier if ....

Reading

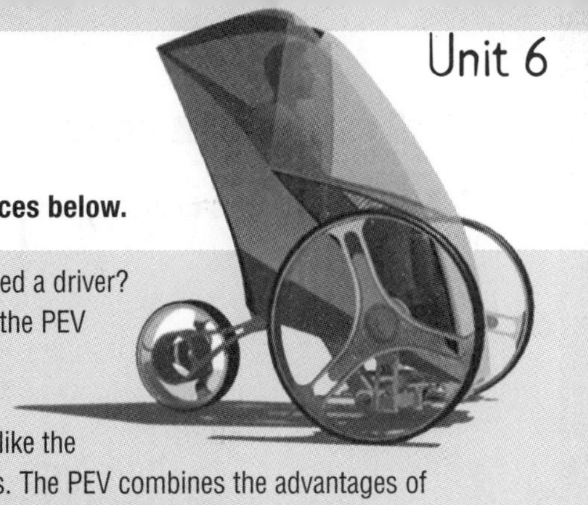

1 Read about the Persuasive Electric Vehicle (PEV). Then complete the sentences below.

The PEV

What form of transport has got three wheels, an electric engine and doesn't need a driver? It's the Persuasive Electric Vehicle (PEV). If project leader Michael Lin is right, the PEV will be one of the main forms of transport in large cities in the future.

Many people around the world are trying to find solutions to traffic and pollution from too many cars in the cities. Some are working on public transport solutions, like the 3D Express Coach. Others are working on personal electric cars with self-driving capabilities. The PEV combines the advantages of public and personal transport. It's an electric three-wheel bicycle with a roof for bad weather and space for bags and other items. PEVs won't be private vehicles – they will belong to the city – but they won't be hard to find because they will come to you.

What is the idea? Imagine you decided to spend a day in the city. If you used a bus, tram or the underground, it wouldn't take you to your precise destination. If you took your car, you would sit in traffic, and then you would also need to look for a parking place. But with a PEV, things will be different. You'll order one with a simple mobile app and it will come to you. To ride to your destination, you can choose to pedal the PEV for exercise or use the electric motor. PEVs won't travel on the road. They'll travel in bicycle lanes, so traffic won't be a problem. At the end of your journey, the PEV will drive itself to the next customer.

In the near future, People are going to test model PEVs in different places around the world. If all goes well, we will see PEVs in our cities soon.

1. The PEV's engine is ....
2. Michael Lin wants people to use PEVs in ....
3. The 3D Express Coach is an example of ....
4. A PEV is better than a bus because it will ....
5. People will order a PEV using a ....

2 Answer the questions.

1. How is a PEV different from other electric bicycles? Give two answers.
   ....
2. Why are people around the world inventing new public and personal vehicles?
   ....
3. Will people buy their own PEVs? Why?
   ....
4. Why is traffic not a problem for a PEV?
   ....
5. Will customers take PEVs to PEV stations after using them? Why?
   ....

Listening

5/11 **3 Listen to a teacher and her students talking about a school trip. How many different forms of transport are mentioned?** ....

5/11 **4 Listen again and tick (✓) the sentences true (T) or false (F). Correct the false sentences.**

	T	F
1. The purpose of the trip is to examine eco-friendly forms of transport.	.....	.....
2. The students are travelling to London by bus.	.....	.....
3. The students are going to talk to passengers at the station.	.....	.....
4. All vehicles going into London pay the congestion charge.	.....	.....
5. The students are going to ride their bikes across the River Thames.	.....	.....
6. The Thames Cable Car is an eco-friendly form of transport.	.....	.....

Thames Cable Car

Vocabulary Verbs

★ **1** **Match the signs to the correct pictures.**

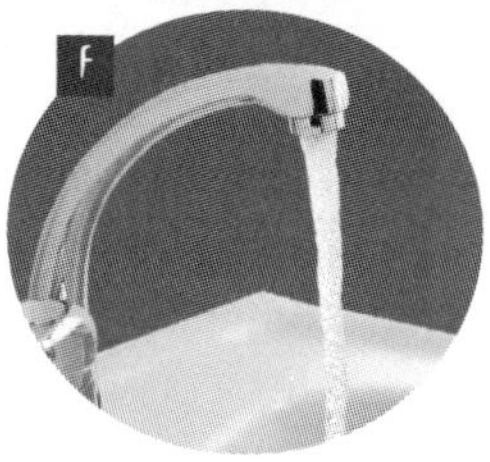

★★ **2** **There are four false sentences below. Find them and correct them by changing the verbs in bold. There may be more than one correct answer.**

1. You can **harm** plastic bags.
   ....
2. You can **damage** rubbish.
   ....
3. You can **destroy** forests.
   ....
4. You can **clean up** energy.
   ....
5. You can **protect** the environment.
   ....
6. You can **throw out** trees.
   ....

★★★ **3** **Complete the text with verbs from Exercises 1 and 2. Use each verb once. There may be more than one possible answer.**

Over a million animals die every year because they eat plastic. How does this happen? We buy food and drinks in plastic bags, boxes or bottles. Some people 1. .... their rubbish and put it in bins, but many people don't. They go to the beach or forest and leave their rubbish on the ground. This 2. .... animals because they find the plastic and think it's food. They eat it and get ill. Many animals die because of this. What can we do to save these animals? We can 3. .... our environment. We must 4. .... our rubbish. We must 5. .... our environment and the animals in it.

English in Use

Match the questions in A to the answers in B to complete the dialogue.

A	B
1. Where are you going?	..... a. I hope so. The local newspaper is going to publish an article about the project, so perhaps people will keep the forest clean.
2. What are you going to do?	..... b. To the forest.
3. Who is doing the project with you?	..... c. Yes, I do. But if everybody comes, it won't take all day.
4. Do you think it'll be difficult?	..... d. We're going to clean up the forest.
5. Will it really help?	..... e. All the students in my class.

Writing Predictions

1 Match the cause in A with the result in B. Then write the sentences using *so*, *as a result* or *for this reason*.

A

1. People will cut down more rainforests.
2. There will be too many people on Earth.
3. People will use electric cars.
4. It won't get dark.

B

..... a. People will wear sunglasses at night.
..... b. Their carbon footprint will be smaller.
..... c. People will build cities on other planets.
..... d. Many animals and plants will disappear.

1. ....
2. ....
3. ....
4. ....

2 Read the model and complete it with suitable connectors of result. There may be more than one possible answer.

The Year 2250

I think life in the year 2250 will be very different from life today. There won't be any petrol on Earth. 1. ...., people will use other forms of energy to travel.

People will use electric types of transport. They will drive electric cars with special batteries. The batteries will be quite small and people will recharge them at home. Buses, motorbikes and scooters will also be electric. There won't be any diesel trains. Trains will be electric, too. People won't have motorboats any more. They will sail yachts or use solar-powered boats during the summer months, when it's hot enough. Many people will choose to walk or ride bicycles to school and work. 2. ...., people will be fitter and healthier.

In my opinion, life in 2250 will be better than it is today. The environment will be less polluted, 3. .... Earth will be a much more pleasant and beautiful place to live.

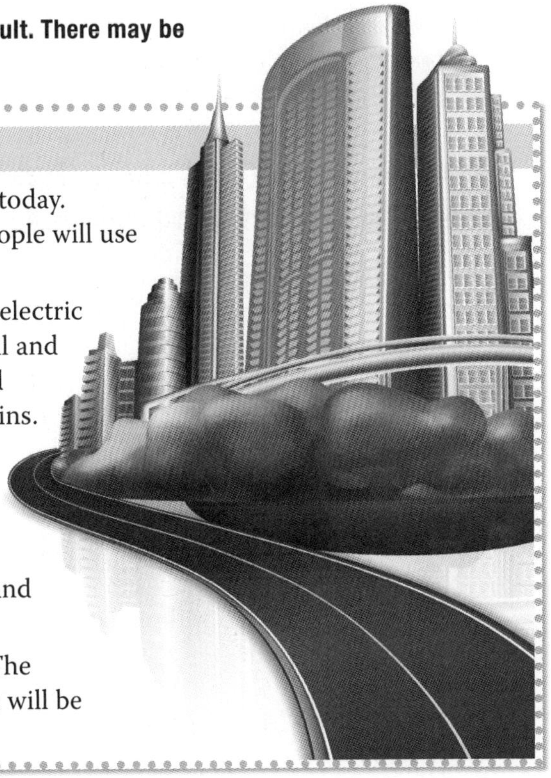

3 Choose a year in the future and one of the topics below and complete the chart.

Year: ....

holidays • transport • school • fashion • homes

Paragraph 1 What we think will happen: .... Reason: ....
Paragraph 2 Details: ....
Paragraph 3 My opinion: ....

4 Write your predictions about the future. Use the chart in Exercise 3 and the model in Exercise 2 to help you.

Check Your Progress

Vocabulary 20 points

1 Complete the sentences with the words below. (10 points)

waste • scooter • unplug • plant • recycle
yacht • tram • ferry • clean up • minivan

1. How many new trees did you .... ?
2. I took my car across the river by ....
3. We are going sailing on a ....
4. You can .... those newspapers.
5. It's important not to .... food.
6. Did you take the .... or the bus?
7. Mrs Green drives a .... because she's got six children.
8. Please .... the kitchen. It's a mess!
9. Can you .... the computer?
10. A .... has got two wheels.

2 Intro 1 2 3 4 5 6 7 8 9 Complete the sentences with a suitable word or phrase. There may be more than one possible answer. (10 points)

1. My g.................................... is 70 years old.
2. We're going to climb the c.................................... .
3. We are going sailing on a y.................................... .
4. It's c.................................... . I'll wear a sweatshirt.
5. Which animals did you see? Did you see a s.................................... ?
6. I'll t .... with my new camera.
7. We sometimes use a c.................................... in maths.
8. When I g.................................... , I'll be a doctor.
9. I can see fish in the s.................................... .
10. The j.................................... listened to the lawyer.

Grammar 30 points

3 Complete the sentences with the verbs below. Use the correct form of *will*. (5 points)

buy • not get • be • rain • not perform

1. Look at the clouds. I think it ....
2. I think I .... a new belt.
3. The test was difficult, so I .... a good mark.
4. .... it .... foggy?
5. I'm sure Tom .... in the band.

4 Choose the correct answer. (5 points)

1. I **am leaving** / **is leaving** / **are leaving** soon.
2. Eva and I **am** / **is** / **are** going to meet later.
3. He **isn't** / **aren't** / **is** travelling to the USA because he went there last year.
4. **Are they** / **They're** / **He is** studying tonight?
5. We **isn't** / **aren't** / **are** going to school tomorrow because we're going on a trip.

5 Complete the sentences with the verbs in brackets. Use the First Conditional. (5 points)

1. If the phone .... (ring), I'll answer it.
2. You .... (catch) the bus if you leave now.
3. If we win the game, we .... (get) a prize.
4. They will come to your party if you .... (invite) them.
5. Unless she .... (want) this book, I'll take it.

6 Complete the sentences with the verbs in brackets. Use the Second Conditional. (5 points)

1. If I .... (get up) ten minutes earlier, I wouldn't be late for school every day.
2. If everyone only used green energy, the air .... (be) cleaner.
3. Jack's marks .... (improve) if he studied harder.
4. If we .... (not have) electricity, we would be bored!
5. I would ride a motorbike if it .... (not be) so dangerous.

7 Intro 1 2 3 4 5 6 7 8 9 Choose the correct answer. (10 points)

1. Cars are **safer than** / **the safest** / **not as safe as** motorbikes.
2. Who **did ride** / **rode** / **ride** your bike yesterday?
3. I **move** / **was moving** / **moved** last week.
4. We always **recycles** / **recycle** / **are recycling** plastic bottles in our house.
5. They **used** / **used to** / **did** have a yacht.
6. Harry **was walking** / **were walking** / **walked** to school when he saw the accident.
7. **Much** / **A** / **Many** people drive cars.
8. If I **be** / **was** / **were** you, I would join the club.
9. They **are doing** / **is doing** / **do** judo now.
10. If you go, I **join** / **am joining** / **will join** you.

Dictation 10 points

5/12 **8 Listen and write the sentences.**

1. ....
2. ....
3. ....
4. ....
5. ....

Speaking 10 points

9 Complete the dialogue with the questions below.

Who is doing the project with you?
What are you going to do there?
Do you think it will be fun?
Where are you going? • Will it really help?

A: 1. ....

B: To the beach.

A: 2. ....

B: We are going to clean up and teach people about protecting the environment.

A: 3. ....

B: All the students in Year 8.

A: That's a lot of people!
4. ....

B: Yes, I do. But I think it will be hard work, too.

A: Yes, I agree. 5. ....

B: Of course. If people want a safe beach, they'll keep it clean.

Writing 10 points

10 Complete the sentences with connectors of result. There may be more than one possible answer.

1. There is a lot of traffic in the city centre. ...., they closed it to cars.
2. Using cars produces pollution. ...., people will use public transport.
3. I missed the bus, ... I'll walk to school today.
4. They closed the underground today. ...., more people are using buses and trams.
5. The car is in the garage, ... we'll take the bus.

Translation 20 points

11 Translate the sentences into English.

1. Si la gente tirase la basura al océano, dañaría el arrecife de coral.
....
2. Voy a ir al colegio en metro mañana.
....
3. Espero que planten más árboles en el parque.
....
4. Vamos a dar una vuelta en todoterreno este fin de semana.
....
5. Ahorrarás energía si desenchufas la televisión.
....

My Scores

Vocabulary __ / 20
Grammar __ / 30
Dictation __ / 10
Speaking __ / 10
Writing __ / 10
Translation __ / 20
My total score: __ / 100

Self-Evaluation

Do the following. Tick (✔) the box if you succeed.

1 Say ...

1. four types of transport. ☐
....
....
2. four verbs related to the environment. ☐
....
....
3. one prediction and one plan using suitable future tenses. ☐
....
....
4. a sentence using the First Conditional. ☐
....
5. a sentence using the Second Conditional. ☐
....

2 Write questions for the answers below. ☐

1. ....
To the recycling centre.
2. ....
We're going to do a recycling project.
3. ....
With my friends John and Adam.
4. ....
No, it'll be fun and easy.

3 Write three predictions for the year 2500. Use connectors of result. ☐

1. ....
2. ....
3. ....

7 Living Your Life

Vocabulary Experiences

★ **1 What can you do with the following items? Write the correct phrase under each picture.**

row a boat • go on a cruise • perform in a circus
take part in a carnival • put out a fire
take lessons in self-defence

1

....

2

....

3

....

4

....

5

....

6

....

★★ **2 Match what the people are saying to their experiences.**

1. I ran faster than all the other athletes.
2. I ate the last biscuit, but I'll say it was Tommy.
3. This is my first time on an aeroplane.
4. I'm not surprised. I didn't study hard enough for this.
5. I didn't remember to call my mum.
6. Where am I? I don't know this street.
7. This is exciting. I hope I reach the other side without falling!
8. I can't believe I gave the elephant an apple and it ate it from my hand!

Experiences

..... a. go abroad
..... b. feed a wild animal
..... c. walk a tightrope
..... d. break a record
..... e. get lost
..... f. fail a test
..... g. tell a lie
..... h. forget things

★★★ **3 Look at pictures from people's albums. Write five sentences about their experiences using phrases from Exercises 1 and 2.**

1. ....
2. ....
3. ....
4. ....
5. ....

Grammar Present Perfect Simple

*** 1 Complete the chart.**

Base Form	Past Simple	Past Participle
1. break	*broke*	*broken*
2.	went	
3.		fed
4. take		
5.	got	
6.		forgotten
7. give		
8.	grew	

**** 2 Complete the sentences with the verbs in brackets. Use the correct form of the Present Perfect Simple. Tick (✓) the sentences that are true for you.**

..... 1. I .... (not be) abroad yet.
..... 2. My friends .... (take) lessons in self-defence this year.
..... 3. I .... always .... (live) in the same house.
..... 4. Bob .... (not eat) sushi yet.
..... 5. I .... just .... (walk) a tightrope.
..... 6. My father .... never .... (forgot) my Mum's birthday.

**** 3 Complete the questions with the verbs below. Use the Present Perfect Simple. Then answer the questions according to the pictures below.**

feed • put out • get • perform

1. .... they .... the fire?
....
2. .... he .... in a circus?
....
3. .... she .... her dog?
....
4. .... they .... lost?
....

**** 4 Choose the correct answer.**

1. Have you taken the dog for a walk **yet** / **ever** / **just**?
2. I have **just** / **already** / **yet** done my homework. I did it yesterday.
3. Have you **ever** / **never** / **yet** been on a cruise?
4. She has **just** / **ever** / **yet** written me an e-mail.
5. They have **yet** / **never** / **ever** taken part in a carnival.
6. I haven't learned to drive **yet** / **already** / **never**.

***** 5 Complete the e-mail with the verbs below. Use the correct form of the Present Perfect Simple.**

take • ride • look • be • not see • row
not buy • return • not do • not rain

Hi Rick,
We're on holiday in Norfolk, in the east of England. We're having a great time. So far, we 1. .... to the coast. We 2. .... for dolphins, but we 3. .... any yet. My dad 4. .... a boat on the Norfolk Broads and I 5. .... my bike along the broads, too. My mum 6. .... much, but she's happy relaxing. I 7. .... any souvenirs yet, but I want to get you something special. The scenery here is beautiful and I 8. .... a lot of amazing photographs. I can't wait to show them to you. Luckily, it 9. .... so far. 10. .... you .... from your holiday yet?
Love,
Mandy

English in Use

Number the sentences in the correct order to make a dialogue.

..... a. I have. I've ridden a unicycle and walked a tightrope.
..... b. Have you ever performed in a circus?
..... c. Have you put out a fire in your mouth, too?
..... d. No, I haven't! That's too dangerous!
..... e. No, I haven't. How about you?

Grammar *for / since*

*** 1 Complete the sentences with *for* or *since*.**

1. She's tired. She hasn't slept .... three days.
2. I haven't spoken to my mum .... this morning.
3. It hasn't snowed here .... six years.
4. We have lived in New York .... 2011.
5. My father has worked at this hospital .... 20 years.
6. He has taken lessons in self-defence .... he was six years old.
7. She has been a detective .... over ten years.

**** 2 Complete the sentences with the Present Perfect Simple and *for* or *since*.**

1. Jim and Nick .... (perform) in a band .... they were ten.
2. She .... (paint) pictures .... she was a young girl.
3. I .... (play) the piano .... seven years.
4. .... you .... (know) Keith .... you were children?
5. Jonny .... (volunteer) at an animal hospital .... more than 10 years.
6. Mr Collins .... (not teach) in our school .... 2010.
7. We .... (not take part) in a carnival .... a long time.

**** 3 Complete the text below. Use the Present Perfect Simple and *for* or *since*.**

Sir Steve Redgrave

Sir Steve Redgrave is a famous British rower. He 1. .... (enjoy) rowing boats 2. .... he was a child. He is an excellent rower and he 3. .... (receive) many awards 4. .... his first one at the age of 17. Redgrave 5. .... (have) diabetes 6. .... over 15 years, but this 7. .... (not stop) him. He 8. .... (carry) the British flag at the opening ceremonies of two Olympic Games and he 9. .... (win) six Olympic medals. He 10. .... (break) an Olympic record, too. Redgrave thinks sport is important for all children. In 2001, he began the Steve Redgrave Fund. It 11. .... (change) the lives of thousands of children in the UK. The fund 12. .... (collect) over £5 million 13. .... 2001. Thanks to the fund, more than 100 schools 14. .... (buy) rowing machines.

**** 4 Write sentences with the phrases below. Use the Present Perfect Simple affirmative or negative and *for* or *since*. Make the sentences true for you.**

study English • use the Internet • go to the beach • buy new clothes • visit relatives

1. ....
2. ....
3. ....
4. ....
5. ....

English in Use

Put the words in the correct order to write questions. Use the Present Perfect Simple. Then answer them about yourself.

1. at / how long / you / this school / be
   ....?
   ....
2. you / know / how long / your best friend
   ....?
   ....
3. live / how long / you / in this country
   ....?
   ....
4. how long / have / a computer / you
   ....?
   ....

Reading

1 Read about Bruce Parry. Then tick (✓) the activities mentioned in the text.

Bruce Parry is a TV presenter and an adventurer. He has organised and led over 15 expeditions and made TV programmes about his adventures. He has travelled across deserts, jungles and mountains. He has taken part in carnivals, has caught wild animals and has even eaten breakfast with cannibals!

In 2002, Parry made his first TV programme in Papua New Guinea. He climbed the Puncak Mandala, a mountain there. Since then, Parry has made many more interesting TV programmes. He has taken children to Borneo to work with monkeys and to Namibia to work with black rhinos. Parry has also lived with isolated tribes in countries all over the world including Brazil, India, Ethiopia and Mongolia. He spent a month with each tribe and learned how to survive with his new friends. In 2008, Parry travelled through Peru and Brazil along the Amazon River and saw how people are destroying rainforests and how this affects the lives of the Amazonian tribes there.

Parry has also walked to the South Pole and more recently he has travelled to the Arctic. The people there have told him how their lives have changed. He has also learned that climate change is a real problem in that region and that it is happening more and more quickly.

Why are Parry's programmes so popular? Many people enjoy learning about the exotic places and cultures on his programmes. Parry also teaches people about the extraordinary lives of different tribes around the world. For now, Parry has stopped travelling. "I'd quite like to start a community and put into practice the things that I've learnt," he said.

..... 1. planned trips to different countries
..... 2. performed in circuses
..... 3. met cannibals
..... 4. climbed a glacier
..... 5. made TV programmes with children
..... 6. learned new languages

2 Answer the questions.

1. What does Bruce Parry do? ....
2. Why did Parry take children to Namibia? ....
3. How long did Parry live with each tribe? ....
4. Why are the lives of the Amazonian tribes changing? ....
5. What did Parry learn in the Arctic? ....
6. Why do people enjoy Parry's programmes? ....

Listening

5/13 **3 Listen to a conversation between a photographer and his friend. Then match A to B to make sentences.**

A	B
1. The Verona Carnival	..... a. is famous for its sophisticated masks.
2. The Venice Carnival	..... b. is in London.
3. The Lan Kwai Fong Street Carnival	..... c. is famous for its excellent food.
4. The Notting Hill Carnival	..... d. is a celebration to remember a historical event.

5/13 **4 Listen again and complete the sentences.**

1. Dan has been out of his country .... times over the last year.
2. The Verona Carnival started about .... years ago.
3. The Verona Carnival takes place in the ....
4. Dan describes .... carnivals in Italy.
5. There are more than .... million visitors at the Venice Carnival each year.
6. Dan .... in Venice because all the streets look the same.
7. The Lan Kwai Fong Street Carnival is in ....

Vocabulary Adjectives

* **1 Write the correct emotion under each picture.**

proud • exhausted • frightened • upset • angry • surprised

** **2 Circle the two words with similar meanings.**

1. rude	ridiculous	silly
2. unique	surprised	unusual
3. exhausted	frightened	tired
4. upset	nasty	unpleasant
5. risky	dangerous	worried

*** **3 Choose the correct answer.**

1. Kim isn't my best friend any more. She was really **nasty** / **silly** / **worried** to me today.
2. Please don't walk the tightrope. It looks **unique** / **risky** / **ridiculous**.
3. I'm talking. It's very **risky** / **unpleasant** / **rude** of you to interrupt me.
4. You can't wear a summer dress on a rainy day! Don't be **ridiculous** / **unpleasant** / **frightened**!
5. Jake hasn't come home from school yet. I'm **upset** / **risky** / **worried** about him.

*** **4 Complete the sentences to show you understand the words in bold. Make them true for you.**

1. I'm sometimes **frightened** when ....
2. It's **rude** to ....
3. The most **ridiculous** thing I've done is ....
4. I get **upset** when ....
5. It's **risky** to ....
6. I'm sometimes **exhausted** after ....

English in Use

Complete the dialogue with the words below.

really worried • wanted to do that • such a risky thing • idea of fun • try it

Sam: Have you ever been cliff diving?

May: No, I haven't, but I've always [1] ....

Sam: Really? That's not my [2] .... Why would you do [3] .... ?

May: I like extreme sports. I'd love to [4] .... , but I think my parents would be [5] ....

Writing A review of a TV programme

1 Rewrite the sentences to include the adjectives and adverbs above each sentence.

ridiculous • quickly • enormous

1. *Wipeout* is a TV game show. Participants must complete an obstacle course to win.

....

well • fantastic • talented

2. *The Voice* is a TV show for singers. Singers must sing to reach the finals.

....

2 Read the review of a TV programme and complete it with the adjectives and adverbs below.

young • suddenly • quite • frightened • nasty • unique

CHANNEL SURFING

TV Programme Review

Pretty Little Liars

Pretty Little Liars is a [1] .... TV drama programme about four best friends – Spencer, Hanna, Aria and Emily. Many [2] .... people have enjoyed watching it since it started in 2010.

In the first episode, the girls' friend, Alison, dies [3] ...., but her friends don't know how. After Alison dies, the girls frequently receive strange messages from "A". Sometimes these unusual messages are [4] .... and the secret writer knows all about the girls. The friends are worried and they try to solve the mystery.

I don't know who "A" is or who killed Alison, but I think *Pretty Little Liars* is a fantastic TV programme. Sometimes it's [5] .... scary and then I'm too [6] .... to watch it on my own!

3 Imagine a TV programme and complete the chart below about your imaginary TV programme.

Paragraph 1
Name of programme: ....
Type of programme: ....

Paragraph 2
Description of programme: ....
....
....

Paragraph 3
My opinion: ....

4 Write a review about your imaginary TV programme. Use the chart in Exercise 3 and the model in Exercise 2 to help you.

Check Your Progress

Vocabulary 20 points

1 Match A to B to make phrases. (5 points)

A		B
1. feed	......	a. a cruise
2. take lessons in	......	b. a carnival
3. break	......	c. a wild animal
4. take part in	......	d. self-defence
5. go on	......	e. a record

2 Complete the sentences with the words below. (5 points)

unpleasant • risky • ridiculous • surprised frightened

1. The film was scary, but I wasn't ....
2. The weather was .... – wet and windy.
3. We made breakfast for our parents this morning. They were really ....
4. You look .... in that old dress.
5. Don't climb that tree. It's too ....

3 Intro 1 2 3 4 5 6 7 8 9 Add a word to each group. (10 points)

1. destroy • waste • ....
2. ferry • scooter • ....
3. witness • lawyer • ....
4. swamp • glacier • ....
5. honest • brave • ....
6. stapler • paintbrush • ....
7. peaceful • pleasant • ....
8. nephew • aunt • ....
9. rain • windy • ....
10. old • fat • ....

Grammar 30 points

4 Put the words below in the correct order to make sentences. Use the Present Perfect Simple. (10 points)

1. a test / Becky / yet / not fail / .
....
2. already / they / that film / see / .
....
3. your / I / birthday / never / forget / .
....
4. you / take part / in a carnival / ever / ?
....
5. just / a new car / buy / your mum / ?
....

5 Complete the sentences with the verbs below and *for* or *since*. Use the Present Perfect Simple. (10 points)

play • not be • not rain • take • live

1. I .... to the cinema .... about a year.
2. Harry .... lessons in self-defence .... he was five years old.
3. My father .... the guitar .... 1990.
4. It .... in London .... last Tuesday.
5. My aunt and uncle .... in New York .... ten years.

6 Intro 1 2 3 4 5 6 7 8 9 Complete the sentences with the correct form of the verb or adjective in brackets. (10 points)

1. I .... (take) a nap at 3.00 yesterday.
2. .... you usually .... (play) the piano in the afternoon?
3. I .... (send) her a text message right now.
4. You aren't as good as I am at skiing. You ski .... (success) I do.
5. If I were you, I .... (not go) there.
6. .... you .... (have) a party next week?
7. Rick .... (have got) a new jacket.
8. Your blue dress is .... (long) your green one. It reaches the floor!
9. If it .... (not rain) tomorrow, we'll go hiking.
10. My dad .... (perform) in a band since he was a teenager.

Dictation 10 points

5/14 **7 Listen and write the sentences.**

1. ....
2. ....
3. ....
4. ....
5. ....

Speaking 10 points

8 Complete the dialogue with the phrases below.

my idea of fun • love to try that • it sounds too too frightened • always wanted to

A: Have you ever taken part in a carnival?

B: No, I haven't. But I'd 1. ....

A: I've 2. .... do that, too. I also want to perform in a circus.

B: Really? That's not 3. ....

A: Why? You can ride horses backwards and walk a tightrope.

B: 4. .... risky to me. I'd be 5. .... to do that!

Writing 10 points

9 Complete the sentences with the adjectives and adverbs in brackets.

1. The .... athlete received his medal .... (proudly, amazing)
2. The .... painter paints .... (talented, beautifully)
3. The .... man rowed across the .... sea. (rough, brave)
4. The .... students left the school .... (quickly, excited)
5. The .... dancer performed .... (excellently, lovely)

Translation 20 points

10 Translate the sentences into English.

1. No nos hemos olvidado de tu cumpleaños.
   ....
2. Él ha actuado en un circo desde que era un niño.
   ....
3. ¿Tus padres han estado preocupados por ti alguna vez?
   ....
4. Nunca me he perdido.
   ....
5. Nunca he dado de comer a un animal salvaje porque tengo demasiado miedo.
   ....

My Scores

Vocabulary __ / 20
Grammar __ / 30
Dictation __ / 10
Speaking __ / 10
Writing __ / 10
Translation __ / 20
My total score: __ / 100

Self-Evaluation

Do the following. Tick (✓) the box if you succeed.

1 Say …

1. four experiences. ☐
   ....
   ....
2. four adjectives. ☐
   ....
   ....
3. one sentence about something interesting you've done and one about something you haven't done but would like to. ☐
   ....
   ....
4. one sentence with *for* and one with *since* in the Present Perfect Simple. ☐
   ....
   ....

2 Write one positive response and one negative response to each of the questions below. ☐

1. Would you like to go bungee jumping?
   ....
   ....
2. Do you want to go on a hike in the mountains?
   ....
   ....

3 Write three sentences from a review of a TV programme. Use adjectives and adverbs. ☐

1. ....
2. ....
3. ....

8 Healthy Choices

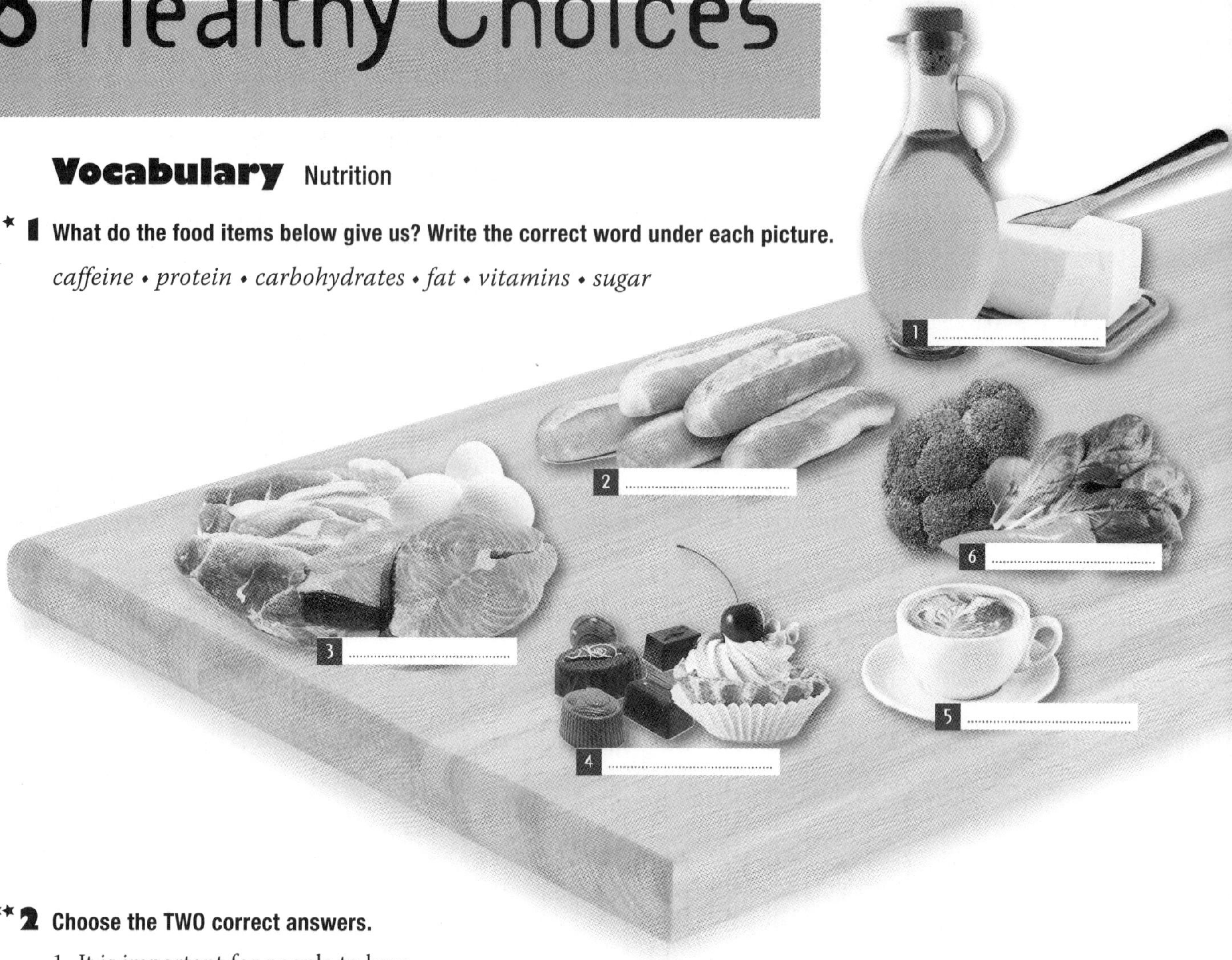

Vocabulary Nutrition

★ **1 What do the food items below give us? Write the correct word under each picture.**

caffeine • protein • carbohydrates • fat • vitamins • sugar

★★ **2 Choose the TWO correct answers.**

1. It is important for people to have ..... .
   a. a healthy lifestyle b. a balanced diet c. processed food
2. Sweets, crisps and chips are ..... .
   a. liquids b. snacks c. junk food
3. Cola and fizzy drinks are ..... .
   a. vitamins b. unhealthy drinks c. liquids
4. There is often unhealthy fat in ..... .
   a. junk food b. caffeine c. processed food
5. Crisps and pizza have got a lot of ..... in them.
   a. calories b. protein c. salt
6. Athletes need ..... .
   a. good nutrition b. carbohydrates c. caffeine

★★★ **3 Look at what Lynn ate yesterday. Write at least five sentences about what is healthy or unhealthy about it. Use as many words from Exercises 1 and 2 as you can.**

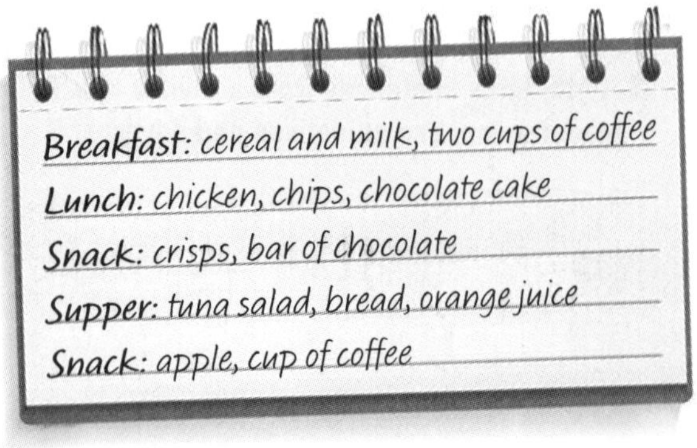

1. ....
2. ....
3. ....
4. ....
5. ....

Grammar Modals

★ 1 Complete the sentences with the modals below.

can • can't • could • couldn't • must • mustn't

1. The baby .... sleep because there was too much noise.
2. We .... stand up when the teacher walks into the room. It's a school rule.
3. .... you come to my house tomorrow?
4. You .... run around the swimming pool. It's dangerous.
5. My grandmother .... swim well when she was young.
6. You're too young. You .... drive.

★ 2 Write sentences with the words below and the correct form of *should*.

1. you / visit / the beautiful Black Forest / in Germany / .
   ....
2. we / eat / lots of junk food / .
   ....
3. I / make potatoes or rice / for dinner / ?
   ....
4. I / drink / too many cups of coffee / every day / .
   ....
5. Lisa / take / vitamin C / ?
   ....

★★ 3 Choose the correct answer to complete the text.

Interesting Food Facts

Broccoli [1] **should / can / must** reduce the risk of cancer. It is one of the healthiest vegetables and we [2] **should / must / could** include it in our diet.

Teenagers [3] **mustn't / couldn't / should** eat no more than a teaspoon of salt a day. We get 75% of the salt we need from everyday foods like bread and cereal, so we [4] **couldn't / can't / shouldn't** add salt to food.

Some people are allergic to specific foods. They [5] **should / mustn't / couldn't** eat these foods because they [6] **can / must / should** die from them.

★★ 4 Complete the sentences with the correct form of *can*, *could*, *should* or *must*.

1. .... you walk when you were two years old?
2. .... you write text messages quickly?
3. We .... complete our nutrition projects by Thursday.
4. .... we have fish or meat for dinner? What do you think?
5. People .... drink a lot of liquid on hot days.
6. We .... bring expensive games to school. It's a rule.
7. My brother is eighteen. He .... drive a car now.
8. I .... swim last year, but now I can.
9. The swimming pool is closed. We .... go swimming today.
10. You .... eat too much sugar. It's unhealthy.

★★★ 5 Rewrite the sentences. Use suitable modals.

1. Try not to drink coffee before going to sleep.
   ....
2. It's a good idea to eat fruit every day.
   ....
3. Some people are allergic to fish.
   ....
4. It's necessary for babies to drink milk every few hours.
   ....
5. It's possible to find a lot of delicious fruit in Thailand.
   ....

English in Use

Complete the sentences about nutrition. Use your own words or words from below.

vitamins • fats • sugar • caffeine • a balanced diet unhealthy food • calories

1. You mustn't ....
2. You shouldn't ....
3. You must ....
4. You can ....
5. You should ....

Grammar Modals

★ **1 Look at the pictures and write sentences with the words below. Use the correct form of *have to*.**

1. 

he / repair / his tyre

....

2. 

she / use / a knife and fork

....

3. 

you / wear / a swimsuit / at the beach

....

4. 

they / drink / some water

....

★ **2 Rewrite the sentences you wrote in Exercise 1. Use the correct form of *need to*.**

1. ....
2. ....
3. ....
4. ....

★ **3 Choose the TWO correct answers.**

1. It's late. We ..... leave soon.
   a. have to
   b. need to
   c. can
2. Luke is allergic to mangoes. He ..... even touch them.
   a. doesn't have to
   b. can't
   c. mustn't
3. Paul ..... have dessert after every meal. It's unhealthy.
   a. must
   b. doesn't need to
   c. doesn't have to
4. There's a problem using this recipe. I ..... find any bananas or strawberries at the supermarket.
   a. couldn't
   b. shouldn't
   c. can't
5. You can have some chocolate cake. You ..... eat healthy food all the time!
   a. don't have to
   b. don't need to
   c. mustn't

★★★ **4 Choose the correct answer.**

PLEASE PLAY!

Today, one in three children in the UK is obese. This is a serious health problem. Obesity 1. **has to / should / can** cause diseases like diabetes. Children 2. **have to / shouldn't / must** eat too much junk food or food with lots of fat. These are very unhealthy. Also, they 3. **need to / don't have to / couldn't** play outside and do sport frequently. But today, children 4. **must / can / have to** spend hours at home without getting bored. They watch television and surf the Internet. TP Activity Toys is a company in the UK. It has produced playground equipment for over 50 years. Now, they 5. **have to / mustn't / can't** make equipment for bigger, heavier children because so many children are obese. Twenty-five years ago, for example, slides 6. **can / must / could** be 21 cm wide, but today, they 7. **have to / could / can** be 32 cm wide, so the children 8. **can / must / have to** go down them. The question is: How 9. **do we have to / can we / do we need to** attract more children to playgrounds? Maybe we 10. **must / have to / should** invent new types of playgrounds, not just ones with bigger equipment.

English in Use

Complete the dialogue with the words and phrases below.

ride my bike • can meet • should • need to stop basketball • have to do

A: Have you got a healthy lifestyle?

B: Yes, I have. I eat a balanced diet. But I 1. .... also 2. .... to school every day and I 3. .... more sport after school. How about you?

A: I usually play 4. .... in the park after school. That's good, but I 5. .... eating so much junk food.

B: Listen! Maybe we 6. .... in the park and play a game of basketball?

A: Sure! Great idea!

Reading

1 Read the article about junk food adverts. Then complete the sentences below.

Junk Food and SPORT

We all know junk food is unhealthy and we shouldn't eat it often. So why do we continue to buy it? One reason is because a lot of people enjoy it, but another is because junk-food companies spend millions of pounds each year trying to sell us their products – with adverts. You can't spend a day without seeing or hearing about a junk-food product or snack on TV, the Internet, the radio or on posters. According to these adverts, we need to have junk food every day! Junk-food companies even advertise their products at sports competitions around the world like the Olympic Games and the World Cup.

Today, one in three children and one in four adults in the UK is obese. The Academy of Medical Royal Colleges thinks that companies must stop advertising at sports competitions. At competitions, people's attention is on the athletes, but they can see the adverts around the stadium. Thousands of people watch the competition at the stadium or on TV and they make a connection between junk food and top athletes. When they see junk food connected to sport, it seems healthier, psychologists say.

No one has investigated the relationship between junk-food adverts at sports competitions and obesity yet. However, psychologist Dr Sheila Keegan believes these adverts can have a direct impact on obesity.

So, will junk-food companies continue to advertise at the Olympic Games? They probably will, because they've got contracts with the International Olympic Committee. But, hopefully, this will change. People need to have healthy lifestyles, so we should advertise good nutrition at sports competitions and not junk food!

1. Junk-food companies create adverts to make us ....
2. We see and hear adverts every day on ....
3. At sports competitions, people watch .... and see .... at the same time.
4. Junk-food companies and the International Olympic Committee have got ....

2 Tick (✓) the sentences true (T) or false (F). Which words or expressions in the text helped you to decide?

	T	F
1. People buy junk food because it tastes good to them.	.....	.....
2. There are more obese children than adults in the UK.	.....	.....
3. When people see junk-food adverts at sporting competitions, they think it's good nutrition.	.....	.....
4. Scientists have done experiments on the connection between advertising junk food at sports competitions and obesity.	.....	.....
5. There will probably be advertisements for junk food at the next Olympics.	.....	.....

Listening

5/15 **3 Listen to Jake and his mother talking about the Mediterranean diet. Tick (✓) the decisions Jake's mother has made.**

They are going to ..... .

..... 1. eat a balanced diet
..... 2. eat a big meal for dinner
..... 3. eat more fresh vegetables
..... 4. eat more meat
..... 5. use more olive oil

5/15 **4 Listen again and match A to B.**

A	B
1. Greek salad	..... a. must walk to school now.
2. Jake's family	..... b. usually eat a big meal in the evening.
3. Olive oil	..... c. has got healthy fat.
4. People eating the Mediterranean diet	..... d. are usually healthier.
5. Jake	..... e. has got vegetables, olives and cheese.

Vocabulary Fitness

★ **1 Write the words under the correct pictures.**

gym • lose weight • team • track • muscle

1 ....

2 ....

3 ....

4 ....

5 ....

★★ **2 Match A to B to make phrases connected to fitness. Then use the phrases to complete the sentences below.**

A	B
1. get	..... a. air
2. fitness	..... b. fit
3. fresh	..... c. weight
4. gain	..... d. trainer

1. My .... teaches me how to exercise safely.
2. It's a lovely day. Let's go for a walk and get some ....
3. I don't want to .... , so I eat 2,200 calories a day.
4. If you exercise every day, you will .... very quickly.

★★ **3 Complete the puzzle according to the clues below.**

Across →

2. This person helps you eat a balanced diet.
4. You run on this.
6. When an athlete gets this, he or she can't compete.
7. an organ in our body

Down ↓

1. These are in your body. They can break.
3. You must do this to stay fit.
5. a place to go and do exercise

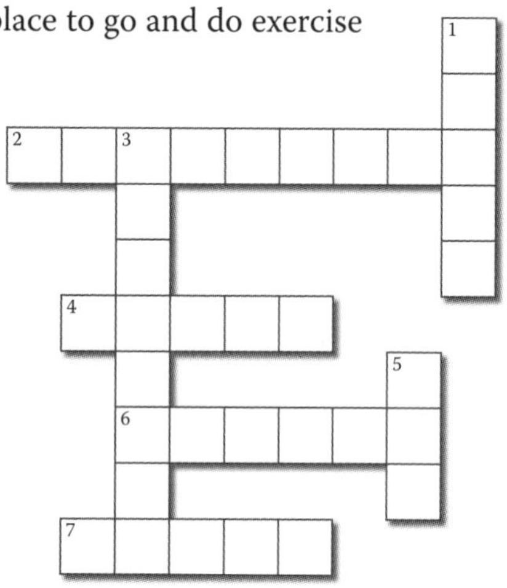

★★★ **4 Write an advert for a gym. Use as many words as you can from Exercises 1, 2 and 3.**

....

....

....

....

....

....

English in Use

Write advice for each of the problems below.

1. I'm always hungry, but I don't want to eat snacks between meals.

....

2. I love sweet drinks, but I know they aren't good for my teeth.

....

3. I want to get fit, but I don't really like sport.

....

4. I can't stop eating pizza and hamburgers, but I know they're not healthy.

....

Writing A news report

1 Complete the sentences with prepositions.

1. Tim Chambers scored the first goal .... the match .... Saturday.
2. Kenton Juniors won the cup .... the second time .... four years.
3. We were winning .... half-time, but we lost the game .... the end.
4. Oli Williams played .... Ryan Todd .... the first tennis match .... the season.
5. Riverside's score went .... 42 .... 61 .... only seven minutes!

2 Read the news report and complete it with correct prepositions.

Sports News 20th January, 2016

Fifteen Year Old Wins Youth Triathlon

Nick Peters has won our 2016 Youth Triathlon 1. .... the first time, making him the youngest winner ever. Last Sunday, hundreds 2. .... people watched the competition.

Two hundred athletes started the race with a 400-metre swim. Nick finished that part of the race 3. .... second place behind Lee Masters. While Lee was getting on his bike 4. .... the second part 5. .... the race, he fell and hurt his arm.

Nick moved 6. .... second 7. .... first place in the 15-km bike race. Nick has loved running since he was a young child and he completed the 5-km run 8. .... a record 22 minutes. The crowd cheered loudly while he was crossing the finishing line. He said, "I've never run so fast in my life!"

3 Complete the chart below about a marathon race with your own ideas.

Paragraph 1
What happened: ....
When: *on Sunday*
Where: *in London*

Paragraph 2
The sequence of events:
1. ....
2. ....
3. ....

Paragraph 3
What happened in the end: ....
....

4 Write a news report about the race. Use the chart in Exercise 3 and the model in Exercise 2 to help you.

Check Your Progress

Vocabulary 20 points

1 Answer the questions with the words below. (10 points)

fitness trainer • track • exercise • carbohydrates gain weight • dietician • muscles • fat • calories vitamins

1. Who can help people to eat a balanced diet? ....
2. Which parts of the body help us to move? ....
3. What can you find in oil? ....
4. What can you find in pasta, bread and potatoes? ....
5. What has every food got? ....
6. What can you find in orange juice? ....
7. Who often works in a gym? ....
8. What do very thin people sometimes need to do? ....
9. Where can you run? ....
10. What can you do at a gym? ....

2 Intro 1 2 3 4 5 6 7 8 9 Write the correct words. (10 points)

1. Your sister's daughter: n .... c .....
2. You can draw circles with it: c .... p ....
3. Smaller than a meal: s ....
4. To create something new: d ..... v ....
5. The opposite of *rough*: c .... m
6. A small river: st ....
7. A weapon: k .... e
8. This type of transport transfers large items on land: l .... y
9. Unusual: u .... q ....
10. Water, oil and coffee are these: l .... s

Grammar 30 points

3 Complete the sentences with the correct form of *can*, *could*, *should* or *must*. (10 points)

1. You .... eat vegetables every day because they give you vitamins.
2. I .... talk now. I'm too busy.
3. People .... eat too much salt.
4. .... you run fast?
5. You .... steal from shops.
6. I .... do it. It was too hard.
7. It's late. I .... go right now!
8. .... I invite Dan? Is that a good idea?
9. He .... speak Chinese excellently.
10. .... you read when you were five?

4 Choose the TWO correct answers. (10 points)

1. **Does Lily need to** / **Could Lily** / **Lily should** help you?
2. Harry **has to** / **must** / **can** wear his uniform for school every day.
3. It's early. You **mustn't** / **don't have to** / **don't need to** hurry.
4. Tom is good at surfing. He **should** / **has to** / **can** teach us how to surf.
5. Lisa **doesn't have to** / **must** / **needs to** leave right now because the shop is closing.

5 Intro 1 2 3 4 5 6 7 8 9 Complete the sentences with one word for each space. There may be more than one possible answer. (10 points)

1. If I .... you, I'd exercise every day.
2. I've never .... here before.
3. We .... drive to the cinema if it rains.
4. Cheetahs are faster .... lions.
5. I'm tired. I think I .... go to bed early tonight.
6. I .... swim when I was seven years old.
7. My mum .... drink fizzy drinks because they aren't healthy.
8. We are .... to school right now.
9. There .... any people at the beach yesterday because it was raining.
10. Milly .... studying at 9.00 last night.

Dictation 10 points

5 16 6 Listen and write the sentences.

1. ....
2. ....
3. ....
4. ....
5. ....

Speaking 10 points

7 Complete the dialogues with the phrases below.

why don't you • it's a good idea
You can either • eat fruit instead
the best thing for you is to join a gym

A: What should I eat for a quick breakfast?
B: 1. .... have some cottage cheese with fruit or muesli with yoghurt.
A: I often eat unhealthy snacks.
B: You should 2. ....
A: I haven't got time to exercise.
B: 3. .... start walking instead of taking the bus?
A: I don't exercise because I'm scared of getting an injury.
B: 4. .... and ask a fitness trainer to help you exercise safely.
A: I'm a vegetarian. What should I eat for protein?
B: I think 5. .... to talk to a dietician.

Writing 10 points

8 Complete the sentences with the correct prepositions.

1. The crowd cheered when the Rangers scored the final points .... the game.
2. Riverside School received the trophy .... the first time.
3. .... the end, the Rangers won the game.
4. Mel Taylor scored six points .... a row.
5. Georgetown was playing .... Kentontown.

Translation 20 points

9 Translate the sentences into English.

1. No debes engordar antes de la carrera.
....
2. No puedo jugar porque tengo una lesión.
....
3. Los atletas no deberían comer grasas poco sanas.
....
4. Tienes que hacer ejercicio porque es bueno para el corazón.
....
5. Los dietistas pueden ayudar a la gente a llevar un estilo de vida saludable.
....

My Scores

Vocabulary __ / 20
Grammar __ / 30
Dictation __ / 10
Speaking __ / 10
Writing __ / 10
Translation __ / 20
My total score: __ / 100

Self-Evaluation

Do the following. Tick (✔) the box if you succeed.

1 Say ...

1. four words connected to nutrition. ☐
....
....
2. four words connected to fitness. ☐
....
....
3. something you couldn't do when you were six years old but can do now, something you have to do today, something you don't need to do today, something you should do soon, and something you mustn't do today. ☐
....
....
....
....
....

2 Write possible solutions to the following problems. ☐

1. It's hard for me to wake up in the morning.
....
2. I find exercise boring.
....
3. I want to exercise but I haven't got enough money to join a gym.
....

3 Write three sentences from a news report. Use different prepositions. ☐

1. ....
2. ....
3. ....

9 Shopping Spree

Vocabulary Fashion

★ **1 Circle the words in the puzzle. Then write them under the correct pictures.**

1 ....

2 ....

3 ....

4 ....

5 ....

6 ....

7 ....

8 ....

9 ....

10 ....

s	r	t	w	w	a	t	c	h	n
u	c	b	w	a	b	w	a	d	e
n	t	k	r	w	l	a	h	h	c
g	i	b	l	a	a	l	o	d	k
l	g	t	e	a	c	l	e	o	l
a	h	i	g	l	n	e	d	t	a
s	t	b	a	d	t	t	l	a	c
s	s	h	o	o	d	i	e	e	e
e	e	a	r	r	i	n	g	s	t
s	i	g	h	a	n	d	b	a	g

★★ **2 Match the definitions in A to the words in B.**

A		B
1. You put your mobile phone in it.	.....	a. purse
2. A woman puts her money in this.	.....	b. make-up
3. This adds colour to your face.	.....	c. nail varnish
4. You wear this on your finger.	.....	d. phone case
5. It's a type of paint. You use it for a manicure.	.....	e. ring

★★ **3 Complete the puzzle according to the clues. Then find the hidden word according to the numbers in the puzzle.**

a. It's sometimes got a diamond.
b. You can see the time here.
c. It's like a sweater with a hat.
d. You can put your purse in it.
e. It's jewellery. You don't wear it on your hand, arm or ear.

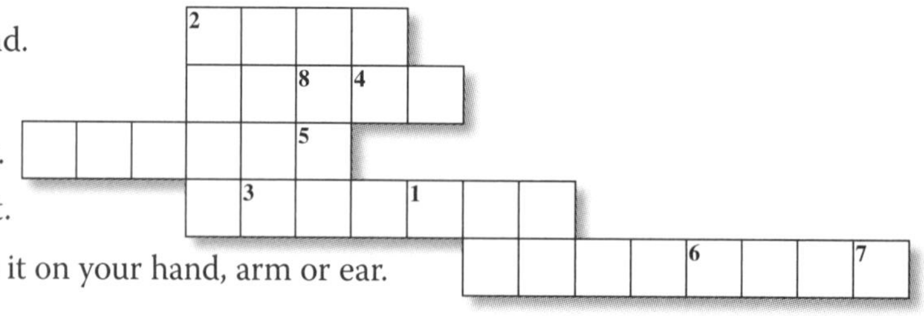

The hidden word is ....
1 2 3 4 5 6 7 8

★★★ **4 Write sentences with words from Exercises 1 and 2. Use at least two of the words in each sentence.**

1. *I keep my purse in my handbag.*
2. ....
3. ....
4. ....
5. ....

Grammar Reported speech

* **1 Choose the correct answer in each sentence in reported speech.**

1. "I can give you a pink phone case," Rose told Laura.
   Rose told Laura that she **could give / can give** her a pink phone case.
2. "I don't need a green handbag," said Mum.
   Mum said that she **don't need / didn't need** a green handbag.
3. "The children will have lots of fun," said Dad.
   Dad said that the children **will have / would have** lots of fun.
4. "Ben is waiting for you at the shoe shop now," Greg told Tony.
   Greg told Tony that Ben **was waiting / is waiting** for him at the shoe shop **there / then**.
5. "I'll phone you," Rob said to Emily.
   Rob told Emily that **he / I** would phone **you / her**.
6. "I want this hoodie in blue," Paul told the shop assistant.
   Paul told the shop assistant that he wanted **this / that** hoodie in blue.
7. "John will probably buy it next week," Mel said.
   Mel said that John would probably buy it **the following week / the previous week**.

** **2 Complete the sentences in reported speech with the words and phrases below.**

wore • was wearing • couldn't wear • would wear bought • could buy • were buying • that day that • there • the next day • then

1. "I'm wearing a new belt today," said Rick.
   Rick said that he .... a new belt ....
2. "You can buy great phone cases here," said Ken.
   Ken said that we .... great phone cases ....
3. "I'll wear my new sunglasses at the beach tomorrow," said Amy.
   Amy said that she .... her new sunglasses at the beach ....
4. "We are buying a watch now," said Michael.
   Michael said that they .... a watch ....
5. "I always buy make-up in this shop," said Kelly.
   Kelly said that she always .... make-up in .... shop.
6. "I wear different earrings every day," said Mel.
   Mel said that she .... different earrings every day.
7. "I can't wear nail varnish at school," said Lauren.
   Lauren said that she .... nail varnish at school.

** **3 Complete the sentences with what the teenagers said. Use reported speech.**

1. "We can't wear earrings at school." – TONY
   Tony said that .... earrings at school.
2. "Fashions will change next year." – AMANDA
   Amanda said that fashions ....
3. "I'm studying fashion design this year." – BRITNEY
   Britney said that she .... fashion design .... year.
4. "I don't save much of my pocket money." – AL
   Al said that he .... much of .... pocket money.
5. "These necklaces and rings look old." – KIM
   Kim said that .... necklaces and rings .... old.

*** **4 Read what Melanie, a teacher, told a reporter about her students and fashion. Then complete what she said in reported speech.**

1. My students don't wear uniforms at school.
2. They can wear jeans and hoodies. They can also wear jewellery.
3. They're learning about fashion in their art class this month.
4. They are working on projects about clothes from different historical periods.
5. The students love these lessons.
6. I'll show you some of their projects.

1. *The teacher said that* ....
2. ....
3. ....
4. ....
5. ....
6. ....

English in Use

Read what each person said to Emma in direct speech. Then complete each sentence in reported speech.

1. "I never wear a watch," said Jack.
   Jack said that ....
2. "I can make a bracelet for Anne," said Sue.
   Sue said that ....
3. "Maybe we'll see the fashion show at the shopping centre," said Emily.
   Emily said that ....

Grammar Gerunds and infinitives

* **1 Complete the sentences with the words below. Use gerunds.**

listen • wear • swim • read • drive

1. My English teacher recommends .... a book every month.
2. Bill likes .... his sunglasses all the time – even at night!
3. I can't stand .... to jazz music.
4. My grandmother is afraid of .... a car.
5. .... in the sea is my dad's favourite activity.

** **2 Complete the sentences with suitable verbs of your own. Use infinitives. Then tick (✔) the sentence which you can also complete with a gerund.**

..... 1. My younger sister is learning .... a bike.

..... 2. I plan .... to exotic places like Madagascar and Thailand one day.

..... 3. I was surprised .... my friends in the park.

..... 4. Mark likes .... on the track near his house.

..... 5. I want .... a lot of money in the future.

** **3 Choose the correct answer.**

1. I can't stand ..... for a swimsuit!
   a. shopping b. to shop
2. Paul keeps ..... his watch at home.
   a. leaving b. to leave
3. You seem ..... a blue T-shirt every day.
   a. wearing b. to wear
4. It's easy ..... nice clothes on these websites.
   a. finding b. to find
5. Do you suggest ..... for earrings for my mum in this shop?
   a. looking b. to look
6. ..... to music is so relaxing.
   a. Dancing b. To dance
7. He's afraid ..... in the rough sea.
   a. surfing b. to surf
8. Are you thinking about ..... a new phone?
   a. getting b. to get

*** **4 Choose the correct answers to complete the text.**

Cornelia's Jewels

The year is 155 BC in Rome. Cornelia is a Roman noblewoman. Today, she and her two sons, Caius and Tiberius, are preparing [1.] **to visit / visiting** an important woman. She is Cornelia's friend and she's lucky [2.] **to be / being** very rich. Her house is enormous and she enjoys [3.] **to wear / wearing** beautiful clothes. Everyone is sitting in the garden. They spend time [4.] **to talk / talking** happily. Then Cornelia's friend decides [5.] **to bring / bringing** a big box outside. She opens it and shows them the jewellery inside the box. Cornelia and her sons see many gold necklaces and beautiful earrings and bracelets. Caius is surprised [6.] **to see / seeing** so much fantastic jewellery. "How many wonderful things can one woman have?" he asks.

Then the rich woman can't help [7.] **to ask / asking** Cornelia, "How much jewellery have you got?" Cornelia isn't rich and she doesn't own any gold necklaces or bracelets, but that isn't important to her. She really doesn't mind [8.] **to not have / not having** any jewellery. Cornelia puts her arms around her two boys and answers, "These are my jewels."

English in Use

Complete the sentences below. Then tick (✔) the ones that express your opinion.

..... 1. I sometimes enjoy ....

..... 2. I'm always happy ....

..... 3. Right now, I feel like ....

..... 4. It was difficult ....

..... 5. I'm planning ....

Reading

1 Read the text about jobs for teenagers. Then complete the sentences with words from the text.

MONEY IDEAS

Do you want to buy a new watch, some bracelets or a phone case? These things cost a lot of money! Many British teenagers have got babysitting jobs to make money, but there are other things they can start doing. Look at some ideas. Do you or your friends do any of these jobs?

1. ROSA

Rosa organises parties for children and recommends trying it if you like children and you're looking for a fun job. She told us that we could plan sports parties or fashion parties. She said that she dressed children in fashion accessories like sunglasses, jewellery and handbags and had a fashion show, and we could also put make-up and nail varnish on the children. But she warned us, "Always ask their parents for permission first."

2. JAKE

Jake explained that dogs could stay home alone for many hours, but it was important for them to go out for a walk two or three times a day. He said that many people worked during the day and couldn't get home to walk their dogs, so his job was to walk those dogs. He said it was fun to be a dog-walker and he enjoyed earning money. He told us that he also took care of dogs, cats and other pets when people went on holiday.

3. SHANA

Shana told us that she loved computers, but some people didn't know much about computers or the Internet. In fact, she said that computers made some people very nervous, so she helped them. Shana gives these people computer lessons and recommends this job to other teens.

1. .... is a popular job for teenagers in Britain.
2. It's important for a party organiser to like ....
3. A party organiser shouldn't put make-up on children before asking ....
4. Dogs need a walk .... every day.
5. People need help with their pets when they ....
6. Some people feel .... using computers.

2 Explain why the words below appear in the text.

1. babysitting: ....
2. sports: ....
3. jewellery: ....
4. stay home alone: ....
5. cats: ....
6. the Internet: ....

Listening

3 Listen to Tim and his mum at a shopping centre. Number the fashion styles below in the order you hear about them.

a. Goth ..... b. Emo ..... c. Skater .....

4 Listen again and tick (✓) the correct column. You may tick more than one column.

	Emos	Goths	Skaters
1. They always wear black clothes.			
2. Their clothes are big.			
3. They sometimes colour their hair pink or blue.			
4. They wear jeans.			
5. They listen to emotional rock music.			
6. They wear black nail varnish.			

Vocabulary Adjectives

* **1 Find seven adjectives in the puzzle and write them under the correct pictures.**

sophisticatedcheapcomfortableformalcasualexpensivetrendy

A

....

....

B

....

....

* **2 Choose the word with the opposite meaning.**

1. expensive
   a. sophisticated (b. cheap) c. trendy
2. second-hand
   a. casual b. practical c. new
3. modern
   a. old-fashioned b. formal c. cool
4. pretty
   a. ugly b. fashionable c. comfortable
5. casual
   a. unusual b. formal c. colourful

** **3 Choose the correct answer.**

1. This handbag is red, blue, green and yellow. It's very **colourful / casual / expensive**.
2. Emma likes fashionable clothes. She wants to look **cheap / formal / trendy**.
3. Tina is pretty and she's got **fashionable / lovely / comfortable** green eyes.
4. Trainers are **sophisticated / pretty / practical** for sport.
5. Bobby doesn't like modern clothes. His clothes usually look **fashionable / old-fashioned / formal**.
6. Andrew dresses like Justin Bieber. He looks **plain / cool / second-hand**!
7. This skirt is too **pretty / modern / plain** for a party. Wear something more fashionable.

*** **4 Imagine you are doing one of the activities below. Write a description of the clothes you are wearing. Use suitable adjectives from Exercise 3.**

flying to London • going to a party
going horse-riding

....

....

....

....

English in Use

Match A to B to make mini-dialogues.

A

1. Maybe we can go shopping in Camden Town this weekend.
2. What do you think of these earrings?
3. How much do you want to spend?
4. What do you want to buy for Gary?
5. This watch is very nice.

B

..... a. They're lovely but they're quite expensive.
..... b. Let's get it!
..... c. That sounds like a good idea!
..... d. About €25.
..... e. Maybe tickets for a concert.

Writing A clothing description

1 Complete the sentences. Use two adjectives of your own in each sentence.

1. There are .... earrings in this shop.
2. We prefer .... skirts.
3. Paula is wearing an .... hat.
4. I've got a .... phone case for my mobile phone.
5. Jack's .... jeans weren't expensive.

2 Read the description about Jenny's father and his clothes. Then complete the description with the adjectives below.

grey • elegant • big • formal

My Dad, the Artist

BY JENNY STONE

My dad is an artist, so he doesn't wear expensive clothes at work. But he's got some cool clothes for going out. What are the clothes in his cupboard like?

Dad wears casual trousers with comfortable 1. .... sweaters on cold days and old T-shirts in the summer. He always gets paint on his clothes, so they are very colourful!

For special occasions, Dad wears fashionable clothes. His favourite item is a trendy 2. .... jacket. He wears it with a 3. .... white shirt, dark trousers and 4. .... black shoes. He loves going dancing with my mum in those shoes! Dad always wears an unusual hat when he goes out. I think he looks cool!

3 Complete the chart below about a friend's or family member's clothing.

Item of clothing	Adjectives describing it	When / Where he / she wears it

4 Write a description of your friend's or family member's clothing. Use the chart in Exercise 3 and the model in Exercise 2 to help you.

Check Your Progress

Vocabulary 20 points

1 Complete the adjective and write the name of the item to make sentences. (10 points)

Those are
e ....
....

There's an
o .... - ....
....

That's a p ....
....

There's some
c ....
....

The .... is
l ....

2 Intro 1 2 3 4 5 6 7 8 9 Follow the instructions. (10 points)

1. Cross out (✗) the animals in the chart.
2. Tick (✓) the nutrition and fitness words.
3. Draw a line (—) through the school items.
4. Circle (O) the types of transport.
5. Draw two lines (=) through the fashion items.

wolf	comfortable	atlas	frog
calories	rabbit	bracelet	tights
tablet	track	tram	belt
ferry	scissors	yacht	muscle

One word is left. What is it?
a. a verb b. an adjective c. a noun

Grammar 30 points

3 Complete the sentences in reported speech. (10 points)

1. "Everything looks cheap in this shop," said Kate.
   Kate said that everything ....
   cheap in .... shop.
2. "I can visit you today," Nick told Mike.
   Nick told Mike that he ....
   him ....
3. "We're leaving London now," Dan said.
   Dan said that they ....
   London ....
4. "It will snow in Moscow tomorrow," Ben said.
   Ben said that it .... in
   Moscow ....
5. "It's raining heavily here," Amy told her mum.
   Amy told her mum that it ....
   heavily ....

4 Choose the correct answer. (10 points)

1. I want **buying** / **to buy** this brown wallet.
2. I'm thinking about **getting** / **to get** earrings.
3. You're lucky **having** / **to have** a fitness trainer.
4. I've decided **giving** / **to give** you this.
5. **Designing** / **To design** accessories is fun!

5 Intro 1 2 3 4 5 6 7 8 9 Choose the correct answer. (10 points)

1. If it **rain** / **rains** / **will rain**, I'll wear this jacket.
2. Have you **ever** / **yet** / **since** coloured your hair?
3. Your dress **looks** / **is looking** / **looking** lovely!
4. At ten o'clock last night, I **put on** / **was putting on** / **were putting on** clothes.
5. If sunglasses were cheaper, I **bought** / **would buy** / **buy** many pairs.
6. You **have to** / **should** / **don't need to** wear a swimming cap at the pool. It's a rule.
7. Brian said that he **can't** / **couldn't** / **isn't** find me.
8. Lily runs **easy** / **easily** / **more easily than** I do.
9. **Ellen used to** / **Ellen didn't use to** / **Did Ellen use to** have black hair?
10. I didn't buy the ring because it was **too expensive** / **not expensive enough** / **more expensive than** for me.

Dictation 10 points

5 18 **6 Listen and write the sentences.**

1. ....
2. ....
3. ....
4. ....
5. ....

Speaking 10 points

7 Complete the dialogue with the words below.

Not a lot • do you think of this • how much quite expensive • How about this one

A: I want to buy a phone case for my mobile phone.
B: 1. .... ? It's very trendy and it costs £20.
A: I don't think so. It's 2. ....
B: Well, 3. .... do you want to spend?
A: 4. .... I've got £20.
B: What 5. .... blue phone case? It's only £7.
A: It's really cool!

Writing 10 points

8 Complete each sentence with two adjectives.

1. I've got a .... necklace.
2. Ken always wears .... hoodies.
3. Do you like .... jeans?
4. Jessica has got some .... earrings.
5. There's a .... jacket in the cupboard.

Translation 20 points

9 Translate the sentences into English.

1. Mike nos dijo que no le gustaba ponerse ropa formal.
....
....
2. Decidí comprarme un vestido sencillo y cómodo.
....
3. Comprar fundas de móvil y bolsos es divertido.
....
4. Bill dijo que no podía llevar una sudadera con capucha al colegio.
....
5. Emma dijo que le haría a Claire una pulsera o un collar por su cumpleaños.
....
....

My Scores

Vocabulary __ / 20
Grammar __ / 30
Dictation __ / 10
Speaking __ / 10
Writing __ / 10
Translation __ / 20
My total score: __ / 100

Self-Evaluation

Do the following. Tick (✓) the box if you succeed.

1 Say ...

1. four fashion accessories. ☐
....
....
2. four adjectives to describe fashion. ☐
....
....
3. two things you said to your friends using reported speech. ☐
....
....
4. something you enjoy doing and something you don't want to do. ☐
....
....

2 Write responses to the questions. ☐

1. How about this belt?
....
2. How much do you want to spend?
....
3. What do you think of trendy sunglasses?
....

3 Write two sentences about the clothes you're wearing. Use two adjectives in each sentence. ☐

1. ....
2. ....

Glossary

Getting Started

adventurous /əd'ventʃərəs/ aventurero/a

amusement park /ə'mjuːzmənt pɑːk/ parque de atracciones

ant /ænt/ hormiga

arcade /ɑː'keɪd/ galería comercial; salón recreativo

armchair /'ɑːmtʃeə/ sillón

athletic /æθ'letɪk/ atlético/a

bank /bæŋk/ banco

bar /bɑː/ bar

basketball /'bɑːskɪtbɔːl/ baloncesto

bat /bæt/ murciélago

bathroom /'bɑːθruːm/ cuarto de baño

beautiful /'bjuːtɪfl/ precioso/a, bonito/a; guapa

bed /bed/ cama

bedroom /'bedruːm/ dormitorio, habitación, cuarto

big /bɪg/ grande

bowling /'bəʊlɪŋ/ bolos

brave /breɪv/ valiente

butterfly /'bʌtəflaɪ/ mariposa

café /'kæfeɪ/ cafetería, café

catch /kætʃ/ coger

chair /tʃeə/ silla

chemist's /'kemɪsts/ farmacia

chicken /'tʃɪkɪn/ gallina; pollo

chimpanzee /tʃɪmpæn'ziː/ chimpancé

church /tʃɜːtʃ/ iglesia

cinema /'sɪnəmə/ cine

clever /'klevə/ listo/a, inteligente

climb /klaɪm/ escalar

clock /klɒk/ reloj

cooker /'kʊkə/ cocina (fogones y horno)

cow /kaʊ/ vaca

creative /kriː'eɪtɪv/ creativo/a

crocodile /'krɒkədaɪl/ cocodrilo

cupboard /'kʌbəd/ armario

curly /'kɜːli/ rizado/a

curtains /'kɜːtɪnz/ cortinas

cycling /'saɪklɪŋ/ ciclismo

dancing /'dɑːnsɪŋ/ baile

dark /dɑːk/ oscuro/a; moreno/a

department store /dɪ'pɑːtmənt stɔː/ grandes almacenes

desk /desk/ escritorio

dining room /'daɪnɪŋ ruːm/ comedor

dolphin /'dɒlfɪn/ delfín

duvet /'duːveɪ/ edredón (nórdico)

elephant /'elɪfənt/ elefante

fat /fæt/ gordo/a

fly /flaɪ/ mosca

football /'fʊtbɔːl/ fútbol

fridge /frɪdʒ/ frigorífico, nevera

frog /frɒg/ rana

funny /'fʌni/ gracioso/a

generous /'dʒenərəs/ generoso/a

giraffe /dʒə'rɑːf/ jirafa

goggles /'gɒglz/ gafas de natación

golf /gɒlf/ golf

good-looking /gʊd'lʊkɪŋ/ guapo/a, atractivo/a

hard-working /hɑːd'wɜːkɪŋ/ trabajador/a

helmet /'helmɪt/ casco

honest /'ɒnɪst/ honrado/a, sincero/a

horse /hɔːs/ caballo

hospital /'hɒspɪtl/ hospital

iguana /ɪ'gwɑːnə/ iguana

karate /kə'rɑːti/ kárate

kitchen /'kɪtʃɪn/ cocina

lamp /læmp/ lámpara

lazy /'leɪzi/ perezoso/a, vago/a

library /'laɪbrəri/ biblioteca

light /laɪt/ claro/a

lion /'laɪən/ león

living room /'lɪvɪŋ ruːm/ cuarto de estar, salón

lizard /'lɪzəd/ lagarto; lagartija

long /lɒŋ/ largo/a

medium height /'miːdiəm haɪt/ de estatura media

mirror /'mɪrə/ espejo

mosquito /mə'skiːtəʊ/ mosquito

museum /mjuː'ziːəm/ museo

old /əʊld/ viejo/a

parrot /'pærət/ loro, papagayo

pillow /'pɪləʊ/ almohada; cojín

police station /pə'liːs steɪʃn/ comisaría

post office /'pəʊst ɒfɪs/ oficina de correos

rabbit /'ræbɪt/ conejo

restaurant /'restrɒnt/ restaurante

rollerblading /'rəʊləbleɪdɪŋ/ patinaje en línea

round /raʊnd/ redondo/a

rug /rʌg/ alfombra

running /'rʌnɪŋ/ correr

scuba diving /'skuːbə daɪvɪŋ/ buceo, submarinismo

shark /ʃɑːk/ tiburón
sheep /ʃiːp/ oveja/s
shelf /ʃelf/ estante, balda
shopping centre /ˈʃɒpɪŋ sentə/ centro comercial
short /ʃɔːt/ corto/a; bajo/a
shower /ˈʃaʊə/ ducha
shy /ʃaɪ/ tímido/a
sink /sɪŋk/ fregadero, pila; lavabo
skiing /ˈskiːɪŋ/ esquí
small /smɔːl/ pequeño/a
snake /sneɪk/ serpiente
sofa /ˈsəʊfə/ sofá
spider /ˈspaɪdə/ araña
sports centre /ˈspɔːts sentə/ polideportivo
straight /streɪt/ liso/a
strong /strɒŋ/ fuerte
surfing /ˈsɜːfɪŋ/ surf
sweet shop /ˈswiːt ʃɒp/ tienda de chucherías
swimming /ˈswɪmɪŋ/ natación
swimming cap /ˈswɪmɪŋ kæp/ gorro de natación
swimming pool /ˈswɪmɪŋ puːl/ piscina
table /ˈteɪbl/ mesa
tall /tɔːl/ alto/a
tennis /ˈtenɪs/ tenis
thin /θɪn/ delgado/a
throw /θrəʊ/ lanzar; tirar
tiger /ˈtaɪgə/ tigre
toilet /ˈtɔɪlət/ baño, servicio, váter
turtle /ˈtɜːtl/ tortuga
ugly /ˈʌgli/ feo/a
volleyball /ˈvɒlibɔːl/ voleibol, balonvolea
weak /wiːk/ débil
weightlifting /ˈweɪtlɪftɪŋ/ levantamiento de peso, halterofilia
whale /weɪl/ ballena
wolf /wʊlf/ lobo
worm /wɜːm/ lombriz, gusano
young /jʌŋ/ joven

Unit 1

art /ɑːt/ arte; dibujo
athlete /ˈæθliːt/ deportista; atleta
atlas /ˈætləs/ atlas
balance /ˈbæləns/ equilibrio
blackboard /ˈblækbɔːd/ pizarra
build models /bɪld ˈmɒdlz/ construir maquetas
calculator /ˈkælkjʊleɪtə/ calculadora
chalk /tʃɔːk/ tiza
champion /ˈtʃæmpiən/ campeón/ona
check e-mails /tʃek ˈiːmeɪlz/ mirar el correo electrónico
compass /ˈkʌmpəs/ compás
computer technology /kəmpjuːtə tekˈnɒlədʒi/ informática
crayon /ˈkreɪən/ lápiz de color
destroy /dɪˈstrɔɪ/ destruir, destrozar
dictionary /ˈdɪkʃənri/ diccionario
disaster zone /dɪˈzɑːstə zəʊn/ zona catastrófica / de desastre
diver /ˈdaɪvə/ saltador/a (de natación)
do experiments /duː ɪkˈsperɪmənts/ hacer experimentos
do judo /duː ˈdʒuːdəʊ/ hacer judo
drama /ˈdrɑːmə/ teatro
English /ˈɪŋglɪʃ/ inglés
flash drive /ˈflæʃ draɪv/ memoria
flood /flʌd/ inundación
French /frentʃ/ francés
geography /dʒiˈɒgrəfi/ geografía
globe /gləʊb/ globo terráqueo
glue /gluː/ pegamento
go horse-riding /gəʊ ˈhɔːsraɪdɪŋ/ ir a montar a caballo; hacer equitación
gold /gəʊld/ oro
government /ˈgʌvənmənt/ gobierno
gymnast /ˈdʒɪmnæst/ gimnasta
hard /hɑːd/ difícil; mucho
history /ˈhɪstri/ historia
hope /həʊp/ esperar
join /dʒɔɪn/ entrar en
laptop /ˈlæptɒp/ ordenador portátil
large /lɑːdʒ/ grande
learn a new language /lɜːn ə njuː ˈlæŋgwɪdʒ/ aprender un idioma nuevo
learn competitive diving /lɜːn kəmˈpetətɪv daɪvɪŋ/ aprender (a hacer) salto (de natación)
literature /ˈlɪtrətʃə/ literatura
look for /ˈlʊk fɔː/ buscar
maths /mæθs/ mates (matemáticas)
microscope /ˈmaɪkrəskəʊp/ microscopio
music /ˈmjuːzɪk/ música
next to /ˈnekst tə/ al lado de
one in (number) /ˈwʌn ɪn/ uno/a de cada (número)
ordinary /ˈɔːdnri/ normal
paintbrush /ˈpeɪntbrʌʃ/ pincel
paint pictures /peɪnt ˈpɪktʃəz/ pintar cuadros
paints /peɪnts/ pinturas
perform in a band /pəˈfɔːm ɪn ə bænd/ tocar en un grupo

Vocabulary Reference

play the piano /pleɪ ðə pi'ænəʊ/ tocar el piano

pleased /pli:zd/ contento/a

potential /pə'tenʃl/ posible, en potencia

proud /praʊd/ orgulloso/a

repair computers /rɪ'peə kəmpju:təz/ arreglar / reparar ordenadores

science /'saɪəns/ ciencia(s)

scissors /'sɪzəz/ tijeras

send text messages /send 'tekst mesɪdʒɪz/ mandar mensajes (de texto)

soon /su:n/ pronto (*How ~ ...?*: ¿Cuánto (se) tarda en...?)

sport /spɔ:t/ deporte, educación física

stapler /'steɪplə/ grapadora

succeed /sək'si:d/ triunfar, tener éxito

supplies /sə'plaɪz/ material/es

tablet /'tæblət/ tableta

take a nap /teɪk ə 'næp/ echarse la / una siesta

take photos /teɪk 'fəʊtəʊz/ hacer fotos

talented /'tæləntɪd/ talentoso/a, con talento

textbook /'tekstbʊk/ libro de texto

train /treɪn/ entrenar (a)

weightlifter /'weɪtlɪftə/ levantador/a de peso, halterófilo/a

Unit 2

attach /ə'tætʃ/ adjuntar; poner, acoplar

(be) born /bi: 'bɔ:n/ nacer

belong to /bɪ'lɒŋ tə/ pertenecer a

bite /baɪt/ morder (a)

borrow /'bɒrəʊ/ pedir / tomar prestado/a

charge /tʃɑ:dʒ/ cargar

clever /'klevə/ ingenioso/a

come out /kʌm 'aʊt/ salir

cross /krɒs/ cruzar, atravesar

demonstrate /'demənstreɪt/ manifestarse; hacer una demostración de

design /dɪ'zaɪn/ modelo, diseño

develop /dɪ'veləp/ desarrollar

die /daɪ/ morir

dwarf /dwɔ:f/ enano/a

evil /'i:vl/ malvado/a

fall in love /fɔ:l ɪn 'lʌv/ enamorarse

fight /faɪt/ pelear / luchar (contra)

freeze /fri:z/ helar(se), congelar(se)

get a job /get ə 'dʒɒb/ conseguir un trabajo

get divorced /get dɪ'vɔ:sd/ divorciarse

get married /get 'mærid/ casarse

go to university /gəʊ tə ju:nɪ'vɜ:səti/ ir a la universidad

GPS tracking device /dʒi:pi:'es trækɪŋ dɪvaɪs/ dispositivo de localización por GPS

graduate from /'grædʒʊeɪt frəm/ graduarse en

grow up /grəʊ 'ʌp/ crecer, criarse

have a child /həv ə 'tʃaɪld/ tener un/a hijo/a

improve /ɪm'pru:v/ mejorar

join /dʒɔɪn/ unirse a (~ *the army*: alistarse en el ejército)

keep warm /ki:p 'wɔ:m/ mantener abrigado/a / caliente a

light /laɪt/ encender, prender

main character /meɪn 'kærəktə/ protagonista

Middle-earth /mɪdl'ɜ:θ/ Tierra Media

move to /'mu:v tə/ mudarse a

prevent /prɪ'vent/ evitar, prevenir; impedir

pull /pʊl/ tirar (de)

reach /ri:tʃ/ alcanzar, llegar a

receive awards /rɪ'si:v əwɔ:dz/ recibir premios

satellite phone /'sætəlaɪt fəʊn/ teléfono por satélite

save /seɪv/ salvar / rescatar (a)

solo /'səʊləʊ/ a solas; solo

steal /sti:l/ robar

survive /sə'vaɪv/ sobrevivir (a)

take (lessons) /teɪk 'lesnz/ recibir / ir a (clases)

top /tɒp/ cumbre, cima

treasure /'treʒə/ tesoro

volunteer /vɒlən'tɪə/ hacer voluntariado, ser voluntario/a

wheel /wi:l/ rueda

Unit 3

bird-watcher /'bɜ:dwɒtʃə/ observador/a de aves

calm /kɑ:m/ tranquilo/a; en calma

canyon /'kænjən/ cañón

carriage /'kærɪdʒ/ coche / carruaje tirado por caballos (*public* ~: diligencia)

cliff /klɪf/ acantilado

coach /kəʊtʃ/ diligencia

coast /kəʊst/ costa

coral reef /'kɒrəl ri:f/ arrecife de coral

course /kɔ:s/ rumbo

dull /dʌl/ aburrido/a, soso/a

east /i:st/ este

elegant /'elɪgənt/ elegante

extraordinary /ɪk'strɔ:dənri/ extraordinario/a

field /fi:ld/ campo

frightening /'fraɪtnɪŋ/ aterrador/a, espantoso/a

frogs' legs /'frɒgz legz/ ancas de rana

glacier /'glæsiə/ glaciar

ground /graʊnd/ suelo, tierra

harbour /ˈhɑːbə/ puerto
holiday resort /ˈhɒlədeɪ rɪzɔːt/ lugar de veraneo
ideal /aɪˈdiːəl/ ideal
isolated /ˈaɪsəleɪtɪd/ aislado/a, apartado/a
jumbo jet /dʒʌmbəʊ ˈdʒet/ Jumbo, avión de fuselaje ancho
lively /ˈlaɪvli/ animado/a, bullicioso/a
location /ləʊˈkeɪʃn/ lugar; situación, ubicación
north /nɔːθ/ norte
pack /pæk/ meter en la maleta
peaceful /ˈpiːsfl/ tranquilo/a
pleasant /ˈpleznt/ agradable
polluted /pəˈluːtɪd/ contaminado/a
rainforest /ˈreɪnfɒrɪst/ selva tropical
relaxing /rɪˈlæksɪŋ/ relajante
rough /rʌf/ agitado/a, encrespado/a, picado/a
safe /seɪf/ seguro/a; a salvo
salt lake /ˈsɔːlt leɪk/ lago de agua salada
scenery /ˈsiːnəri/ paisaje
smelly /ˈsmeli/ maloliente
snail /sneɪl/ caracol
south /saʊθ/ sur
steam train /ˈstiːm treɪn/ tren de vapor
stream /striːm/ arroyo
swamp /swɒmp/ pantano
tasteless /ˈteɪstləs/ soso/a, insípido/a
terrible /ˈterəbl/ espantoso/a, terrible
unreliable /ʌnrɪˈlaɪəbl/ poco fiable
useless /ˈjuːsləs/ inútil, inservible
wake up to /weɪk ˈʌp tə/ despertar(se) con
west /west/ oeste
wonderful /ˈwʌndəfl/ maravilloso/a, precioso/a
worry /ˈwʌri/ preocupación

Review 1

bend back /bend ˈbæk/ doblar hacia atrás
backboard /ˈbækbɔːd/ tablero
blow out /bləʊ ˈaʊt/ apagar (con un soplo)
bounce off /baʊns ˈɒf/ rebotar
freezing /ˈfriːzɪŋ/ helado/a, congelado/a
half-court shot /ˈhɑːfkɔːt ʃɒt/ tiro (a canasta) desde mitad de la cancha
light /laɪt/ encender
shoot /ʃuːt/ tirar (a canasta)
three-pointer /θriːˈpɔɪntə/ triple
trophy /ˈtrəʊfi/ trofeo

Unit 4

aunt /ɑːnt/ tía
cave /keɪv/ cueva
cloudy /ˈklaʊdi/ nublado/a
cold /kəʊld/ frío/a
cool /kuːl/ fresco/a
cousin /ˈkʌzn/ primo/a
daughter /ˈdɔːtə/ hija
daytime /ˈdeɪtaɪm/ de día
dry /draɪ/ seco/a, árido/a
earth /ɜːθ/ tierra
entry /ˈentri/ entrada, comentario, nota
flood /flʌd/ inundar
foggy /ˈfɒgi/ brumoso/a, con niebla
get around /get əˈraʊnd/ moverse, desplazarse
go away /gəʊ əˈweɪ/ irse (de vacaciones)
granddaughter /ˈgrændɔːtə/ nieta
grandfather /ˈgrænfɑːðə/ abuelo
grandmother /ˈgrænmʌðə/ abuela
grandson /ˈgrænsʌn/ nieto
heating /ˈhiːtɪŋ/ calefacción
hike (n) /haɪk/ caminata
hike (v) /haɪk/ hacer senderismo, dar una caminata
hot /hɒt/ caluroso/a, cálido/a (*it's* ~: hace calor)
husband /ˈhʌzbənd/ marido, esposo
lightning /ˈlaɪtnɪŋ/ rayo/s, relámpago/s
mat /mæt/ colchoneta
monsoon /mɒnˈsuːn/ monzónico/a
nephew /ˈnefjuː/ sobrino
niece /niːs/ sobrina
outdoors /aʊtˈdɔːz/ al aire libre, fuera
parents /ˈpeərənts/ padres
pipe /paɪp/ tubería
rain /reɪn/ lluvia
snow /snəʊ/ nieve
son /sʌn/ hijo
spotlight /ˈspɒtlaɪt/ centro de atención
stilt /stɪlt/ pilote, pilar
stormy /ˈstɔːmi/ tormentoso/a (*it's* ~: hay tormenta)
sunny /ˈsʌni/ soleado/a (*it's* ~: hace sol)
tent /tent/ tienda de campaña
thunder /ˈθʌndə/ trueno/s
uncle /ˈʌŋkl/ tío
warm /wɔːm/ cálido/a, templado/a
wet /wet/ lluvioso/a; mojado/a
wife /waɪf/ mujer, esposa
windy /ˈwɪndi/ ventoso/a, de mucho viento (*it's* ~: hace viento)

Unit 5

arrest /ə'rest/ arrestar (a)

burglar /'bɜːglə/ ladrón/ona

close off /kləʊz 'ɒf/ cerrar al público / tráfico

clue /kluː/ pista

court /kɔːt/ tribunal, juzgado

criminal /'krɪmɪnl/ criminal

detective /dɪ'tektɪv/ detective

drop /drɒp/ dejar caer (sin querer)

evidence /'evɪdəns/ pruebas

expert /'ekspɜːt/ experto/a, especialista

fingerprint /'fɪŋgəprɪnt/ huella dactilar / digital

forensic scientist /fə'rensɪk saɪəntɪst/ investigador/a forense

forger /'fɔːdʒə/ falsificador/a

get in /get 'ɪn/ entrar, meterse

gun /gʌn/ pistola, revólver

helpful /'helpfl/ útil

hijack /'haɪdʒæk/ secuestrar

hurry /'hʌri/ darse prisa (para llegar a)

investigate /ɪn'vestɪgeɪt/ investigar

judge /dʒʌdʒ/ juez/a

jury /'dʒʊəri/ jurado

knife /naɪf/ cuchillo

lawyer /'lɔːjə/ abogado/a

loud /laʊd/ fuerte

murder /'mɜːdə/ asesinato

next door /nekst 'dɔː/ de al lado

plan /plæn/ plano

police officer /pə'liːs ɒfɪsə/ policía

prison /'prɪzn/ prisión, cárcel

prisoner /'prɪznə/ detenido/a; acusado/a; preso/a, reo/a

return /rɪ'tɜːn/ devolver

robbery /'rɒbəri/ robo

scene /siːn/ lugar, escenario

security guard /sɪ'kjʊərəti gɑːd/ guarda jurado/a, guardia de seguridad

shocked /ʃɒkt/ estupefacto/a

smell /smel/ olor

suspect /'sʌspekt/ sospechoso/a

thief /θiːf/ ladrón/ona

towel /'taʊəl/ toalla

victim /'vɪktɪm/ víctima

weapon /'wepən/ arma

witness /'wɪtnəs/ testigo

Unit 6

aeroplane /'eərəpleɪn/ avión

air pollution /'eə pəluːʃn/ contaminación del aire / atmosférica

bottom /'bɒtəm/ fondo

clean up /kliːn 'ʌp/ limpiar

coach /kəʊtʃ/ autocar, autobús

cruise ship /'kruːz ʃɪp/ crucero

cut down /kʌt 'daʊn/ talar, deforestar

damage /'dæmɪdʒ/ dañar, perjudicar

destroy /dɪ'strɔɪ/ destruir, destrozar

disastrous /dɪ'zɑːstrəs/ catastrófico/a

ferry /'feri/ transbordador, *ferry*

harm /hɑːm/ dañar

helicopter /'helɪkɒptə/ helicóptero

in order to /ɪn 'ɔːdə tə/ para, a fin de

increase /ɪn'kriːs/ aumentar

indoors /ɪn'dɔːz/ en un lugar cubierto, dentro

jeep /dʒiːp/ todoterreno

law /lɔː/ ley

lorry /'lɒri/ camión

major /'meɪdʒə/ principal

make a difference /meɪk ə 'dɪfrəns/ cambiar las cosas, causar un impacto positivo

minivan /'mɪnivæn/ monovolumen

motorbike /'məʊtəbaɪk/ motocicleta, moto

motorboat /'məʊtəbəʊt/ (lancha) motora

pick up /pɪk 'ʌp/ coger, recoger

plant /plɑːnt/ plantar

power /'paʊə/ energía

protect /prə'tekt/ proteger

rally /'ræli/ concentración

recycle /riː'saɪkl/ reciclar

replace /rɪ'pleɪs/ sustituir

resource /rɪ'sɔːs/ recurso

reuse /riː'juːz/ reutilizar, volver a usar

room /ruːm/ sitio, espacio; habitación, cuarto

save /seɪv/ ahorrar; salvar

scooter /'skuːtə/ vespa, *scooter*

source /sɔːs/ fuente, origen

throw out /θrəʊ 'aʊt/ tirar

tram /træm/ tranvía

underground /'ʌndəgraʊnd/ metro

unplug /ʌn'plʌg/ desenchufar, desconectar

waste /weɪst/ derrochar

yacht /jɒt/ yate

Review 2

ark /ɑːk/ arca

climb out /klaɪm 'aʊt/ salir trepando

dig (for) /'dɪg fɔː/ excavar (en busca de)

pull up /pʊl 'ʌp/ levantar, subir

raider /'reɪdə/ ladrón/ona

Raiders of the Lost Ark /reɪdəz əv ðə lɒst 'ɑːk/ *En busca del arca perdida*

rope /rəʊp/ cuerda, soga

torch /tɔːtʃ/ antorcha

Unit 7

amaze /ə'meɪz/ asombrar

angry /'æŋgri/ enfadado/a

break a record /breɪk ə 'rekɔːd/ batir un récord

build up (someone's) confidence /bɪld ʌp sʌmwʌnz 'kɒnfɪdəns/ dar más confianza en sí mismo/a (a alguien)

exhausted /ɪg'zɔːstɪd/ exhausto/a, agotado/a

face-to-face /feɪstə'feɪs/ cara a cara

fail the test /feɪl ðə 'test/ suspender el examen

feed a wild animal /fiːd ə waɪld 'ænɪml/ dar de comer a un animal salvaje

few /fjuː/ pocos/as

forget things /fə'get θɪŋz/ olvidar cosas

frightened /'fraɪtnd/ asustado/a (*be* ~: tener miedo)

get lost /get 'lɒst/ perderse

go abroad /gəʊ ə'brɔːd/ ir(se) al extranjero

go on a cruise /gəʊ ɒn ə 'kruːz/ ir de / hacer un crucero

juggle /'dʒʌgl/ hacer juegos malabares

Latin /'lætɪn/ latino/a

look back /lʊk 'bæk/ mirar hacia atrás; pensar en el pasado

nasty /'nɑːsti/ desagradable

perform in a circus /pəfɔːm ɪn ə 'sɜːkəs/ actuar en un circo

performer /pə'fɔːmə/ artista

profile /'prəʊfaɪl/ perfil

proud /praʊd/ orgulloso/a

put out a fire /pʊt aʊt ə 'faɪə/ apagar / extinguir un fuego / incendio

reality TV /ri'æləti tiː viː/ (de) telerrealidad

ridiculous /rɪ'dɪkjələs/ ridículo/a, absurdo/a (*Don't be ~!:* ¡No digas tonterías!)

risky /'rɪski/ arriesgado/a

row a boat /rəʊ ə 'bəʊt/ remar en una barca / un bote

rude /ruːd/ grosero/a

silly /'sɪli/ tonto/a, absurdo/a

social networking site /səʊʃl 'netwɜːkɪŋ saɪt/ página / sitio web de redes sociales

surprised /sə'praɪzd/ sorprendido/a

take away from /teɪk ə'weɪ frəm/ restar

take lessons in self-defence /teɪk lesnz ɪn self dɪ'fens/ ir a clases de defensa personal

take part in a carnival /teɪk pɑːt ɪn ə 'kɑːnɪvl/ participar en un carnaval

tell lies /tel 'laɪz/ decir mentiras

text /tekst/ enviar mensajes de texto

unicycle /'juːnɪsaɪkl/ monociclo

unique /juː'niːk/ único/a, excepcional

unpleasant /ʌn'pleznt/ desagradable

upset /ʌp'set/ disgustado/a; molesto/a

walk a tightrope /wɔːk ə 'taɪtrəʊp/ andar por la cuerda floja

worried /'wʌrid/ preocupado/a

youth /juːθ/ juvenil, de jóvenes

Unit 8

balanced diet /bælənst 'daɪət/ dieta equilibrada

befriend /bɪ'frend/ confraternizar con, tratar con amistad a

bone /bəʊn/ hueso

break out /breɪk 'aʊt/ estallar

caffeine /'kæfiːn/ cafeína

calories /'kæləriz/ calorías

carbohydrates /kɑːbəʊ'haɪdreɪts/ carbohidratos

cheer /tʃɪə/ dar vítores

die in action /daɪ ɪn 'ækʃn/ morir en combate / acción (de guerra)

diet /'daɪət/ estar a régimen, hacer dieta

dietician /daɪə'tɪʃn/ médico especialista en dietética, dietista

egg-white /'egwaɪt/ de clara de huevo

exercise /'eksəsaɪz/ hacer ejercicio

fat /fæt/ grasa

fight back /faɪt 'bæk/ contraatacar

fitness trainer /'fɪtnəs treɪnə/ entrenador/a

fresh air /freʃ 'eə/ aire fresco

gain weight /geɪn 'weɪt/ ganar peso, engordar

get fit /get 'fɪt/ ponerse en forma

go crazy /gəʊ 'kreɪzi/ ponerse como loco/a

gym /dʒɪm/ gimnasio

healthy lifestyle /helθi 'laɪfstaɪl/ estilo de vida sano / saludable

heart /hɑːt/ corazón

in a row /ɪn ə 'rəʊ/ seguido/a, consecutivo/a

injury /'ɪndʒəri/ lesión

junk food /'dʒʌŋk fu:d/ comida basura
liquid /'lɪkwɪd/ líquido
long jump /lɒŋ 'dʒʌmp/ salto de longitud
lose weight /lu:z 'weɪt/ perder peso, adelgazar
meal /mi:l/ comida
medal /'medl/ medalla
muscle /'mʌsl/ músculo
nutrition /nju:'trɪʃn/ nutrición
omelette /'ɒmlət/ tortilla
pancake /'pænkeɪk/ tortita
porridge /'pɒrɪdʒ/ avena cocida
processed food /'prəʊsest fu:d/ comida procesada
protein /'prəʊti:n/ proteína
remain /rɪ'meɪn/ seguir, continuar
salt /sɔ:lt/ sal
score /skɔ:/ marcar
slice /slaɪs/ rebanada
snack /snæk/ tentempié
sort /sɔ:t/ clase, tipo
sugar /'ʃʊgə/ azúcar
take the lead /teɪk ðə 'li:d/ tomar la delantera
team /ti:m/ (de) equipo
track /træk/ pista
unhealthy /ʌn'helθi/ poco sano/a
vitamins /'vɪtəmɪnz/ vitaminas

Unit 9

animal rights /'ænɪməl raɪts/ derechos de los animales
bearskin /'beəskɪn/ gorro militar de piel de oso
belt /belt/ cinturón
best man /best 'mæn/ padrino
bracelet /'breɪslət/ pulsera
bright /braɪt/ fuerte, vivo/a
casual /'kæʒʊəl/ informal, de *sport*
cheap /tʃi:p/ barato/a
colourful /'kʌləfl/ colorido/a, de colores vivos
comfortable /'kʌmftəbl/ cómodo/a
cool /ku:l/ guay (*be* ~: molar)
Crown Jewels /kraʊn 'dʒu:əlz/ joyas de la Corona
curriculum /kə'rɪkjələm/ plan de estudios
device /dɪ'vaɪs/ dispositivo, aparato
earrings /'ɪərɪŋz/ pendientes
expensive /ɪk'spensɪv/ caro/a
fashionable /'fæʃnəbl/ moderno/a, a la / de moda
finance /'faɪnæns/ finanzas, asuntos financieros
formal /'fɔ:ml/ formal; de etiqueta
fur /fɜ:/ (de) piel
groom /gru:m/ novio
handbag /'hændbæg/ bolso (de mano)
hoodie /'hʊdi/ sudadera con capucha
kilt /kɪlt/ falda escocesa
leather /'leðə/ de cuero / piel
lovely /'lʌvli/ precioso/a, bello/a
make-up /'meɪkʌp/ maquillaje
manage /'mænɪdʒ/ administrar
modern /'mɒdn/ moderno/a
nail varnish /'neɪl vɑ:nɪʃ/ esmalte de uñas, pintaúñas
necklace /'nekləs/ collar
old-fashioned /əʊld'fæʃnd/ anticuado/a, pasado/a de moda
pattern /'pætn/ diseño, estampado
phone case /'fəʊn keɪs/ funda de teléfono
plain /pleɪn/ sencillo/a; liso/a
practical /'præktɪkl/ práctico/a
pretty /'prɪti/ bonito/a
purse /pɜ:s/ monedero
ring /rɪŋ/ anillo
ruling /'ru:lɪŋ/ reinante
save /seɪv/ ahorrar (~ *for a "rainy day"*: ahorrar para cuando lleguen tiempos peores)
second-hand /sekənd'hænd/ de segunda mano
shamrock /'ʃæmrɒk/ trébol
sophisticated /sə'fɪstɪkeɪtɪd/ sofisticado/a
spending /'spendɪŋ/ gastos
square /skweə/ cuadro, cuadrado
sunglasses /'sʌnglɑ:sɪz/ gafas de sol
thistle /'θɪsl/ cardo
tights /taɪts/ pantis, medias
trendy /'trendi/ moderno/a, a la moda
understanding /ʌndə'stændɪŋ/ conocimiento/s
wallet /'wɒlɪt/ cartera, billetera
warder /'wɔ:də/ celador/a
watch /wɒtʃ/ reloj (de pulsera)
wool /wʊl/ lana

Review 3

belly /'beli/ barriga
buck /bʌk/ dólar
celery /'seləri/ apio
deal /di:l/ trato, acuerdo
delight /dɪ'laɪt/ deleite, placer
eggplant (Am. Eng.) /'egplɑ:nt/ berenjena
hand /hænd/ dar (en mano)
string beans (Am. Eng.) /strɪŋ 'bi:nz/ judías verdes

Speaking Glossary

Greetings and introductions

Are you new here? /ɑ: ju: 'nju: hɪə/ ¿Eres nuevo/a aquí?

This is my friend ... . /ðɪs ɪz maɪ 'frend/ Este/a es mi amigo/a... .

Is this ... ? /'ɪz ðɪs/ ¿Este es el...?

Can I please speak to ... ? /kən aɪ 'pli:z spi:k tə/ ¿Puedo hablar con..., por favor?

Hi, welcome to our school. /haɪ 'welkəm tə ɑ: sku:l/ Hola, bienvenido/a a nuestro colegio.

Sorry, ... isn't here. /'sɒri ... ɪznt hɪə/ Lo siento, ... no está aquí.

Thanks, my name's ... . Nice to meet you. /θæŋks maɪ neɪmz '... naɪs tə 'mi:t ju:/ Gracias, me llamo... . Encantado/a de conocerte.

Yes, it is. Who's calling? /jes ɪt 'ɪz. hu:z 'kɔ:lɪŋ/ Sí. ¿Quién llama / es?

Yes, I'm from ... . /'jes aɪm frɒm/ Sí, soy de... .

Hi, I'm ... . /'haɪ aɪm/ Hola, soy... .

Hello, ... This is ... . /hə'ləʊ ... ðɪs ɪz/ Hola, ... Soy... .

Call again later, ... /kɔ:l əgen 'leɪtə/ Vuelve a llamar luego / más tarde, ...

Classroom language

Listen carefully. /lɪsn 'keəfli/ Escucha/d con atención.

Can you explain this to me, please? /kən ju: ɪk'spleɪn ðɪs tə mi pli:z/ ¿Puede explicarme esto, por favor?

Where is your homework? /weə ɪz jɔ: 'həʊmwɜ:k/ ¿Dónde están tus deberes?

I'm sorry I'm late. /aɪm 'sɒri aɪm leɪt/ Siento llegar tarde.

Can you spell this word? /kən ju: 'spel ðɪs wɜ:d/ ¿Puede deletrear esta palabra?

Can I borrow a ... , please? /kən aɪ 'bɒrəʊ ə ... pli:z/ ¿Puedo tomar prestado/a / Me prestas un/a..., por favor?

Who knows the answer to this question? /hu: nəʊz ði: 'ɑ:nsə tə ðɪs kwestʃən/ ¿Quién sabe la respuesta a esta pregunta?

When is the ... exam? /wen ɪz ðə '... ɪgzæm/ ¿Cuándo es el examen de...?

What page are we on? /wɒt 'peɪdʒ ɑ: wi ɒn/ ¿En qué página estamos?

Describing a picture

There are ... . /'ðeə ɑ:/ Hay... .

The ... looks ... . /ðə '... lʊks/ El / La... parece... .

There's a ... and a ... in the picture. /ðeəz ə '... ənd ə '... ɪn ðə pɪktʃə/ Hay un/a... y un/a... en la imagen.

I can see ... and they're ... . /aɪ kæn si: '... ənd ðeə/ Veo / Puedo ver... y están... .

In this picture, ... is ... . /ɪn 'ðɪs pɪktʃə ... ɪz/ En esta imagen, ... está... .

The ... are ... . /ðə '... ɑ:/ Los/as... son / están... .

Discussing biographies

When was ... born? /wen wəz ... 'bɔ:n/ ¿Cuándo nació...?

Where was ... born? /weə wɒz ... 'bɔ:n/ ¿Dónde nació...?

What did ... do? /wɒt dɪd ... 'du:/ ¿Qué hizo / hacía...?, ¿En qué trabajó / trabajaba...?

Why was ... famous? /waɪ wɒz ... 'feɪməs/ ¿Por qué fue / era famoso/a...?

When did ... get married? /wen dɪd ... get 'mærid/ ¿Cuándo se casó...?

Did ... have children? /dɪd ... həv 'tʃɪldrən/ ¿... tuvo / tenía hijos?

When did ... die? /wen dɪd ... 'daɪ/ ¿Cuándo murió...?

Where did ... die? /weə dɪd ... 'daɪ/ ¿Dónde murió...?

Planning a holiday

What kind of holiday do you want? /wɒt kaɪnd əv 'hɒlədeɪ də ju: wɒnt/ ¿Qué tipo de vacaciones quieres?

Where do you want to go? /weə də ju: wɒnt tə 'gəʊ/ ¿Adónde quieres ir?

When do you want to go? /wen də ju: wɒnt tə 'gəʊ/ ¿Cuándo quieres ir?

How long do you want to be away? /haʊ 'lɒŋ də ju: wɒnt tə bi: əweɪ/ ¿Cuánto tiempo quieres estar fuera?

What do you want to do there? /wɒt də ju: wɒnt tə 'du: ðeə/ ¿Qué quieres hacer allí?

What do you think of ... ? /wɒt də ju: 'θɪŋk əv/ ¿Qué piensas / opinas de...?

A personal interview

How many ... have you got? /haʊ meni '... hæv juː gɒt/ ¿Cuántos/as... tienes?

What are your favourite ... ? /wɒt ɑː jɔː 'feɪvərɪt/ ¿Cuáles son tus... favoritos/as?

What ... do you do? /wɒt '... də juː də/ ¿Qué... haces?

How often do you ... ? /haʊ 'ɒfn də juː/ ¿Con qué frecuencia...?

Where does ... work? /weə dʌz '... wɜːk/ ¿Dónde trabaja...?

What's the weather like where you live? /wɒts ðə 'weðə laɪk weə juː lɪv/ ¿Cómo es el tiempo donde vives?

Investigating a crime

What were you doing on ... at ... last night? /wɒt wɜː juː 'duːɪŋ ɒn ... ət ... lɑːst naɪt/ ¿Qué estaba haciendo en... anoche a las...?

What happened? /wɒt 'hæpənd/ ¿Qué ocurrió / pasó?

What did you do? /wɒt dɪd juː 'duː/ ¿Qué hizo?

Can you describe the ... ? /kæn juː 'dɪskraɪb ðə/ ¿Puede describir (a) el / la...?

What was ... wearing? /wɒt wəz ... 'weərɪŋ/ ¿Qué llevaba puesto...?

Can you give us any more information? /kæn juː gɪv əs eni mɔː ɪnfə'meɪʃn/ ¿Nos puede dar más información?

Talking about plans

Where are you going? /weə ɑː juː 'gəʊɪŋ/ ¿Adónde vas?

What are you going to do? /wɒt ɑː juː gəʊɪŋ tə 'duː/ ¿Qué vas a hacer?

Who is doing the project with you? /huː ɪz duːɪŋ ðə 'prɒdʒekt wɪð juː/ ¿Quién está haciendo el proyecto contigo?

Do you think it'll be difficult? /duː juː θɪŋk ɪtl biː 'dɪfɪkəlt/ ¿Crees que será difícil?

Will it really help? /wɪl ɪt rɪəli 'help/ ¿De verdad servirá?

Talking about experiences

I'd love to try that, wouldn't you? /aɪd 'lʌv tə traɪ ðæt wʊdnt juː/ Me encantaría probar / intentar eso, ¿a ti no? / ¿y a ti?

But why would I do such a risky thing? /bət waɪ wʊd aɪ duː sʌtʃ ə 'rɪski θɪŋ/ Pero ¿por qué haría yo algo tan arriesgado?

That's not my idea of fun. /ðæts 'nɒt maɪ aɪdɪə əv fʌn/ Esa no es mi idea de diversión.

My parents would be really worried. /maɪ peərənts wʊd biː rɪəli 'wʌrid/ Mis padres estarían muy preocupados.

I'd be too frightened. /aɪd biː tuː 'fraɪtnd/ Estaría demasiado asustado/a.

It sounds like a ridiculous idea to me. /ɪt saʊndz laɪk ə rɪ'dɪkjələs aɪdɪə tə miː/ Me parece una idea absurda.

What a silly thing to do. /wɒt ə 'sɪli θɪŋ tə duː/ Qué tontería.

I've always wanted to do that, haven't you? /aɪv 'ɔːlweɪz wɒntɪd tə duː ðæt hævnt juː/ Siempre he querido hacer eso, ¿tú no? / ¿y tú?

Giving advice

What should I do? /wɒt ʃəd aɪ 'duː/ ¿Qué debería hacer / hago?

The best thing for you to do is ... . /ðə 'best θɪŋ fə juː tə duː ɪz/ Lo mejor que puedes hacer es... .

I think you need to ... . /aɪ 'θɪŋk juː niːd tə/ Creo que tienes que... .

Maybe you should ... . /'meɪbi juː ʃʊd/ Tal vez deberías... .

I think it's a good idea to ... . /aɪ θɪŋk ɪts ə gʊd aɪd'ɪə tə/ Creo que es buena idea... .

Why don't you ... ? /waɪ 'dəʊnt juː/ ¿Por qué no...?

You can either ... or ... . /juː kən 'aɪðə ... ɔː/ Puedes... o... .

Buying a gift

Does that sound like a good idea? /dʌz ðæt saʊnd laɪk ə gʊd aɪ'dɪə/ ¿(Te) Parece una buena idea?

How much do you want to spend? /haʊ 'mʌtʃ də juː wɒnt tə spend/ ¿Cuánto quieres gastarte?

Let's get ... ! /lets 'get/ ¡Vamos a comprar / Compremos...!

Let's buy ... ! /lets 'baɪ/ ¡Vamos a comprar / Compremos...!

It's quite ... . /ɪts 'kwaɪt/ Es bastante... .

How about getting this ... ? /'haʊ əbaʊt getɪŋ ðɪs/ ¿Qué tal si compro / compramos este/a...?

What a great idea! /wɒt ə greɪt aɪ'dɪə/ ¡Qué buena idea!

I don't think so. /aɪ dəʊnt 'θɪŋk səʊ/ Me parece / Creo que no.

What do you want to buy for ... ? /wɒt də juː wɒnt tə 'baɪ fɔː/ ¿Qué quieres comprar para...?

These are very ... . /'ðiːz ɑː veri/ Estos/as son muy... .

I agree. /aɪ ə'griː/ Estoy de acuerdo.

What do you think of ... ? /wɒt də juː 'θɪŋk əv/ ¿Qué piensas / opinas de...?

That looks ... . /ðæt 'lʊks/ (Eso) Parece / Está... .

Thinking / Answering

I'm pretty sure ... /aɪm 'prɪti ʃʊə/ Estoy bastante seguro/a de...

I have no idea. /aɪ hæv nəʊ aɪ'dɪə/ No tengo ni idea.

I think so. /aɪ 'θɪŋk səʊ/ Eso creo., Creo que sí.

Agreeing and disagreeing

That's true. /ðæts 'truː/ Eso es verdad / cierto.

That's wrong. /ðæts 'rɒŋ/ Eso es incorrecto / está mal.

That's false. /ðæts 'fɔːls/ Eso es falso.

No way! /nəʊ 'weɪ/ ¡Ni hablar!, ¡De ninguna manera!

Asking questions

Who / What / Where / Why ... ? /huː/wɒt/weə/waɪ/ ¿Quién/enes...? / ¿Qué...?, ¿Cuáles...? / ¿Dónde...?, ¿Adónde...? / ¿Por qué...?

Which ... ? /wɪtʃ/ ¿Cuál/es…?, ¿Qué…?

How / How many / How long ... ? /haʊ/haʊ 'meni/ haʊ 'lɒŋ/ ¿Cómo…? / ¿Cuántos/as…? / ¿Cuánto tiempo…?

Asking for clarification

Can you repeat that? /kən juː rɪ'piːt ðæt/ ¿Puedes repetir eso?

How do you spell that? /haʊ də juː 'spel ðæt/ ¿Cómo se deletrea eso?

How many? /haʊ 'meni/ ¿Cuántos/as?

When was that? /wen wəz 'ðæt/ ¿Cuándo fue eso?

Asking for more information

Why do you think that? /waɪ duː juː 'θɪŋk ðæt/ ¿Por qué piensas eso?

What else? /wɒt 'els/ ¿Qué más?

Tell me more. /tel miː 'mɔː/ Cuéntame más (cosas).

Making suggestions

Let's ... /lets/ Vamos / Vayamos a…

What do you think of ... ? /wɒt də juː 'θɪŋk əv/ ¿Qué piensas / opinas de…?

How about ... ? /haʊ ə'baʊt/ ¿Qué tal si…?, ¿Qué hay de…?

Answering questions

I'm quite sure. /aɪm 'kwaɪt ʃʊə/ Estoy totalmente seguro/a.

That's easy. /ðæts 'iːzi/ Eso es fácil.

I'm really not sure. /aɪm 'riːəli nɒt ʃʊə/ La verdad es que no estoy seguro/a.

Comparing

So do I. /səʊ duː 'aɪ/ Yo / A mí también.

Me, too. /miː 'tuː/ Yo / A mí también.

Not me. /nɒt 'miː/ Yo / A mí no.

Thinking back

Let me think. /let miː 'θɪŋk/ Déjame pensar / que piense.

I really don't remember. /aɪ 'riːəli dəʊnt rɪmembə/ La verdad es que no me acuerdo.

I'm not sure. /aɪm nɒt 'ʃʊə/ No estoy seguro/a.

Answering questions

I think ... /aɪ 'θɪŋk/ Creo…

Definitely. /'defɪnətli/ Seguro., Sin duda.

Not really. /nɒt 'rɪəli/ No mucho., La verdad es que no.

I'm quite sure. /aɪm 'kwaɪt ʃʊə/ Estoy totalmente seguro/a.

Predicting plans

probably /'prɒbəbli/ probablemente

definitely /'defɪnətli/ decididamente, definitivamente

maybe /'meɪbi/ tal vez, quizá/s

Reacting

How boring! /haʊ 'bɔːrɪŋ/ ¡Qué aburrido/a!

Aren't you exaggerating? /ɑːnt juː ɪg'zædʒəreɪtɪŋ/ ¿No estás exagerando?

That's a nice idea. /ðæts ə naɪs aɪ'dɪə/ Esa es una buena idea.

Comparing experiences

How about you? /haʊ əbaʊt 'juː/ ¿Y tú?, ¿Qué hay de ti?

And you? /ənd 'juː/ ¿Y tú?

Me, too. /miː 'tuː/ Yo / A mí también.

Me neither. /miː 'naɪðə/ Yo / A mí tampoco.

Showing surprise

No way! /nəʊ 'weɪ/ ¡Ni hablar!, ¡De ninguna manera!

Are you crazy? /ɑː juː 'kreɪzi/ ¿Estás loco/a?

Are you kidding? /ɑː juː 'kɪdɪŋ/ ¿Estás bromeando / de broma?

Of course. /əv 'kɔːs/ Por supuesto.

Thinking

Um ... /ʌm/ Eh…

I'm not sure. /aɪm nɒt 'ʃʊə/ No estoy seguro/a.

Let me think. /let miː 'θɪŋk/ Déjame pensar / que piense.

Solving problems

Perhaps ... /pə'hæps/ Tal vez / Quizá/s…

It seems to me (that) ... /ɪt siːmz tə 'miː ðæt/ Me parece (que)…

In my opinion, ... /ɪn maɪ ə'pɪnjən/ En mi opinión, …

Saying when

in the past /ɪn ðə 'pɑːst/ en el pasado

the other day /ðə 'ʌðə deɪ/ el otro día

a while ago /ə 'waɪl əgəʊ/ hace rato, hace un tiempo

Reacting

Do you? /'duː juː/ ¿Sí?

That's too bad. /ðæts 'tuː bæd/ Qué pena / lástima.

Yes, we are. /'jes wiː ɑː/ Sí.

Grammar Appendix

Getting Started

Los pronombres personales sujeto

I	yo	**it**	ello
you	tú, usted	**we**	nosotros/as
he	él	**you**	vosotros/as, ustedes
she	ella	**they**	ellos/as

- Hacen de sujeto y nunca pueden faltar para que la oración sea correcta y tenga sentido.
  I have got a new notebook. ***It*** *is blue.*
  (Tengo un cuaderno nuevo. Es azul.)
- Recuerda que ***I*** siempre se escribe en mayúscula y que ***it*** (que se refiere a cosas o animales) no se suele traducir.

Los adjetivos posesivos

my	mi, mis
your	tu, tus, su, sus (de usted)
his	su, sus (de él)
her	su, sus (de ella)
its	su, sus (de cosa o animal)
our	nuestro/a, nuestros/as
your	vuestro/a, vuestros/as, su, sus (de ustedes)
their	su, sus (de ellos/as)

- Indican de quién es algo.
- Siempre van delante del sustantivo que indica lo que se posee, sin importar el género ni el número que tenga: ***my*** *class*, ***my*** *books* (mi clase, mis libros).
- En la 3ª persona del singular hay tres formas, dependiendo de si el poseedor es de género masculino (***his***), femenino (***her***) o neutro (***its***).

Los pronombres posesivos

mine	mío/a, míos/as
yours	tuyo/a, tuyos/as, suyo/a, suyos/as (de usted)
his	suyo/a, suyos/as (de él)
hers	suyo/a, suyos/as (de ella)
ours	nuestro/a, nuestros/as
yours	vuestro/a, vuestros/as, suyo/a, suyos/as (de ustedes)
theirs	suyo/a, suyos/as (de ellos/as)

- Sustituyen al sustantivo que indica lo que se posee y concuerdan con el poseedor.
  The red schoolbag is ***yours****.* (La mochila roja es tuya.)
- Al traducirlos, se pueden acompañar estos pronombres con el artículo determinado.
  The green book isn't ***mine****. It's* ***yours****.*
  (El libro verde no es (el) mío. Es (el) tuyo.)
- En la 3ª persona del singular hay dos formas: masculina (***his***) y femenina (***hers***). No hay forma neutra.

El genitivo sajón

- Se emplea para indicar posesión y se usa con personas, animales o países. Para formarlo, añadimos un apóstrofo (***'***) y una ***s***.
  *Lucy****'s*** *hair* (el pelo de Lucy)
  *the cat****'s*** *legs* (las patas del gato)
  *Spain****'s*** *food* (la comida de España)
- Si el sustantivo es un plural regular o acaba en ***s***, se añade solo ***'***, pero si es un plural irregular se añade ***'s***.
  the boys' school (el colegio de los niños)
  *the women****'s*** *photo* (la foto de las mujeres)
- Si el nombre propio acaba en ***s***, se puede añadir ***'*** o ***'s***.
  *James' / James****'s*** *car* (el coche de James)
- Con las cosas se usa ***of***, no el genitivo sajón.
  the colour ***of*** *the pencil* (el color del lápiz)

El verbo *to be*

El verbo ***to be*** significa principalmente "ser" o "estar".

- **Afirmativa:** sujeto + ***am*** / ***is*** / ***are***. Es el único verbo que tiene tres formas distintas en el presente. Las formas contraídas se usan más en la conversación.
  She ***is*** *very clever.* (Ella es muy inteligente.)
- **Negativa:** sujeto + ***am*** / ***is*** / ***are*** + la partícula ***not*** o la contracción ***n't*** (que se puede añadir a ***is*** y a ***are***, pero no a ***am***).
  You ***aren't*** *funny.* (No sois graciosos.)
- **Interrogativa:** ***Am*** / ***Is*** / ***Are*** + sujeto.
  Is *he a singer?* (¿Él es cantante?)
- **Respuestas breves:** se pone el pronombre personal sujeto + el verbo ***to be***, sin contraer en afirmativa o contraído en negativa.
  Is *Woody a toy? Yes, he* ***is****. / No, he* ***isn't****.*
  (¿Woody es un juguete? Sí. / No.)

Los usos del verbo *to be*

Definiciones y hechos generales	*Bristol* ***is*** *in England.* (Bristol está en Inglaterra.)
Sentimientos y estados	*We* ***are*** *very happy.* (Estamos muy contentos.)
Edad	*She* ***is*** *twelve years old.* (Ella tiene doce años.)
Profesiones, religiones y nacionalidades	*Johnny Depp* ***is*** *an actor.* (Johnny Depp es un actor.)
Precios	*How much* ***is*** *it? It's 5 euros.* (¿Cuánto es? Son 5 euros.)
Medidas	*It's 2 metres long.* (Mide 2 metros de largo.)
Tiempo atmosférico	*It* ***is*** *windy.* (Hace viento.)

El verbo *have got*

El verbo ***have got*** significa "tener". Expresa lo que poseemos o las características de alguien o algo cuando lo describimos.

- **Afirmativa:** sujeto + ***have*** (*'ve*) ***got*** o ***has*** (*'s*) ***got***.
  *I **have got** a famous friend.*
  (Tengo una amiga famosa.)
- **Negativa:** sujeto + ***have*** / ***has*** + ***not*** (*n't*) + ***got***.
  *She **hasn't got** curly hair.*
  (Ella no tiene el pelo rizado.)
- **Interrogativa:** ***Have*** / ***Has*** + sujeto + ***got***.
  ***Have** you **got** an adventurous brother?*
  (¿Tienes un hermano aventurero?)
- **Respuestas breves:** se pone el pronombre personal sujeto + ***have*** / ***has*** o ***haven't*** / ***hasn't*** (sin ***got***).
  ***Has** he **got** small ears? Yes, he **has**. / No, he **hasn't**.*
  (¿Él tiene las orejas pequeñas? Sí. / No.)

Los pronombres personales objeto

me	me (a mí)
you	te (a ti), lo, la, le, se (a usted)
him	lo, le, se (a él)
her	la, le, se (a ella)
it	lo, la (una cosa)
us	nos (a nosotros/as)
you	os (a vosotros/as), los, las, les (a ustedes)
them	los, las, les, se (a ellos/as)

- Hacen las funciones de objeto, es decir, de complemento directo, indirecto o preposicional.
  *I met **him** last month.*
  (Lo / Le conocí el mes pasado.)
  *They gave **me** a present yesterday.*
  (Me dieron un regalo ayer.)
  *I sang for **them**.* (Canté para ellos.)
- Si en la frase hay un complemento directo y otro indirecto en su forma de pronombre, se ponen en este orden: CD + preposición + CI.
  *Sue needed a book about art and I gave **it** to **her**.*
  (Sue necesitaba un libro sobre arte y yo se lo di.)

El *Present Simple*

- **Afirmativa:** es como la forma base del verbo (infinitivo sin ***to***) en todas las personas menos en la 3ª del singular, en la que se añade ***-s***.
  *He **walks** the dog every day.*
  (Él pasea al perro todos los días.)

  En los siguientes casos, se añade ***-es*** en vez de *-s*:
  - Si acaba en ***ss***, ***sh***, ***ch*** y ***x***:
    pass - passes *wash - washes* *mix - mixes*
  - Si acaba en ***o***:
    do - does *go - goes*
  - Si acaba en **consonante** + ***y***, se cambia la ***y*** por una ***i***:
    study - studies *carry - carries*
- **Negativa:** sujeto + ***do*** / ***does*** + ***not*** (*n't*) + verbo en la forma base.
  *My mother **doesn't cook**.* (Mi madre no cocina.)
- **Interrogativa:** ***Do*** / ***Does*** + sujeto + verbo.
  ***Do** you **study** with friends?* (¿Estudias con amigos?)
- **Respuestas breves:** se pone el pronombre personal sujeto + ***do*** / ***does*** o ***don't*** / ***doesn't***.
  ***Does** she **watch** TV? Yes, she **does**. / No, she **doesn't**.*
  (¿Ella ve la televisión? Sí. / No.)
- Con el *Present Simple* se suelen usar las siguientes **expresiones temporales:** ***every day*** / ***week*** / ***year*** (todos/as los días / semanas / años), ***once*** / ***twice a year*** (una / dos veces al año), ***on*** + día de la semana en plural, ***at night*** (por la noche), ***in the morning*** (por la mañana), ***in the summer*** (en verano), etc. Todas pueden ir al principio o al final de la frase, pero se suelen poner al final.
  *She **plays** football **twice a year**.*
  (Ella juega al fútbol dos veces al año.)
- También se utilizan estos **adverbios de frecuencia:** ***always*** (siempre), ***usually*** (normalmente), ***often*** (a menudo), ***sometimes*** (algunas veces, a veces), ***rarely*** (rara vez) y ***never*** (nunca). Estos se colocan delante del verbo, pero si acompañan al verbo ***to be*** se sitúan detrás.
  *We **often go** there.* (A menudo vamos allí.)
  *She **is always** funny.* (Ella siempre es graciosa.)

Los usos del *Present Simple*

Verdades generales y descripciones	*The sun **sets** in the west.* (El sol se pone por el oeste.)
Hechos habituales o cotidianos	*Do you **play** football?* (¿Juegas al fútbol?)
Gustos y opiniones	*She **likes** sport.* (Le gustan los deportes.)
Programas y horarios	*We **get up** at 7.30.* (Nos levantamos a las 7:30.)

El *Present Continuous*

Expresa lo que está ocurriendo en el momento de hablar o en el periodo de tiempo presente.

- **Afirmativa:** sujeto + ***am*** / ***is*** / ***are*** + un verbo terminado en ***-ing***.
  *He **is visiting** the house.* (Él está visitando la casa.)

  En los siguientes casos, hay que fijarse en estas reglas ortográficas para añadir ***-ing*** al verbo:
  - Si acaba en ***e*** muda, se pierde la ***e***:
    live - living
  - Si es de 1 sílaba y acaba en **1 vocal** + **1 consonante** que no sea ***w***, ***x*** o ***y***, se dobla esta consonante:
    run - running *sit - sitting*
  - Si es de 2 sílabas y tiene el acento en la última, se dobla la última consonante:
    refer - referring *begin - beginning*
  - Si acaba en ***l***, se dobla esa letra:
    travel - travelling
  - Si acaba en ***ie***, se cambia ***ie*** por una ***y***:
    lie - lying *die - dying*

- **Negativa:** sujeto + ***am / is / are*** + la partícula ***not*** o la contracción ***n't*** (que se puede añadir a ***is*** y a ***are***, pero no a ***am***) + un verbo terminado en ***-ing***. En conversación suele usarse la forma contraída.
  *We **aren't driving** my car.*
  (No estamos conduciendo mi coche.)
- **Interrogativa:** ***Am / Is / Are*** + sujeto + un verbo terminado en ***-ing***.
  ***Is** she **sleeping** at the moment?*
  (¿Ella está durmiendo en este momento?)
- **Respuestas breves:** se pone el pronombre personal sujeto + el verbo ***to be***, sin contraer en afirmativa o contraído en negativa.
  ***Are** you **walking** in the forest? Yes, I **am**. / No, I'**m not**.* (¿Estás andando por el bosque? Sí. / No.)
- El *Present Continuous* se suele usar para describir fotos, ya que se habla de la escena como si fuera algo que está ocurriendo ahora.
  *In the photo, there is a man. He **is sitting** on a chair.*
  (En la foto hay un hombre. Está sentado en una silla.)
- Con el *Present Continuous* se suelen usar las siguientes expresiones temporales: ***now*** (ahora), ***at the moment*** (en este momento), ***right now*** (justo ahora, ahora mismo), ***today*** (hoy), ***these days*** (hoy en día), ***this week*** (esta semana), etc.
  Todas pueden ir al principio o al final de la frase, pero se suelen poner al final.
  *I **am buying** a bus ticket **now**.*
  (Estoy comprando un billete de autobús ahora.)

Unit 1

Contraste *Present Simple / Present Continuous*

El *Present Simple* expresa hábitos, mientras que el *Present Continuous* indica lo que está ocurriendo en el momento de hablar.

*I usually **study** at home, but today I'**m studying** at my friend's house.* (Normalmente estudio en casa, pero hoy estoy estudiando en casa de mi amigo.)

Los verbos "estáticos"

Los verbos estáticos se utilizan para expresar gustos, sentimientos y deseos, actividades de la mente, posesión y percepción. Se refieren a estados en lugar de a acciones, por lo que no se suelen utilizar con el *Present Continuous*.

*She **likes** the film.* (A ella le gusta la película.)
*I **don't know** the answer.* (No sé la respuesta.)

There is / There are

	Contables	No contables
Afirmativa	**There is** a house. **There are** rooms.	**There is** rubbish.
Negativa	**There isn't** a toilet. **There aren't** beds.	**There isn't** tea.
Interrogativa	**Is there** a fridge? **Are there** tables?	**Is there** money?
Respuestas breves	Yes, **there is**. / No, **there isn't**. Yes, **there are**. / No, **there aren't**.	

- **Afirmativa:** ***There is*** va seguido de nombres contables en singular o no contables. ***There are*** va seguido de nombres contables en plural. Ambos se traducen como "Hay...".
- **Negativa:** ***There is / There are*** + la partícula ***not*** (***There is not / There are not***) o la contracción ***n't*** (***There isn't / There aren't***).
- **Interrogativa:** las preguntas empiezan por ***Is / Are + there***.
- **Respuestas breves:** se vuelve al orden normal y en la negativa se usan las formas contraídas.

Artículos y cuantificadores

a / an	Con nombres contables en singular. Se usan delante de un nombre que no es conocido por el hablante.	
	un/a	***a** picture, **an** orange* pero ***a** uniform*
the	Con nombres contables y no contables. Se usa delante de un nombre que es conocido por el hablante.	
	el, la, los/as	*I have got a house. **The** house has got a garden.*
some	Frases afirmativas: Con nombres contables en plural y no contables. Frases interrogativas: Cuando la pregunta expresa una oferta o petición y se espera que la respuesta sea afirmativa.	
	unos/as algunos/as algo de un poco de (o no se traduce)	*There are **some** trees.* *We've got **some** fruit.* *Would you like **some** tea?*
any	Frases negativas e interrogativas: Con nombres contables en plural y no contables.	
	ningún/una nada de (o no se traduce)	*I haven't got **any** sisters.* *She hasn't got **any** money.*
	algún/una algunos/as algo de (o no se traduce)	*Are there **any** biscuits?* *Have you got **any** water?*
a lot of / lots of	Con nombres contables en plural y no contables.	
	mucho/a/os/as un montón de	***A lot of** children study here.* *I have got **a lot of** homework.* ***Lots of** people enjoy films.*
many	Con nombres contables en plural.	
	muchos/as	***Many** students play football.*
much	Frases negativas e interrogativas: Con nombres no contables.	
	mucho/a	*I haven't got **much** money.* *Was there **much** smoke?*

How many / How much

Usamos **How many** y **How much** para preguntar por la cantidad de algo.

How many ...? ¿Cuántos/as...?	Nombres contables en plural. *How many rooms are there?*
How much ...? ¿Cuánto/a...?	Nombres no contables. Cuando va con el verbo ***to be*** sirve para preguntar el precio de una cosa. *How much water do you need?* *How much is it?*

Unit 2

El *Past Simple*

Afirmativa	Negativa	Forma contraída
I **washed**	I **did not wash**	I **didn't wash**
You **washed**	You **did not wash**	You **didn't wash**
He **washed**	He **did not wash**	He **didn't wash**
She **washed**	She **did not wash**	She **didn't wash**
It **washed**	It **did not wash**	It **didn't wash**
We **washed**	We **did not wash**	We **didn't wash**
You **washed**	You **did not wash**	You **didn't wash**
They **washed**	They **did not wash**	They **didn't wash**

Interrogativa	Respuestas breves	
	Afirmativa	Negativa
Did I **wash** ...?	Yes, I **did**.	No, I **didn't**.
Did you **wash** ...?	Yes, you **did**.	No, you **didn't**.
Did he **wash** ...?	Yes, he **did**.	No, he **didn't**.
Did she **wash** ...?	Yes, she **did**.	No, she **didn't**.
Did it **wash** ...?	Yes, it **did**.	No, it **didn't**.
Did we **wash** ...?	Yes, we **did**.	No, we **didn't**.
Did you **wash** ...?	Yes, you **did**.	No, you **didn't**.
Did they **wash** ...?	Yes, they **did**.	No, they **didn't**.

- **Afirmativa:** se forma añadiendo ***-ed*** a los verbos regulares y es igual en todas las personas. Los verbos irregulares no siguen ninguna regla y por eso hay que aprenderlos de memoria. Puedes consultar la lista de las páginas 107-108.
  *I **visited** Larry last night.* (Visité a Larry anoche.)

  En los siguientes casos, hay que fijarse en estas reglas ortográficas para añadir ***-ed*** al verbo:

  - Si es de 1 sílaba y acaba en **1 vocal** + **1 consonante** que no sea ***w***, ***x*** o ***y***, se dobla esta consonante:
    stop** - stopp**ed ***drop** - dropp**ed***
  - Si es de 2 sílabas y tiene el acento en la última, se dobla la última consonante:
    prefer** - preferr**ed ***permit** - permitt**ed***
  - Si acaba en ***l***, se dobla esa letra:
    travel** - travell**ed
  - Si acaba en **consonante** + ***y***, se cambia la ***y*** por una ***i***:
    worry** - worri**ed ***try** - tri**ed***
  - Si acaba en ***e*** muda, solo se añade ***-d***:
    bake** - bake**d ***live** - live**d***

- **Negativa:** sujeto + ***did not*** o ***didn't*** + un verbo en la forma base.
  *She **didn't go** there.* (Ella no fue allí.)
- **Interrogativa:** ***Did*** + sujeto + un verbo en la forma base.
  ***Did** you **call** her last night?* (¿La llamaste anoche?)
- **Respuestas breves:** se pone el pronombre personal sujeto + ***did*** o ***didn't***.
  ***Did** she **go** to the party? Yes, she **did**. / No, she **didn't**.*
  (¿Ella fue a la fiesta? Sí. / No.)
- Con el *Past Simple* se suelen usar estas **expresiones temporales**: las que llevan ***ago*** (hace) al final de la expresión, ***last night / week*** (anoche, la semana pasada), ***at*** + una hora, ***on*** + un día / fecha, ***in*** + un año, ***in the past*** (en el pasado), ***yesterday*** (ayer), etc. Pueden ir al principio o al final de la frase, pero se suelen poner al final.
  *Three days **ago**, they **came**.* (Vinieron hace tres días.)
  *He **created** the company **in** 1989.*
  (Él creó la empresa en 1989.)

Los usos del *Past Simple*

Expresar acciones pasadas	*We **watched** that film.* (Vimos esa película.)
Decir qué se hizo en un momento concreto	*They **went** home yesterday.* (Se fueron a casa ayer.)
Contar acciones pasadas consecutivas	*I **visited** the tower. Then I **went** to the museum.* (Visité la torre. Luego fui al museo.)
Contar cómo eran las cosas en otro tiempo	*In the past, people **worked** more hours.* (En el pasado, la gente trabajaba más horas.)

There was / There were

	Contables	No contables
Afirmativa	**There was** a house. **There were** rooms.	**There was** rubbish.
Negativa	**There wasn't** a toilet. **There weren't** beds.	**There wasn't** tea.
Interrogativa	**Was there** a fridge? **Were there** tables?	**Was there** money?
Respuestas breves	Yes, **there was**. / No, **there wasn't**. Yes, **there were**. / No, **there weren't**.	

- **Afirmativa:** *There was* va seguido de nombres contables en singular o no contables. *There were* va seguido de nombres contables en plural.
  Son las formas de pasado de *There is* y *There are* y, por lo tanto, significan "Había..." o "Hubo...".
- **Negativa:** *There was* / *There were* + la partícula ***not*** (*There was not* / *There were not*) o la contracción ***n't*** (*There wasn't* / *There weren't*).
- **Interrogativa:** las preguntas empiezan por *Was* / *Were* + *there*.
- **Respuestas breves:** se vuelve al orden normal y en la negativa se usan las formas contraídas.

used to

Used to expresa hechos o estados que eran habituales en otro tiempo y luego dejaron de serlo. Solo tiene la forma de pasado y va seguido de otro verbo en la forma base. Se traduce como el pretérito imperfecto del verbo "soler" o del verbo que lo sigue.

- **Afirmativa:** sujeto + ***used to*** + un verbo en la forma base.
  *We **used to go** to the swimming pool every day.*
  (Solíamos ir / Íbamos a la piscina todos los días.)
- **Negativa:** sujeto + ***did not / didn't*** + ***use to*** (sin "d") + un verbo en la forma base.
  *He **didn't use to buy** vegetables.* (No solía comprar / compraba verduras.)
- **Interrogativa:** ***Did*** + sujeto + ***use to*** (sin "d") + un verbo en la forma base.
  ***Did** you **use to play** tennis on Sundays?*
  (¿Solías ir / Ibas a jugar al tenis los domingos?)
- **Respuestas breves:** se pone el pronombre personal sujeto + ***did*** o ***didn't***.
  ***Did** she **use to travel** abroad? Yes, she **did**. / No, she **didn't**.* (¿Solía viajar / Viajaba al extranjero? Sí. / No.)

Unit 3

El comparativo de los adjetivos

Para comparar dos cosas, animales o personas se utilizan los adjetivos en grado comparativo.

- El comparativo de **superioridad** (más... que) se usa para comparar dos cosas, animales o personas cuando una supera a la otra en algún aspecto. Para formarlo hay que fijarse en la longitud del adjetivo:

  1. Si tiene 1 sílaba, o 2 y termina en *y*, el adjetivo se considera corto y se le añade la terminación *-er*. Detrás se pone la partícula ***than***.
  *A crocodile is **bigger than** a lizard.*
  (Un cocodrilo es más grande que un lagarto.)

  En los siguientes casos, el adjetivo cambia al añadirle *-er*:

  - Si tiene 1 sílaba y acaba en **1 vocal + 1 consonante**, se dobla esa consonante:
    *th**in** - thi**nner*** *b**ig** - bi**gger***
  - Si acaba en **consonante** + *y*, se cambia la *y* por una *i*:
    *craz**y** - craz**ier*** *dr**y** - dr**ier***
  - Si acaba en *l*, se duplica esa letra:
    *crue**l** - crue**ller***
  - Si acaba en *e* muda, solo se añade *-r*:
    *nic**e** - nice**r***

  2. Si tiene 2 sílabas o más, el adjetivo se considera largo y la comparativa se forma con ***more*** + adjetivo + ***than***.
  *Wolves are **more dangerous than** zebras.*
  (Los lobos son más peligrosos que las cebras.)

- El comparativo de **inferioridad** se forma con ***less*** + adjetivo + ***than*** (menos... que).
  *Chimpanzees are **less frightening than** gorillas.*
  (Los chimpancés dan menos miedo que los gorilas.)

El superlativo de los adjetivos

- Se usa para comparar más de dos cosas, animales o personas y decir que una destaca sobre las demás. También hay que tener en cuenta la longitud del adjetivo:

  1. Si es corto, se pone delante ***the*** y se le añade la terminación ***-est*** según las mismas reglas que para formar el comparativo con ***-er***.
  *This is **the cheapest** necklace in the shop.*
  (Este es el collar más barato de la tienda.)

  2. Si es largo, se pone delante ***the most***.
  *This forest is **the most pleasant** place in the area.*
  (Este bosque es el lugar más agradable de la zona.)

- El superlativo puede ir seguido de las preposiciones ***in***, ***of*** y ***on***.
  *Spring is **the most colourful** season **of** the year.*
  (La primavera es la estación más colorida del año.)
- Para indicar que alguien o algo es inferior que el resto en algún aspecto se utiliza la estructura ***the least*** + adjetivo.
  *Deserts are **the least noisy** places in the world.* (Los desiertos son los lugares menos ruidosos del mundo.)

Los adjetivos irregulares

Al no seguir ninguna regla, hay que aprender sus formas comparativa y superlativa de memoria.

Adjetivo	Comparativo	Superlativo
good (bueno/a)	**better**	**best**
bad (malo/a)	**worse** /wɜːʳs/	**worst** /wɜːʳst/ peor
far (lejano/a)	**farther / further**	**farthest / furthest**
little (poco/a)	**less**	**least**

/fa:ðə/ /fa:ðest/

(not) as ... as / too ... / (not) ... enough

- El comparativo de **igualdad** se forma con (***not***) ***as*** + adjetivo + ***as*** ((no) tan... como).
  *This table is **as heavy as** an elephant.*
  (Esta mesa es tan pesada como un elefante.)
  *Mount Aneto is **not as high as** Mount Everest.*
  (El Aneto no es tan alto como el Everest.)
- ***Too*** va delante del adjetivo e indica que la cualidad expresada por este es excesiva. Significa "demasiado".
  *These earrings are **too expensive** for me.*
  (Estos pendientes son demasiado caros para mí.)
- En cambio, ***enough*** se pone detrás del adjetivo y significa "(lo) bastante" o "(lo) suficientemente".
  *This pub is **lively enough** for us.* (Este bar es (lo) bastante / suficientemente animado para nosotros.)

  Y ***not*** + adjetivo + ***enough*** significa "no (lo) bastante" o "no (lo) suficientemente".
  *This place is **not peaceful enough** to study.* (Este lugar no es (lo) bastante tranquilo para estudiar.)
  *I **didn't** feel **full enough** after the meal.* (No me sentí (lo) suficientemente lleno después de la comida.)

Cat nap -sista

Unit 4

Subject / Object Questions

Las partículas interrogativas ***who***, ***what***, ***which***, ***where***, ***when***, ***why*** y ***how often*** se utilizan para hacer preguntas sobre el sujeto, el complemento directo o el complemento circunstancial de la oración.

- Para pedir información sobre el sujeto utilizamos ***who*** o ***what***. El orden de las palabras en la pregunta es igual que el de una frase afirmativa y siempre se pone el verbo en la 3ª persona del singular, pero la respuesta puede ir en singular o en plural.
  *Who **works** in this company? He **works** in this company.* (¿Quién trabaja en esta empresa? Él trabaja en esta empresa.)
  *What **makes** you feel happy? Babies **make** me feel happy.* (¿Qué te hace sentir feliz? Los bebés me hacen sentir feliz.)
- Para pedir información sobre el complemento directo utilizamos ***who***, ***what*** o ***which***. El orden de las palabras en la pregunta es igual que el de una frase interrogativa, así que siempre hay que invertir el orden sujeto-verbo o emplear ***do***, ***does*** o ***did***.
  *What **do** you **prefer**?* (¿Qué prefieres?)
  *Which sport **do** you **play**?* (¿A qué deporte juegas?)
  Cuando el verbo rige una preposición, esta se pone al final de la pregunta.
  *Who **did** you **play** baseball **with**?*
  (¿Con quién jugaste al béisbol?)
- Para pedir información sobre el complemento circunstancial (lugar, tiempo, causa o frecuencia) utilizamos ***where***, ***when***, ***why*** o ***how often***. El orden de las palabras en la pregunta es igual que el de una frase interrogativa, así que hay que invertir el orden sujeto-verbo o emplear ***do***, ***does*** o ***did***.
  *Where **does** she **have** lunch?* (¿Dónde come ella?)
  *When **did** they **arrive**?* (¿Cuándo llegaron?)
  *Why **is** Beth **crying**?* (¿Por qué está llorando Beth?)
  *How often **does** it **rain**?* (¿Con qué frecuencia llueve?)

Los adverbios de modo

- Los adverbios de modo describen la forma en que se realiza la acción. Con ellos se responde a las preguntas que empiezan con ***How ... ?*** (¿Cómo...?).
- La mayoría son regulares y se forman añadiendo la terminación ***-ly*** al adjetivo correspondiente.
  *They eat **slowly**.* (Comen despacio.)
  Si el adjetivo acaba en **consonante** + ***y***, se cambia la ***y*** por una ***i*** y luego se añade ***-ly***.
  *It all ended **happily**.* (Todo acabó felizmente.)
- Algunos son irregulares y, o bien no se parecen nada al adjetivo, o bien son iguales.
  *She sings very **well**.* (Ella canta muy bien.)

El comparativo de los adverbios

- Sirve para comparar dos acciones y se forma así: ***more*** / ***less*** + adverbio + ***than***.
  *You listened to it **more carefully than** I did.*
  (Lo escuchaste con más atención que yo.)
- Con ***as*** + adverbio + ***as*** se indica que dos acciones se realizan de la misma forma.
  *We ran **as fast as** you.* (Corrimos tan deprisa como tú.)

Los adverbios irregulares

Al no seguir ninguna regla, hay que aprender de memoria estos adverbios y su forma comparativa.

Adjetivo	Adverbio	Forma comparativa
fast (rápido/a)	**fast** (rápidamente, deprisa)	**faster than**
hard (duro/a; difícil)	**hard** (duro, mucho)	**harder than**
high (alto/a)	**high** (alto)	**higher than**
far (lejano/a)	**far** (lejos)	**farther / further than**
good (bueno/a)	**well** (bien)	**better than**
bad (malo/a)	**badly** (mal)	**worse than**

Unit 5

El *Past Continuous*

Afirmativa	Negativa
I **was eating**	I **was not / wasn't eating**
You **were eating**	You **were not / weren't eating**
He **was eating**	He **was not / wasn't eating**
She **was eating**	She **was not / wasn't eating**
It **was eating**	It **was not / wasn't eating**
We **were eating**	We **were not / weren't eating**
You **were eating**	You **were not / weren't eating**
They **were eating**	They **were not / weren't eating**

Interrogativa	Respuestas breves	
	Afirmativa	Negativa
Was I **eating**?	Yes, I **was**.	No, I **wasn't**.
Were you **eating**?	Yes, you **were**.	No, you **weren't**.
Was he **eating**?	Yes, he **was**.	No, he **wasn't**.
Was she **eating**?	Yes, she **was**.	No, she **wasn't**.
Was it **eating**?	Yes, it **was**.	No, it **wasn't**.
Were we **eating**?	Yes, we **were**.	No, we **weren't**.
Were you **eating**?	Yes, you **were**.	No, you **weren't**.
Were they **eating**?	Yes, they **were**.	No, they **weren't**.

- **Afirmativa:** sujeto + ***was*** / ***were*** + un verbo terminado en ***-ing***.
  *I **was cooking** in the kitchen.*
  (Estaba cocinando en la cocina.)
  Las reglas para añadir ***-ing*** se encuentran en la pág. 95.
- **Negativa:** sujeto + ***was*** / ***were*** + la partícula ***not*** o la contracción ***n't*** + un verbo terminado en ***-ing***.
  *They **weren't playing** tennis.*
  (No estaban jugando al tenis.)
- **Interrogativa:** ***Was*** / ***Were*** + sujeto + un verbo terminado en ***-ing***.
  ***Was** Sue **taking** pictures?* (¿Sue estaba haciendo fotos?)
- **Respuestas breves:** se pone el pronombre personal sujeto + ***was*** / ***were***, sin contraer en afirmativa o contraído en negativa.
  ***Was** it **raining** yesterday? Yes, it **was**. / No, it **wasn't**.*
  (¿Estuvo lloviendo ayer? Sí. / No.)

- Con el *Past Continuous* se suelen usar estas **expresiones temporales**: las que llevan ***ago*** (hace) al final de la expresión, ***at*** + una hora, ***yesterday morning / afternoon*** (ayer por la mañana / tarde), ***last night*** (anoche), etc. Pueden ir al principio o al final de la frase, pero se suelen poner al final.
  *They **were watching** a match **at six o'clock yesterday**.*
  (Estaban viendo un partido ayer a las seis en punto.)

Los usos del *Past Continuous*

Expresar lo que estaba ocurriendo en el pasado	*At eight o'clock last night, we **were swimming**.* (Anoche a las ocho en punto, estábamos nadando.)
Describir dos o más acciones prolongadas y simultáneas en el pasado, unidas por ***while*** o ***as***	*She **was talking** to her friend **while / as** she **was driving**.* (Ella estaba hablando con su amiga mientras estaba conduciendo.)

Contraste *Past Continuous / Past Simple*

- El *Past Simple* indica que la acción ocurrió y terminó en el tiempo indicado en la frase, mientras que el *Past Continuous* habla de acciones prolongadas que estaban ocurriendo en el pasado.
  *He **did** his homework last Monday.*
  (Hizo los deberes el lunes pasado.)
  *He **was doing** his homework yesterday afternoon.*
  (Estuvo haciendo los deberes ayer por la tarde.)
- Con el *Past Simple* se suele utilizar ***when*** y con el *Past Continuous* las conjunciones ***while*** o ***as***.
  *We were listening to the news **when** he **arrived**.*
  (Estábamos escuchando las noticias cuando llegó.)
  ***While / As** we **were listening** to the news, he arrived.*
  (Llegó mientras estábamos escuchando las noticias.)

Unit 6

El futuro con *will*

Afirmativa	Forma contraída
I **will read**	I**'ll read**
You **will read**	You**'ll read**
He **will read**	He**'ll read**
She **will read**	She**'ll read**
It **will read**	It**'ll read**
We **will read**	We**'ll read**
You **will read**	You**'ll read**
They **will read**	They**'ll read**
Negativa	**Forma contraída**
I **will not read**	I **won't read**
You **will not read**	You **won't read**
He **will not read**	He **won't read**
She **will not read**	She **won't read**
It **will not read**	It **won't read**
We **will not read**	We **won't read**
You **will not read**	You **won't read**
They **will not read**	They **won't read**

Interrogativa	Respuestas breves	
	Afirmativa	Negativa
Will I **read** ...?	Yes, I **will**.	No, I **won't**.
Will you **read** ...?	Yes, you **will**.	No, you **won't**.
Will he **read** ...?	Yes, he **will**.	No, he **won't**.
Will she **read** ...?	Yes, she **will**.	No, she **won't**.
Will it **read** ...?	Yes, it **will**.	No, it **won't**.
Will we **read** ...?	Yes, we **will**.	No, we **won't**.
Will you **read** ...?	Yes, you **will**.	No, you **won't**.
Will they **read** ...?	Yes, they **will**.	No, they **won't**.

- **Afirmativa:** sujeto + el auxiliar ***will*** + verbo en la forma base. Es igual en todas las personas.
  En la conversación, ***will*** se contrae con el sujeto (***'ll***) y se pronuncia como una sola "l".
  *We **will win** the match.* (Ganaremos el partido.)
- **Negativa:** sujeto + ***will*** + la partícula ***not*** (o la contracción ***won't***) + verbo en la forma base.
  *They **won't score** another goal.* (No marcarán otro gol.)
- **Interrogativa:** ***Will*** + sujeto + verbo en la forma base.
  ***Will** Jess **play** today?* (¿Jess jugará hoy?)
- **Respuestas breves:** se pone el pronombre personal sujeto + ***will*** o ***won't***.
  ***Will** pollution **increase**? Yes, it **will**. / No, it **won't**.*
  (¿Aumentará la contaminación? Sí. / No.)
- Con ***will*** se suelen usar **expresiones temporales** como ***later*** (más tarde, luego), ***soon*** (pronto, dentro de poco), ***in an hour*** (dentro de una hora), ***next month / year*** (el mes / año que viene / próximo), ***tomorrow*** (mañana), etc. También se usan otras que indican un futuro lejano: ***in ten years*** (dentro de diez años), ***in*** + un año, ***one day*** (algún día), ***in the future*** (en el futuro), etc. Todas pueden ir al principio o al final de la frase, pero se suelen poner al final.
  ***One day**, I **will become** a doctor.*
  (Algún día llegaré a ser médico.)

Los usos del futuro con *will*

Anunciar acciones o hechos futuros	*Messi **will score** a goal.* (Messi marcará un gol.)
Predecir lo que se cree que ocurrirá	*I think it **will rain** tomorrow.* (Creo que lloverá mañana.)
Expresar decisiones repentinas	*It's cold. I**'ll take** my coat.* (Hace frío. Cogeré el abrigo.)

El futuro con *be going to*

Afirmativa	Forma contraída
I **am going to run**	I**'m going to run**
You **are going to run**	You**'re going to run**
He **is going to run**	He**'s going to run**
She **is going to run**	She**'s going to run**
It **is going to run**	It**'s going to run**
We **are going to run**	We**'re going to run**
You **are going to run**	You**'re going to run**
They **are going to run**	They**'re going to run**

Negativa y forma contraída
I **am not** / I**'m not going to run**
You **are not** / You **aren't** / You**'re not going to run**
He **is not** / He **isn't** / He**'s not going to run**
She **is not** / She **isn't** / She**'s not going to run**
It **is not** / It **isn't** / It**'s not going to run**
We **are not** / We **aren't** / We**'re not going to run**
You **are not** / You **aren't** / You**'re not going to run**
They **are not** / They **aren't** / They**'re not going to run**

Interrogativa	Respuestas breves	
	Afirmativa	Negativa
Am I **going to run**?	Yes, I **am**.	No, I**'m not**.
Are you **going to run**?	Yes, you **are**.	No, you **aren't**.
Is he **going to run**?	Yes, he **is**.	No, he **isn't**.
Is she **going to run**?	Yes, she **is**.	No, she **isn't**.
Is it **going to run**?	Yes, it **is**.	No, it **isn't**.
Are we **going to run**?	Yes, we **are**.	No, we **aren't**.
Are you **going to run**?	Yes, you **are**.	No, you **aren't**.
Are they **going to run**?	Yes, they **are**.	No, they **aren't**.

Significa "ir a" + infinitivo.

- **Afirmativa:** sujeto + ***to be*** en presente + ***going to*** + verbo en la forma base.
  *He **is going to have** a party.* (Él va a hacer una fiesta.)
- **Negativa:** sujeto + ***to be*** en presente + ***not*** (***n't***) + ***going to*** + verbo en la forma base.
  *They **aren't going to order** pizza.* (No van a pedir pizza.)
- **Interrogativa:** ***to be*** en presente + sujeto + ***going to*** + verbo en la forma base.
  ***Is** she **going to take** a trip?* (¿Ella va a hacer un viaje?)
- **Respuestas breves:** se pone el pronombre personal sujeto + el verbo ***to be***, sin contraer en afirmativa o contraído en negativa.
  ***Are** you **going to go** hiking? Yes, I **am**. / No, I**'m not**.*
  (¿Vas a ir a dar una caminata? Sí. / No.)
- Con ***be going to*** se suelen usar las siguientes **expresiones temporales**: ***later*** (más tarde, luego), ***soon*** (pronto, dentro de poco), ***this afternoon / evening*** (esta tarde), ***tonight*** (esta noche), ***tomorrow*** (mañana), ***in*** + un año, ***next week / month / year*** (la semana / el mes / el año que viene / próximo/a), ***in the future*** (en el futuro), ***on*** + un día de la semana o fecha, etc. Todas pueden ir al principio o al final de la frase, pero se suelen poner al final.
  *I **am going to visit** my relatives **later**.*
  (Voy a visitar a mis parientes luego.)
  ***Next month**, I**'m going to go** to a concert.*
  (El mes que viene voy a ir a un concierto.)

Los usos del futuro con *be going to*

Hablar de intenciones, planes o decisiones	*I**'m going to visit** Ireland.* (Voy a visitar Irlanda.)
Expresar lo que va a suceder porque vemos indicios de ello	*I am very tired. I **am going to sleep** late.* (Estoy muy cansada. Voy a levantarme tarde.)

El *Present Continuous* con valor de futuro

- El *Present Continuous* (como ya se ha visto en la unidad introductoria) se usa para expresar lo que está ocurriendo en el momento de hablar. Se forma con ***to be*** + un verbo terminado en ***-ing***, y se deben seguir unas reglas ortográficas para añadir correctamente esa terminación.
- Pero, además, el *Present Continuous* tiene "valor de futuro" porque se usa para anunciar acciones fijadas con antelación o planes concretos que ocurrirán en el futuro cercano.
  *I **am visiting** my cousins next week.*
  (Visito / Visitaré a mis primos la semana que viene.)
- La diferencia con el *Present Continuous* normal está en que el que tiene valor de futuro debe llevar una **expresión temporal** de futuro que indique cuándo va a ocurrir la acción: ***next week*** (la semana que viene / próxima), ***this afternoon / evening*** (esta tarde), ***on*** + un día de la semana o una fecha, ***in*** + un mes o un año, ***at*** + una hora, ***in ten minutes*** (dentro de diez minutos), ***tomorrow*** (mañana), etc.
  *The library **is opening in one hour**.*
  (La biblioteca abre / abrirá dentro de una hora.)
- La diferencia con ***be going to*** es que no se trata solo de una intención, sino de algo que va a ocurrir con toda seguridad porque ya se ha fijado de antemano. Con este valor se usan principalmente los verbos de movimiento.
  *She **is running** in a race tomorrow.*
  (Ella corre / correrá en una carrera mañana.) [seguro]

El primer condicional

Se usa para hablar de acciones que ocurrirán si se cumple la condición señalada.

- **Afirmativa:** la condición (oración subordinada) se expresa con ***if*** + *Present Simple*, y el resultado (oración principal) suele ir en futuro con ***will***.
  *He **will win** the medal **if** he **runs** faster.*
  (Él ganará la medalla si corre más deprisa.)
  Si la condición va primero, se pone una coma entre la oración principal y la subordinada.
  ***If** he **runs** faster, he **will win** the medal.*
  (Si él corre más deprisa, ganará la medalla.)
- **Negativa:** se puede negar el verbo en presente, el verbo en futuro o ambos.
  ***If** he **doesn't go**, I **will stay** at home.*
  (Si él no va, me quedaré en casa.)
  ***If** he **goes**, I **won't stay** at home.*
  (Si él va, no me quedaré en casa.)
  ***If** he **doesn't go**, I **won't stay** at home.*
  (Si él no va, no me quedaré en casa.)
- **Interrogativa:** ***Will*** + sujeto + predicado de la oración principal + oración subordinada.
  ***Will** they **go** skiing **if** it **is** stormy?*
  (¿Irán a esquiar si hay tormenta?)
- **Respuestas breves:** se pone el pronombre personal sujeto + ***will*** o ***won't***.
  ***Will** you **come** to the beach **if** it **is** sunny? Yes, I **will**. / No, I **won't**.* (¿Vendrás a la playa si hace sol? Sí. / No.)

Para expresar que algo ocurrirá o no ocurrirá si no se cumple la condición, la subordinada es introducida por la conjunción ***unless***, que equivale a ***if not*** ("a no ser que", "a menos que", "si no"). Esta conjunción se usa con bastante asiduidad en el primer condicional, pero es menos frecuente en el segundo.

__Unless__ you __train__ us, we __will lose__ the next match.
(A no ser que nos entrenes / Si no nos entrenas, perderemos el próximo partido.)

El segundo condicional

Se usa para hablar de acciones hipotéticas referidas al presente (es decir, que es poco probable que ocurran) y también para dar consejos.

- **Afirmativa:** la condición se forma con *if* + *Past Simple*, y el resultado con ***would*** (o la contracción ***'d***) + el verbo en la forma base.
  __If there were__ more policemen, people __would feel__ safe.
  (Si hubiera más policías, la gente se sentiría segura.)
  En lugar de ***would***, podemos usar el verbo modal ***could*** en el resultado, pero este indica que la probabilidad de que se cumpla la hipótesis es aún menor. Equivale al verbo "poder" en condicional o a las expresiones "tal vez" o "quizá/s" + condicional.
  __If__ I __had__ money, I __could buy__ a new car. (Si yo tuviera dinero, tal vez compraría un coche nuevo.)
  Si el verbo de la condición es ***to be***, se suele usar ***were*** en todas las personas del singular y del plural.
  __If__ he __were__ home, he__'d open__ the door.
  (Si él estuviera en casa, abriría la puerta.)
  Para dar consejos se emplea la fórmula ***If I were***.
  __If I were__ you, I__'d go__ to the new market.
  (Si yo fuera tú, iría al mercado nuevo.)
- **Negativa:** se puede negar la condición, el resultado o ambos.
  __If__ I __didn't have__ a car, I __would go__ by bus.
  (Si yo no tuviera un coche, iría en autobús.)
  __If__ I __had__ a car, I __wouldn't go__ by bus.
  (Si yo tuviera un coche, no iría en autobús.)
  __If__ I __didn't have__ a car, I __wouldn't go__ by bus.
  (Si yo no tuviera un coche, no iría en autobús.)
- **Interrogativa:** ***Would*** + sujeto + predicado de la oración principal + oración subordinada.
  __Would__ you __buy__ a house in the city __if__ you __had__ money?
  (¿Comprarías una casa en la ciudad si tuvieras dinero?)
- **Respuestas breves:** se pone el pronombre personal sujeto + ***would*** o ***wouldn't***.
  __Would__ you __do__ volunteer work __if__ you __had__ free time? Yes, I __would__. / No, I __wouldn't__. (¿Trabajarías como voluntario si tuvieras tiempo libre? Sí. / No.)

Unit 7

El *Present Perfect Simple*

Afirmativa	Forma contraída
I **have played**	**I've played**
You **have played**	You**'ve played**
He **has played**	He**'s played**
She **has played**	She**'s played**
It **has played**	It**'s played**
We **have played**	We**'ve played**
You **have played**	You**'ve played**
They **have played**	They**'ve played**
Negativa	**Forma contraída**
I **have not played**	I **haven't played**
You **have not played**	You **haven't played**
He **has not played**	He **hasn't played**
She **has not played**	She **hasn't played**
It **has not played**	It **hasn't played**
We **have not played**	We **haven't played**
You **have not played**	You **haven't played**
They **have not played**	They **haven't played**

Interrogativa	Respuestas breves	
	Afirmativa	Negativa
Have I **played** ...?	Yes, I **have**.	No, I **haven't**.
Have you **played** ...?	Yes, you **have**.	No, you **haven't**.
Has he **played** ...?	Yes, he **has**.	No, he **hasn't**.
Has she **played** ...?	Yes, she **has**.	No, she **hasn't**.
Has it **played** ...?	Yes, it **has**.	No, it **hasn't**.
Have we **played** ...?	Yes, we **have**.	No, we **haven't**.
Have you **played** ...?	Yes, you **have**.	No, you **haven't**.
Have they **played** ...?	Yes, they **have**.	No, they **haven't**.

- **Afirmativa:** sujeto + ***has*** / ***have*** + un verbo en participio. El participio se forma añadiendo ***-ed*** a los verbos regulares y es igual en todas las personas. Los verbos irregulares no siguen ninguna regla y por eso hay que aprenderlos de memoria. Puedes consultar la lista de las páginas 107-108.
  We __have milked__ the cows. (Hemos ordeñado las vacas.)
- **Negativa:** sujeto + ***has*** / ***have*** + la partícula ***not*** o la contracción ***n't*** + un verbo en participio.
  Megan __hasn't swum__ with sharks.
  (Megan no ha nadado con tiburones.)
- **Interrogativa:** ***Has*** / ***Have*** + sujeto + un verbo en participio.
  __Have__ you __had__ any unusual pets?
  (¿Has tenido alguna mascota poco común?)
- **Respuestas breves:** se pone el pronombre personal sujeto + ***has*** / ***have***, sin contraer en afirmativa o contraído con la partícula ***not*** en negativa.
  __Have__ they __discovered__ anything? Yes, they __have__. / No, they __haven't__. (¿Han descubierto algo? Sí. / No.)

- Con el *Present Perfect Simple* se suelen usar los siguientes **adverbios** y **expresiones**:

ever	interrogativa: "alguna vez"	*Have you **ever** held a snake?*
	negativa: "nunca", "jamás"	*I haven't **ever** fed lions.*
never	afirmativa: "nunca"	*She has **never** trained dogs.*
always	"siempre"	*They've **always** had that car.*
already	afirmativa: "ya"	*We've **already** been to Berlin.*
just	afirmativa: "acabar de"	*We have **just** met them.*
yet	negativa: "aún", "todavía"	*She hasn't tried your cake **yet**.*
	interrogativa: "ya"	*Have you watched that film **yet**?*
recently	"recientemente"	*Have they been here **recently**?*
lately	"últimamente"	*He hasn't been to the gym **lately**.*
several times	"varias veces"	*They have volunteered there **several times**.*
so far	"hasta el momento"	*How much of the country have you explored **so far**?*

Hay que tener en cuenta que ***just***, ***already***, ***always***, ***ever*** y ***never*** se ponen entre el auxiliar ***have*** y el participio del verbo principal. ***Yet*** se coloca al final de la frase. El resto pueden ir al principio o al final de la frase, pero se suelen poner al final.

for / since

Con el *Present Perfect Simple* también se utilizan las **expresiones temporales** que comienzan con:

- La preposición ***for*** seguida de un periodo de tiempo que indica la duración de la acción. Se traduce como "durante" o no se traduce.
  *Your sister has lived in the USA **for** one year.*
  (Tu hermana ha vivido en EE. UU. durante un año.)
  (Tu hermana ha vivido un año en EE. UU.)
- La preposición ***since***, que indica el momento en que empezó la acción. Se traduce como "desde".
  *I haven't seen him **since** Tuesday.*
  (No lo he visto desde el martes.)

Los usos del *Present Perfect Simple*

Acciones que empezaron en el pasado y aún continúan (lleva ***for*** o ***since*** y se traduce en presente)	*Sam **has volunteered** at the Red Cross **since** 1998.* (Sam es voluntario de la Cruz Roja desde 1998.)
Acciones pasadas que afectan al presente o tienen consecuencias en el momento actual	*I **have rowed** for hours. I'm very tired now.* (He remado durante horas. Ahora estoy muy cansado.)
Acciones pasadas sin especificar cuándo ocurrieron	*I **have parachuted** once.* (He saltado en paracaídas una vez.)
Acciones muy recientes (lleva ***just*** y se traduce "acabar de"+ infinitivo)	*The aeroplane **has just landed**.* (El avión acaba de aterrizar.)

Unit 8

can

Afirmativa	Negativa	
I **can play**	I **cannot** / **can't play**	
You **can play**	You **cannot** / **can't play**	
He **can play**	He **cannot** / **can't play**	
She **can play**	She **cannot** / **can't play**	
It **can play**	It **cannot** / **can't play**	
We **can play**	We **cannot** / **can't play**	
You **can play**	You **cannot** / **can't play**	
They **can play**	They **cannot** / **can't play**	
Interrogativa	**Respuestas breves**	
	Afirmativa	**Negativa**
Can I **play**?	Yes, I **can**.	No, I **can't**.
Can you **play**?	Yes, you **can**.	No, you **can't**.
Can he **play**?	Yes, he **can**.	No, he **can't**.
Can she **play**?	Yes, she **can**.	No, she **can't**.
Can it **play**?	Yes, it **can**.	No, it **can't**.
Can we **play**?	Yes, we **can**.	No, we **can't**.
Can you **play**?	Yes, you **can**.	No, you **can't**.
Can they **play**?	Yes, they **can**.	No, they **can't**.

El verbo modal ***can*** significa "saber" o "poder".

- **Afirmativa:** sujeto + ***can*** + verbo en la forma base. Como es un verbo modal, no se añade *-s* en la 3ª persona del singular.
  *She **can play** football.* (Ella sabe jugar al fútbol.)
- **Negativa:** sujeto + ***cannot*** o la contracción ***can't*** + verbo en la forma base.
  *My brother **can't ride** a bike.*
  (Mi hermano no sabe / puede montar en bici.)
- **Interrogativa:** ***Can*** + sujeto + verbo en la forma base.
  ***Can** you **throw** me the ball?*
  (¿Puedes lanzarme la pelota?)
- **Respuestas breves:** se pone el pronombre personal sujeto + ***can*** o ***can't***.
  ***Can** they **play** today? Yes, they **can**. / No, they **can't**.*
  (¿Pueden jugar hoy? Sí. / No.)

Los usos de *can*

Habilidad o capacidad para hacer algo: "saber"	*I **can speak** Spanish.* (Sé hablar español.)
Posibilidad de hacer algo: "poder"	*I **can meet** you tomorrow.* (Puedo quedar contigo mañana.)
Petición de permiso o favores: "poder"	***Can** you close the door?* (¿Puedes cerrar la puerta?)

could

Afirmativa	Negativa
I **could go**	I **couldn't go**
You **could go**	You **couldn't go**
He **could go**	He **couldn't go**
She **could go**	She **couldn't go**
It **could go**	It **couldn't go**
We **could go**	We **couldn't go**
You **could go**	You **couldn't go**
They **could go**	They **couldn't go**

Interrogativa	Respuestas breves	
	Afirmativa	Negativa
Could I **go**?	Yes, I **could**.	No, I **couldn't**.
Could you **go**?	Yes, you **could**.	No, you **couldn't**.
Could he **go**?	Yes, he **could**.	No, he **couldn't**.
Could she **go**?	Yes, she **could**.	No, she **couldn't**.
Could it **go**?	Yes, it **could**.	No, it **couldn't**.
Could we **go**?	Yes, we **could**.	No, we **couldn't**.
Could you **go**?	Yes, you **could**.	No, you **couldn't**.
Could they **go**?	Yes, they **could**.	No, they **couldn't**.

- **Afirmativa:** sujeto + *could* + verbo en la forma base. Como es un verbo modal, no se añade *-s* en la 3ª persona del singular.
  *When I was five, I **could speak** two languages.*
  (Cuando tenía cinco años, sabía hablar dos idiomas.)
  *In the past, people **could drive** fast on this road.*
  (En el pasado, la gente podía conducir deprisa en esta carretera.)
- **Negativa:** sujeto + ***could not*** o la contracción ***couldn't*** (la más habitual es la segunda) + verbo en la forma base.
  *They **couldn't find** any ghosts in the house.*
  (No pudieron encontrar ningún fantasma en la casa.)
- **Interrogativa:** *Could* + sujeto + verbo en la forma base.
  ***Could** they **give** you any explanation?*
  (¿Pudieron darte alguna explicación?)
- **Respuestas breves:** se pone el pronombre personal sujeto + *could* o *couldn't*.
  ***Could** they **do** it? Yes, they **could**. / No, they **couldn't**.*
  (¿Pudieron hacerlo? Sí. / No.)

Los usos de *could*

Habilidad o capacidad para hacer algo en el pasado	*Sam **could read** at the age of six.* (Sam sabía leer con seis años.)
Posibilidad de hacer algo en el pasado	*I **couldn't refuse** to do it.* (No pude negarme a hacerlo.)
Petición formal de permiso o favores	***Could** you **pick** me **up**?* (¿Podrías recogerme?)

must

Afirmativa	Negativa
I **must run**	I **mustn't run**
You **must run**	You **mustn't run**
He **must run**	He **mustn't run**
She **must run**	She **mustn't run**
It **must run**	It **mustn't run**
We **must run**	We **mustn't run**
You **must run**	You **mustn't run**
They **must run**	They **mustn't run**

El verbo modal ***must*** en **afirmativa** significa "deber" y expresa la obligación o la necesidad grande de hacer algo.

En **negativa**, en cambio, tiene un significado totalmente distinto: expresa prohibición, que algo no está permitido o que no se debe hacer porque no es conveniente o correcto.

- **Afirmativa:** sujeto + *must* + verbo en la forma base. Como es un verbo modal, no se añade *-s* en la 3ª persona del singular.
  *In the UK, you **must drive** on the left.*
  (En el Reino Unido, debes conducir por la izquierda.)
- **Negativa:** sujeto + ***must not*** o la contracción ***mustn't*** (la más habitual es la segunda) + verbo en la forma base.
  *You **mustn't kick** the basketball.* (No debes darle una patada al balón de baloncesto.) [está prohibido]
  *You **mustn't shout** at the other players.* (No debes gritar a los otros jugadores.) [no es correcto]
- **Interrogativa:** *Must* + sujeto + verbo en la forma base. En este caso, ***must*** expresa obligación o necesidad, aunque este verbo modal no se suele usar en la forma interrogativa.
  ***Must** I **bring** water?* (¿Debo llevar agua?)
- **Respuestas breves:** se pone el pronombre personal sujeto + *must*.
  ***Must** you **leave** now? Yes, I **must**.*
  (¿Debes irte ahora? Sí.)

should

Afirmativa	Negativa
I **should try**	I **shouldn't try**
You **should try**	You **shouldn't try**
He **should try**	He **shouldn't try**
She **should try**	She **shouldn't try**
It **should try**	It **shouldn't try**
We **should try**	We **shouldn't try**
You **should try**	You **shouldn't try**
They **should try**	They **shouldn't try**

catch: coger, pillar, atrapar

Interrogativa	Respuestas breves	
	Afirmativa	Negativa
Should I **try**?	Yes, I **should**.	No, I **shouldn't**.
Should you **try**?	Yes, you **should**.	No, you **shouldn't**.
Should he **try**?	Yes, he **should**.	No, he **shouldn't**.
Should she **try**?	Yes, she **should**.	No, she **shouldn't**.
Should it **try**?	Yes, it **should**.	No, it **shouldn't**.
Should we **try**?	Yes, we **should**.	No, we **shouldn't**.
Should you **try**?	Yes, you **should**.	No, you **shouldn't**.
Should they **try**?	Yes, they **should**.	No, they **shouldn't**.

- **Afirmativa:** sujeto + ***should*** + verbo en la forma base. Como es un verbo modal, no se añade *-s* en la 3ª persona del singular.
  You ***should have*** *a balanced diet.*
  (Deberías llevar una dieta equilibrada.)
- **Negativa:** sujeto + ***should not*** o la contracción ***shouldn't*** (la más habitual es la segunda) + verbo en la forma base.
  You ***shouldn't eat*** *junk food.*
  (No deberías comer comida basura.)
- **Interrogativa:** ***Should*** + sujeto + verbo en la forma base.
  Should *I* ***be*** *worried?* (¿Debería estar preocupado?)
- **Respuestas breves:** se pone el pronombre personal sujeto + ***should*** o ***shouldn't***.
  Should *I* ***lose*** *weight? Yes, you* ***should****. / No, you* ***shouldn't****.* (¿Debería adelgazar? Sí. / No.)

Los usos de *should*

Dar consejos	*You* ***should*** *go now. It's late.* (Deberías irte ya. Es tarde.)
Decir lo que se debería o no hacer	*They* ***shouldn't shout*** *here.* (No deberían gritar aquí.)

have to

Afirmativa	Negativa
I **have to go**	I **don't have to go**
You **have to go**	You **don't have to go**
He **has to go**	He **doesn't have to go**
She **has to go**	She **doesn't have to go**
It **has to go**	It **doesn't have to go**
We **have to go**	We **don't have to go**
You **have to go**	You **don't have to go**
They **have to go**	They **don't have to go**

Interrogativa	Respuestas breves	
	Afirmativa	Negativa
Do I **have to go**?	Yes, I **do**.	No, I **don't**.
Do you **have to go**?	Yes, you **do**.	No, you **don't**.
Does he **have to go**?	Yes, he **does**.	No, he **doesn't**.
Does she **have to go**?	Yes, she **does**.	No, she **doesn't**.
Does it **have to go**?	Yes, it **does**.	No, it **doesn't**.
Do we **have to go**?	Yes, we **do**.	No, we **don't**.
Do you **have to go**?	Yes, you **do**.	No, you **don't**.
Do they **have to go**?	Yes, they **do**.	No, they **don't**.

- **Afirmativa:** sujeto + ***have / has to*** + verbo en la forma base. Significa "tener que" y expresa, como ***must***, la obligación o necesidad de hacer algo. La diferencia es que ***have to*** sí se conjuga y, por eso, se usa en los tiempos que ***must*** no tiene.
  We ***have to send*** *her an e-mail right now.* (Tenemos que enviarle un correo electrónico ahora mismo.)
- **Negativa:** sujeto + ***don't / doesn't have to*** + verbo en la forma base. Significa "no tener que / por qué".
  He ***doesn't have to buy*** *her a present.*
  (No tiene que / por qué comprarle un regalo.)

  Recuerda que ***have to*** significa lo mismo que ***must***, pero ***don't have to*** y ***mustn't*** no son equivalentes.
  You ***don't have to*** *go.*
  (No tienes que / por qué ir.) [no es necesario]
  You ***mustn't*** *go.*
  (No debes ir.) [está prohibido]
- **Interrogativa:** ***Do / Does*** + sujeto + ***have to*** + verbo en la forma base.
  Do *you* ***have to do*** *any homework this afternoon?*
  (¿Tienes que hacer deberes esta tarde?)
- **Respuestas breves:** se pone el pronombre personal sujeto + ***do / does*** o ***don't / doesn't***.
  Does *she* ***have to leave*** *now? Yes, she* ***does****. / No, she* ***doesn't****.* (¿Tiene que irse ahora? Sí. / No.)

need to

Afirmativa	Negativa
I **need to call**	I **don't need to call**
You **need to call**	You **don't need to call**
He **needs to call**	He **doesn't need to call**
She **needs to call**	She **doesn't need to call**
It **needs to call**	It **doesn't need to call**
We **need to call**	We **don't need to call**
You **need to call**	You **don't need to call**
They **need to call**	They **don't need to call**

Interrogativa	Respuestas breves	
	Afirmativa	Negativa
Do I **need to call**?	Yes, I **do**.	No, I **don't**.
Do you **need to call**?	Yes, you **do**.	No, you **don't**.
Does he **need to call**?	Yes, he **does**.	No, he **doesn't**.
Does she **need to call**?	Yes, she **does**.	No, she **doesn't**.
Does it **need to call**?	Yes, it **does**.	No, it **doesn't**.
Do we **need to call**?	Yes, we **do**.	No, we **don't**.
Do you **need to call**?	Yes, you **do**.	No, you **don't**.
Do they **need to call**?	Yes, they **do**.	No, they **don't**.

Need to significa "tener que" y expresa, como ***have to***, la obligación o necesidad de hacer algo. Se puede conjugar, así que puede usarse en todos los tiempos verbales.

- **Afirmativa:** sujeto + ***need / needs to*** + verbo en la forma base.
  *I **need to rest** for a few days because I'm tired.* (Tengo que descansar unos días porque estoy cansada.)
- **Negativa:** sujeto + ***don't / doesn't need to*** + verbo en la forma base.
  *You **don't need to help** me.* (No tienes que ayudarme.)
- **Interrogativa:** ***Do / Does*** + sujeto + ***need to*** + verbo en la forma base.
  ***Do** you **need to buy** something for dinner?*
  (¿Tienes que comprar algo para la cena?)
- **Respuestas breves:** se pone el pronombre personal sujeto + ***do / does*** o ***don't / doesn't***.
  ***Does** he **need to come** home soon? Yes, he **does**. / No, he **doesn't**.* (¿Tiene que venir pronto a casa? Sí. / No.)

Unit 9

El estilo indirecto

- Se utiliza para contar lo que ha dicho alguien sin repetir exactamente sus palabras. Para ello, se usa el verbo ***say*** y la conjunción ***that*** (esta se suele omitir en inglés hablado), se quitan las comillas y se cambian el pronombre sujeto y la persona del verbo.
  "Many people use watches," Alice says.
  *Alice **says that** many people **use** watches.*
  (Alice dice que mucha gente utiliza relojes.)
- Pero lo normal es contarlo en pasado. Por lo tanto, se usa ***said*** y, además, el verbo de la oración introducida por ***that*** da un salto atrás en el tiempo.

Estilo directo	Estilo indirecto
Present Simple	**Past Simple**
*"I always **recycle** newspapers," Beth said.* *Beth said that she always **recycled** newspapers.* (Beth dijo que siempre reciclaba los periódicos.)	
Present Continuous	**Past Continuous**
*"She **is giving** a talk at school," Paul said.* *Paul said that she **was giving** a talk at school.* (Paul dijo que ella estaba dando una charla en el colegio.)	
will	**would**
*"I **will visit** all the museums in Oslo," Jane said.* *Jane said that she **would visit** all the museums in Oslo.* (Jane dijo que visitaría todos los museos de Oslo.)	
can	**could**
*"You **can** buy green products," he said.* *He said that we **could** buy green products.* (Él dijo que podíamos comprar productos ecológicos.)	

- El cambio de estilo directo a indirecto también afecta a las expresiones de tiempo y de lugar, a los demostrativos y a los posesivos:

Estilo directo	Estilo indirecto
now, today, tonight	then, that day, that night
tomorrow	the next / following day, the day after
next week / year	the following week / year, the week / year after
here	there
this, these	that, those
my	his / her, etc.

Reporting verbs

- Son los que introducen el estilo indirecto, como ***say*** y ***tell***, que transmiten el mensaje sin añadir más información en cuanto a la intención o tono del hablante. El verbo ***tell*** va siempre seguido de un complemento indirecto. El verbo ***say*** puede llevar o no llevar complemento indirecto, pero si lo lleva, debe ir precedido de ***to***.
  tell + c. indirecto ***say*** (+ ***to*** + c. indirecto)
  "I throw the newspapers in the recycling bin," he said.
  *He **said (to us) / told us that** he threw the newspapers in the recycling bin.* (Él nos dijo que tiraba los periódicos al contenedor de reciclaje.)

El gerundio y el infinitivo

El gerundio

Es la forma verbal terminada en ***-ing***, que funciona como sustantivo en los siguientes casos:

- Como sujeto de la oración cuando se habla de acciones o hechos en general.
  ***Visiting** Beijing was an amazing experience.*
  (Visitar Pekín fue una experiencia increíble.)
- Como complemento directo de algunos verbos: ***finish***, ***enjoy***, ***avoid***, ***miss***, ***recommend***, ***suggest***, ***imagine***, ***regret***, ***keep***, ***mind***, ***spend***, etc.
  *She **enjoys eating** food from different countries.*
  (Ella disfruta comiendo comida de distintos países.)
- Detrás de las preposiciones.
  *He is thinking **about learning** Chinese.*
  (Él está pensando en aprender chino.)
- Detrás de algunas formas verbales: ***can't stand***, ***feel like***, ***don't mind***, ***it's no use***, ***look forward to***, etc.
  *I **don't mind walking** to work.*
  (No me importa ir andando al trabajo.)

El infinitivo

Es la forma verbal precedida de ***to*** y se emplea en estos casos:

- Detrás de verbos como ***decide***, ***want***, ***promise***, ***hope***, ***pretend***, ***refuse***, ***offer***, ***agree***, ***seem***, ***appear***, ***choose***, ***expect***, ***learn***, ***plan***, ***wish***, ***allow***, ***wait***, etc.
  *Paul **has promised to take** her dog to the vet.*
  (Paul ha prometido llevar su perro a la veterinaria.)
  *She **decided to wear** the red tights.*
  (Decidió ponerse las medias rojas.)
- Detrás de adjetivos tales como ***easy***, ***happy***, ***sad***, ***lucky***, ***hard***, ***surprised*** y ***nice***.
  *I'm **happy to volunteer**.*
  (Estoy contenta de ser voluntaria.)

Verbos seguidos de gerundio y de infinitivo

Algunos verbos (***like***, ***love***, ***hate***, ***prefer***, ***begin***, ***start***, ***continue***, etc.) pueden ir seguidos de gerundio o de infinitivo sin que su significado varíe.
*They **like going / to go** to summer camps.*
(Les gusta ir a los campamentos de verano.)

Irregular Verb List

BASE FORM (V1)	PAST SIMPLE (V2)	PAST PARTICIPLE (V3)	CASTELLANO
be /biː/	was/were /wɒz/wɜː/	been /biːn/	ser, estar
beat /biːt/	beat /biːt/	beaten /'biːtn/	golpear
become /bɪ'kʌm/	became /bɪ'keɪm/	become /bɪ'kʌm/	llegar a ser, convertirse
begin /bɪ'gɪn/	began /bɪ'gæn/	begun /bɪ'gʌn/	empezar
bend /bend/	bent /bent/	bent /bent/	doblar(se)
bet /bet/	bet /bet/	bet /bet/	apostar
bite /baɪt/	bit /bɪt/	bitten /'bɪtn/	morder
bleed /bliːd/	bled /bled/	bled /bled/	sangrar
blow /bləʊ/	blew /bluː/	blown /bləʊn/	soplar
break /breɪk/	broke /brəʊk/	broken /'brəʊkən/	romper
bring /brɪŋ/	brought /brɔːt/	brought /brɔːt/	traer
build /bɪld/	built /bɪlt/	built /bɪlt/	construir
burn /bɜːn/	burnt/burned /bɜːnt/bɜːnd/	burnt/burned /bɜːnt/bɜːnd/	quemar
buy /baɪ/	bought /bɔːt/	bought /bɔːt/	comprar
catch /kætʃ/	caught /kɔːt/	caught /kɔːt/	coger, agarrar
choose /tʃuːz/	chose /tʃəʊz/	chosen /'tʃəʊzn/	elegir
come /kʌm/	came /keɪm/	come /kʌm/	venir
cost /kɒst/	cost /kɒst/	cost /kɒst/	costar
cut /kʌt/	cut /kʌt/	cut /kʌt/	cortar
dig /dɪg/	dug /dʌg/	dug /dʌg/	cavar
do /duː/	did /dɪd/	done /dʌn/	hacer
draw /drɔː/	drew /druː/	drawn /drɔːn/	dibujar
dream /driːm/	dreamt/dreamed /dremt/driːmd/	dreamt/dreamed /dremt/driːmd/	soñar
drink /drɪŋk/	drank /dræŋk/	drunk /drʌŋk/	beber
drive /draɪv/	drove /drəʊv/	driven /'drɪvn/	conducir
eat /iːt/	ate /eɪt/	eaten /'iːtn/	comer
fall /fɔːl/	fell /fel/	fallen /'fɔːlən/	caer(se)
feed /fiːd/	fed /fed/	fed /fed/	alimentar
feel /fiːl/	felt /felt/	felt /felt/	sentir(se)
fight /faɪt/	fought /fɔːt/	fought /fɔːt/	luchar, pelear
find /faɪnd/	found /faʊnd/	found /faʊnd/	encontrar
fly /flaɪ/	flew /fluː/	flown /fləʊn/	volar
forget /fə'get/	forgot /fə'gɒt/	forgotten /fə'gɒtn/	olvidar
forgive /fə'gɪv/	forgave /fə'geɪv/	forgiven /fə'gɪvn/	perdonar
freeze /friːz/	froze /frəʊz/	frozen /'frəʊzn/	congelar(se)
get /get/	got /gɒt/	got /gɒt/	conseguir; llegar
give /gɪv/	gave /geɪv/	given /'gɪvn/	dar
go /gəʊ/	went /went/	gone /gɒn/	ir
grow /grəʊ/	grew /gruː/	grown /grəʊn/	crecer; cultivar
hang /hæŋ/	hanged/hung /hæŋd/hʌŋ/	hanged/hung /hæŋd/hʌŋ/	colgar
have /hæv/	had /hæd/	had /hæd/	tener; haber
hear /hɪə/	heard /hɜːd/	heard /hɜːd/	oír
hide /haɪd/	hid /hɪd/	hidden /'hɪdn/	esconder(se)
hit /hɪt/	hit /hɪt/	hit /hɪt/	golpear, pegar
hold /həʊld/	held /held/	held /held/	sujetar
hurt /hɜːt/	hurt /hɜːt/	hurt /hɜːt/	herir, hacer daño; doler
keep /kiːp/	kept /kept/	kept /kept/	guardar, mantener
know /nəʊ/	knew /njuː/	known /nəʊn/	saber, conocer
lay /leɪ/	laid /leɪd/	laid /leɪd/	poner; extender
lead /liːd/	led /led/	led /led/	guiar, conducir

BASE FORM (V1)	PAST SIMPLE (V2)	PAST PARTICIPLE (V3)	CASTELLANO
learn /lɜːn/	learnt/learned /lɜːnt/lɜːnd/	learnt/learned /lɜːnt/lɜːnd/	aprender
leave /liːv/	left /left/	left /left/	dejar; irse, salir
lend /lend/	lent /lent/	lent /lent/	prestar
let /let/	let /let/	let /let/	permitir, dejar
lie /laɪ/	lay /leɪ/	lain /leɪn/	tumbarse, echarse
lie /laɪ/ (regular verb)	lied /laɪd/	lied /laɪd/	mentir
light /laɪt/	lit /lɪt/	lit /lɪt/	encender
lose /luːz/	lost /lɒst/	lost /lɒst/	perder
make /meɪk/	made /meɪd/	made /meɪd/	hacer, fabricar
mean /miːn/	meant /ment/	meant /ment/	significar, querer decir
meet /miːt/	met /met/	met /met/	conocer a; quedar con
pay /peɪ/	paid /peɪd/	paid /peɪd/	pagar
put /pʊt/	put /pʊt/	put /pʊt/	poner
read /riːd/	read /red/	read /red/	leer
ride /raɪd/	rode /rəʊd/	ridden /'rɪdn/	montar
ring /rɪŋ/	rang /ræŋ/	rung /rʌŋ/	llamar (por teléfono)
rise /raɪz/	rose /rəʊz/	risen /'rɪzn/	elevarse, alzarse
run /rʌn/	ran /ræn/	run /rʌn/	correr
say /seɪ/	said /sed/	said /sed/	decir
see /siː/	saw /sɔː/	seen /siːn/	ver
sell /sel/	sold /səʊld/	sold /səʊld/	vender
send /send/	sent /sent/	sent /sent/	enviar
set /set/	set /set/	set /set/	colocar
shake /ʃeɪk/	shook /ʃʊk/	shaken /'ʃeɪkən/	agitar
shine /ʃaɪn/	shone /ʃɒn/	shone /ʃɒn/	brillar
shoot /ʃuːt/	shot /ʃɒt/	shot /ʃɒt/	disparar
show /ʃəʊ/	showed /ʃəʊd/	shown /ʃəʊn/	mostrar, enseñar
shut /ʃʌt/	shut /ʃʌt/	shut /ʃʌt/	cerrar
sing /sɪŋ/	sang /sæŋ/	sung /sʌŋ/	cantar
sink /sɪŋk/	sank /sæŋk/	sunk /sʌŋk/	hundirse
sit /sɪt/	sat /sæt/	sat /sæt/	sentarse
sleep /sliːp/	slept /slept/	slept /slept/	dormir(se)
smell /smel/	smelt/smelled /smelt/smeld/	smelt/smelled /smelt/smeld/	oler
speak /spiːk/	spoke /spəʊk/	spoken /'spəʊkən/	hablar
spell /spel/	spelt/spelled /spelt/speld/	spelt/spelled /spelt/speld/	deletrear
spend /spend/	spent /spent/	spent /spent/	gastar; pasar (tiempo)
stand /stænd/	stood /stʊd/	stood /stʊd/	estar de pie
steal /stiːl/	stole /stəʊl/	stolen /'stəʊlən/	robar
stick /stɪk/	stuck /stʌk/	stuck /stʌk/	pegar
sweep /swiːp/	swept /swept/	swept /swept/	barrer
swim /swɪm/	swam /swæm/	swum /swʌm/	nadar
take /teɪk/	took /tʊk/	taken /'teɪkən/	coger; llevar
teach /tiːtʃ/	taught /tɔːt/	taught /tɔːt/	enseñar
tear /teə/	tore /tɔː/	torn /tɔːn/	romper, desgarrar
tell /tel/	told /təʊld/	told /təʊld/	decir, contar
think /θɪŋk/	thought /θɔːt/	thought /θɔːt/	pensar
throw /θrəʊ/	threw /θruː/	thrown /θrəʊn/	tirar; lanzar
understand /ʌnde'stænd/	understood /ʌnde'stʊd/	understood /ʌnde'stʊd/	comprender, entender
wake up /weɪk 'ʌp/	woke up /wəʊk 'ʌp/	woken up /wəʊkən 'ʌp/	despertar(se)
wear /weə/	wore /wɔː/	worn /wɔːn/	llevar puesto; ponerse
win /wɪn/	won /wʌn/	won /wʌn/	ganar
write /raɪt/	wrote /rəʊt/	written /'rɪtn/	escribir

Writing Guide

Antes de escribir

Brainstorming

- Asegúrate de que comprendes el tema sobre el que vas a escribir.
- Haz una lista de ideas relacionadas con ese tema y anota todas las que se te ocurran sin preocuparte por la gramática ni la ortografía.
- Luego lee esa lista de ideas y elige las importantes.

History of Tennis

Major Walter Wingfield invented the game in 1873.

He gave it the name *Sphairistike*.

~~People play tennis on tennis courts.~~

The first world tennis competition at Wimbledon was in 1877.

In 1877, there were 22 players and 200 spectators.

~~People wear tennis shoes when they play tennis.~~

Spencer Gore won the first competition.

In 1884, women started competing in Wimbledon.

Estructura del párrafo

Paragraph structure

Un párrafo tiene tres partes:

- La primera oración (*opening sentence*), que presenta la idea principal.
- El cuerpo del párrafo (*body of paragraph*), que amplía la idea principal con información importante.
- La última oración (*closing sentence*), que resume la idea principal y la repite con otras palabras.

I love music.	opening sentence
I use my phone on the way to school. I download songs from the Internet onto my phone and I listen to it all the time. I like many types of music: hip-hop, Latin, jazz and pop, too.	body of paragraph
When there is good music, I'm happy.	closing sentence

Repasa lo escrito

Checking your writing

Las mayúsculas
(Capital letters)

Se escriben con mayúscula:

- los nombres y títulos de las personas: *Mrs Sandra Bennett, Dr Perry, Ray Mears*
- los nombres de lugares como ciudades, países, continentes, edificios famosos, museos, etc.: *London, Italy, Asia, the Eiffel Tower, the Guggenheim Museum*
- las nacionalidades: *English, Chinese, American*
- los días: *Saturday, Tuesday, Friday*
- los meses: *January, July, October*
- la primera palabra de una oración: *My sister is thirteen years old.*
- el pronombre personal ***I***: *I go ice skating and I play the guitar.*
- los idiomas: *French, Thai, Arabic*
- las palabras importantes de los títulos de libros y películas, canciones, festividades y juegos de ordenador: *A Tale of Two Cities, Avatar, California Dreamin', Christmas, SimCity*

Las preposiciones de tiempo
(Prepositions of time)

Se usan distintas preposiciones delante de las horas y los periodos de fiesta, los días y las fechas, los meses, las estaciones, los años y las partes del día. Es muy importante que sepas utilizar la correcta en cada caso. Presta atención a estos ejemplos:

• ***at***	horas:	*at two o'clock* (a las 2 en punto)
	festividades:	*at Christmas* (en navidad)
• ***on***	días de la semana:	*on Sunday* el domingo
	fechas:	*on 10th May*
		on Christmas Day
• ***in***	meses:	*in June*
	estaciones:	*in winter*
	años:	*in 2010*
	partes del día:	*in the evening* en la tarde
Excepciones:		*at the weekend* (el fin de semana)
		at night (por la noche)

at prep. lugar concreto
tiempo at night → por la noche
- en navidad : en
- para las horas : a
- velocidad a
- precio en

La puntuación
(Punctuation)

- El punto (.) va al final de las oraciones afirmativas y negativas.
  Mary is fourteen years old.
- La coma (,) se usa para separar palabras o ideas. Normalmente no se pone delante de ***and***.
  I've got maths, English and science today.
- El signo de interrogación (?) se pone sólo al final de las preguntas.
  Do you like sport?
- El signo de exclamación (!) también se pone sólo al final de la frase y sirve para expresar una emoción o un sentimiento y para hacer hincapié en algo.
  I love football!

El orden de las palabras: sujeto - verbo
(Word order: Subject – Verb)

El sujeto de la oración se pone delante del verbo.

David walks to school.
s v

David is riding a new bike.
s v

Pero en las preguntas va detrás del verbo o entre el auxiliar y el verbo principal.

Where is my swimming cap?
v s

Does David walk to school?
aux s v

El orden de las palabras: las expresiones temporales
(Word order: Time expressions)

Las expresiones temporales pueden ir al principio o al final de la frase, aunque es más habitual ponerlas al final.

Tom Hanks started acting in the 1980s.
time expr.

Si van al principio, se separan de la oración principal con una coma.

In the 1980s, Tom Hanks started acting.
time expr.

El orden de las palabras: los adjetivos
(Word order: Adjectives)

- Normalmente van delante de los sustantivos.
  warm sweater
  adj n
  Y también detrás del verbo ***to be***.
  The sweater is warm.
  v adj
- Si hay varios adjetivos, suelen ir en este orden: opinión, tamaño, color.
  She's got a beautiful, tiny black kitten.
  o s c

El orden de las palabras: los adverbios
(Word order: Adverbs)

- Los adverbios de intensidad y de modo van detrás del verbo.
  Anna is sitting very quietly.
  adverb of degree / adverb of manner
- Los adverbios de frecuencia van delante del verbo en las oraciones afirmativas.
  He always acts in comedies.
  adv v
  Pero si el verbo es ***to be***, el adverbio va detrás.
  Celebrities are usually very rich.
  v adv

Las conjunciones
(Linking words)

Son palabras que unen dos o más ideas.

- ***and*** (y) une dos oraciones o ideas.
  *I sailed to Greece **and** I flew to Australia last year.*
- ***or*** (o) une dos ideas distintas.
  *We walk to school **or** we go on a bus.*
- ***but*** (pero) contrasta dos ideas.
  *David likes travelling **but** he doesn't like flying.*
- ***because*** (porque) expresa la razón o causa de algo.
  *Janice doesn't go on a motorboat **because** she doesn't like water.*
- ***so*** (así que) expresa el resultado de lo que se ha dicho anteriormente.
  *I forgot my textbook, **so** my teacher will be angry.*

Los conectores de secuencia
(Connectors of sequence)

Cuando contamos una serie de hechos usamos estas palabras para mostrar el orden en que ocurrieron:

- ***first*** (primero, en primer lugar)
- ***next*** (a continuación)
- ***then*** (luego, entonces)
- ***after that*** (luego, después [de eso])
- ***finally*** (finalmente, para terminar)

First indica lo primero que pasó y ***finally*** lo último.

My grandfather came to England sixty years ago. ***First,*** *he worked in a restaurant.* ***Next,*** *he studied science at university.* ***Then,*** *he became a chemist and opened a chemist's.* ***After that,*** *he met my grandmother and they got married. He worked for many years, but* ***finally,*** *he sold his shop and he and my grandmother went to live near the sea.*

Los conectores temporales en la narración
(Narrative linkers)

Los conectores temporales, como ***when***, ***suddenly*** o ***a minute later***, se utilizan para unir ideas y dar cohesión a la narración.

I was in the shop ***when*** *the robbery took place.*

Suddenly, *a man started shouting.*

A police officer came ***a minute later*** *and arrested the man.*

Las conjunciones y locuciones consecutivas
(Connectors of result)

Las conjunciones y locuciones consecutivas, como ***for this reason, as a result*** y ***so***, se usan para presentar una situación y su resultado o consecuencia.

Travelling by tram is very slow. ***For this reason,*** *people prefer to take the underground.*

We waste too much water. ***As a result,*** *there won't be enough water for everyone in the near future.*

I don't need these plastic bottles, ***so*** *I'm going to recycle them.*

Las preposiciones
(Prepositions)

Las preposiciones acompañan a un sustantivo, pronombre o sintagma nominal y su función varía según lo que se quiere expresar: pueden servir para mostrar dirección, posición o tiempo, así como para introducir un complemento.

Es difícil aprender a utilizar las preposiciones correctamente en un idioma extranjero. Muchos sustantivos, verbos y adjetivos se usan con determinadas preposiciones, pero a veces no se puede saber cuál es la preposición correcta y es necesario aprender las expresiones de memoria.

He is coming ***at*** *3 o'clock.*

We were standing ***at*** *the door.*

She was born ***on*** *9th July.*

The books are ***on*** *the table.*

The keys are ***in*** *my pocket.*

I usually have a shower ***in*** *the morning.*

In *the end, Redhill won the match.*

We played ***against*** *the Timberwolves.*

He is the captain ***of*** *the Timberwolves.*

Who is running ***with*** *the ball right now?*

She received an injury ***to*** *her leg.*

The shop is open ***from*** *Monday* ***to*** *Friday.*

The score went ***from*** *12* ***to*** *44.*

He fell ***in*** *the last minute* ***of*** *the game.*

We won the competition ***for*** *the fifth time* ***in*** *a row.*

Writing Plan 1

Write a photo description.

1 Choose a photo.

2 Complete the charts below about the photo.

Person: ....
Description: ....
Where in photo: ....
Activity: ....

Person: ....
Description: ....
Where in photo: ....
Activity: ....

Person: ....
Description: ....
Where in photo: ....
Activity: ....

3 Use the information in the charts to write your photo description.

....
....
....
....
....
....
....

Check Yourself ✔

Content – I included

- ☐ descriptions of the people / things
- ☐ where they are in the photo
- ☐ what the people are doing

Language – I used

- ☐ adjectives correctly
- ☐ prepositions of place correctly
- ☐ linking words correctly

Useful Language

There is / There are ... in the photo.
They're at ...
The boy / girl in the ... is ...
The boy's / girl's name is ...
He / She is standing next to / between ...
Can you see ... ?

Writing Guide, Workbook, page 110

Writing Plan 2

Write a biography of a famous person.

1 **Choose a person.**

2 **Complete the chart below about the person.**

Name: ....

Birth: ....

Job: ....

Famous because: ....

....

Marriage: ....

....

Children: ....

....

Death: ....

3 **Use the information in the chart to write a biography.**

....

....

....

....

....

....

....

Check Yourself ✓

Content – I included

- ☐ important dates
- ☐ facts about the person's jobs and achievements
- ☐ facts about the person's family

Language – I used

- ☐ the Past Simple correctly
- ☐ connectors of sequence correctly

Useful Language

... was a ...
He / She was born in ... on ...
In ... , he / she ...
When ... was ... , he / she ...
He / She got married in ...
He / She had ... children.
... died on / in ...

Writing Guide, Workbook, page 110

Writing Plan 3

Write a report about a travel destination.

1 **Choose a travel destination.**

2 **Complete the chart below about the destination.**

Paragraph 1
Name of place: ....
Where it is: ....
General information: ....
Paragraph 2 ....
Description of the place: ....
....
Things to see and do: ....
....
Paragraph 3 ....
Opinion of the place: ....

3 **Use the information in the chart to write a report about a travel destination. Organise your ideas into paragraphs according to the chart above.**

Paragraph 1 ....
....
....
....

Paragraph 2 ....
....
....
....

Paragraph 3 ....
....

Check Yourself ✓

Content – I included

- ☐ basic information about the destination
- ☐ a description and suggestions for activities
- ☐ an opinion of the place
- ☐ information organised in paragraphs

Language – I used

- ☐ the correct tenses
- ☐ adjectives to describe the place

Useful Language

... is a ... in ...
It's easy to get there by ...
The climate is ...
It's got ...
Visitors come to ...
It's popular for ...
A holiday in ... can be ...
It's the perfect destination for ...

Writing Guide, Workbook, page 110

Writing Plan 4

Write a personal profile.

1 Complete the chart below about yourself.

Paragraph 1

Personal details: ....

Family members: ....

Paragraph 2

Summer activities: ....

....

Winter activities: ....

....

Paragraph 3

Feelings: ....

2 Use the information in the chart to write your personal profile. Organise your ideas into paragraphs according to the chart above.

Paragraph 1 ....

....

....

Paragraph 2 ....

....

....

Paragraph 3 ....

....

....

Check Yourself

Content – I included

- ☐ personal details
- ☐ information about my family
- ☐ activities we do
- ☐ my feelings about my life

Language – I used

- ☐ adverbs of frequency correctly
- ☐ time expressions correctly
- ☐ correct word order

Useful Language

My name is ...
I'm ... (years old)
I've got ...
I live in ...
It's got ...
In the summer, ...
In the winter, ...
I like / love ...

Writing Guide, Workbook, page 110

Writing Plan 5

Write a narrative.

1 **Choose an incident you read about or saw on TV or imagine an incident.**

2 **Complete the chart below about the incident.**

Paragraph 1

The incident: ....

When: ....

Where: ....

Paragraph 2

The sequence of events:

....

....

....

Paragraph 3

What happened in the end: ....

3 **Use the information in the chart to write your narrative. Organise your ideas into paragraphs according to the chart above.**

Paragraph 1 ....

....

....

Paragraph 2 ....

....

....

Paragraph 3 ....

....

Check Yourself ✓

Content – I included
- ☐ background information
- ☐ the sequence of events
- ☐ the ending

Language – I used
- ☐ narrative linkers correctly
- ☐ the Past Continuous and the Past Simple correctly

Useful Language

On ... , while I was ... , there was ...
Suddenly, ...
People were ...
After that, ...
In the end, ...

Writing Guide, Workbook, page 110

Writing Plan 6

Write predictions about life in the year 2222.

1 Complete the chart below about your predictions.

Paragraph 1

What we think will happen: ....

Reason: ....

Paragraph 2

Details: ....

....

....

Paragraph 3

My opinion: ....

2 Use the information in the chart to write your predictions. Organise your ideas into paragraphs according to the chart above.

Paragraph 1 ....

....

....

Paragraph 2 ....

....

....

Paragraph 3 ....

....

Check Yourself ✓

Content – I included

- ☐ predictions
- ☐ reason for predictions
- ☐ details about the predictions
- ☐ my opinion about the future

Language – I used

- ☐ connectors of result correctly
- ☐ expressions of opinion correctly

Useful Language

In my opinion, life in the year 2222 will be ...

There will be ...

There won't be ...

The ... will look like ...

It will probably be ...

Life in the future ...

I think ...

Writing Guide, Workbook, page 110

Writing Plan 7

Write a review of a TV programme.

1 Think of a reality TV programme you watch.

2 Complete the chart below about the programme.

Paragraph 1

Name of programme: ....

Type of programme: ....

Paragraph 2

Description of programme: ....

....

Paragraph 3

Your opinion: ....

3 Use the information in the chart to write a review of a TV programme. Organise your ideas into paragraphs according to the chart above.

Paragraph 1 ....

....

....

Paragraph 2 ....

....

....

Paragraph 3 ....

....

....

Check Yourself ✔

Content – I included

- ☐ the name and type of programme
- ☐ a description of the programme
- ☐ my opinion of the programme

Language – I used

- ☐ a variety of adjectives and adverbs
- ☐ correct word order

Useful Language

... is a reality TV programme.
The participants / characters ...
There are ...
Sometimes, ...
In my opinion, ...
Check out ...
It's a ... programme to watch.

Writing Guide, Workbook, page 110

Writing Plan 8

Write a news report.

1 Choose a real or imaginary match or competition.

2 Complete the chart below about the match or competition.

Paragraph 1

What happened: ....

When: ....

Where: ....

Paragraph 2

The sequence of events: ....

....

....

Paragraph 3

What happened in the end: ....

3 Use the information in the chart to write your news report. Organise your ideas into paragraphs according to the chart above.

Paragraph 1 ....

....

....

Paragraph 2 ....

....

....

Paragraph 3 ....

....

....

Check Yourself ✓

Content – I included

- ☐ basic information
- ☐ the sequence of events
- ☐ the ending

Language – I used

- ☐ tenses correctly
- ☐ prepositions correctly

Useful Language

... has won the ...
On ... , ... at ...
The teams / players ...
Then, ...
... took the lead.
The score was ...
In the last minute, ...
The crowd ...
The final score was ...

Writing Guide, Workbook, page 110

Writing Plan 9

Write a clothing description.

1 Complete the chart below about your clothing.

Paragraph 1

General introduction about types of clothing: ....

Paragraph 2

Details about clothing for school: ....

....

Opinion of clothing: ....

Paragraph 3

Details about clothing outside school: ....

....

Opinion of clothing: ....

2 Use the information in the chart to write your clothing description. Organise your ideas into paragraphs according to the chart above.

Paragraph 1 ....

....

....

Paragraph 2 ....

....

....

Paragraph 3 ....

....

....

Check Yourself ✓

Content – I included

- ☐ general introduction about types of clothing
- ☐ details about clothing for school and outside school
- ☐ opinion of types of clothing

Language – I used

- ☐ correct adjective order

Useful Language

I wear ... for ...
I've got ... pairs of ...
I love ...
Some are ...
There are ... in my cupboard.
When it's hot / cold, ...

Writing Guide, Workbook, page 110

Learning Competences

Student Learning Record:

Competence in initiative and entrepreneurship

First and family name: ....

Address: .... (street)

.... (city)

Date of birth: ....

Country of birth: ....

Nationality / Nationalities: ....

Language/s I know well: ....

Language/s I am learning: ....

School: ....

Year: ....

English teacher: ....

Tick (✓) the sentences that are true for you.

I learn English at ...

- school. ☐
- a private language school. ☐
- a summer language school. ☐

It's important for me to learn English because ...

- I want to do well at school. ☐
- I want to understand the words of songs. ☐
- I want to read magazines and books in English. ☐
- I want to study at university. ☐
- I want to surf the web easily. ☐
- I want to chat online. ☐
- I want to travel to English-speaking countries. ☐

My English Experience:

Competence in learning to learn skills

My English Learning Biography	
I started learning English in:	(year)
I used these books: (Write the titles you remember.)	
My mark last year was:	

I use English when I ...	Never	Sometimes	Often
travel and meet English-speaking people.			
watch TV or films in English.			
write e-mails.			
read adverts in English.			
listen to / sing English songs.			
surf the web or chat online.			

My Marks in 2nd of ESO							
	Diagnostic Test	Term 1	Term 2	Term 3	Final Exam 1	Final Exam 2	Final Mark
Reading							
Speaking							
Listening							
Writing							
Grammar							
Vocabulary							
Teacher's observations							

English and Me:

Competence in learning to learn skills

Use this scale:

1	2	3	4	5
with difficulty		OK		easily

Things I can do in English:	Term 1	Term 2	Term 3
Reading			
I can read and understand short texts from different genres.			
I can understand the instructions in my English book.			
I can understand simple messages (letters, e-mails, text messages, etc.).			
I can read signs in English.			
I can understand graded readers / stories in English.			
I can read and understand simple songs, poems and comics.			
I can use an English dictionary.			
Speaking			
I can speak to my friends or my teacher in English.			
I can say some of the expressions in my book and use them in appropriate conversations.			
I can have dialogues with friends or my teacher and I can do simple role-plays / acting in English using expressions in my book.			
I can give information, ask questions about things in class and talk about my personal details (where I live, etc.).			
I can respond when people speak to me and I can use a variety of simple phrases.			
I can talk about my experiences and routines and I can give instructions.			
Listening			
I can understand my teacher's instructions and expressions / phrases about people and places I know.			
I can understand short messages about things in class when people speak to me clearly.			
I can understand the recording when I listen carefully.			
I can understand conversations in English or when English people speak in films, or on videos / DVDs in my English lesson.			
Writing			
I can complete charts in English.			
I can write notes and send messages to friends in English (text messages / e-mails, etc.).			
I can write short sentences.			
I can write my own short texts using similar texts as a model.			
I can write short texts for my teacher about things I know.			
I can write texts of one or two paragraphs with linking words like *and* or *because* and connectors of sequence (*first*, *then*, *next*, *finally*, etc.).			

My Strategies for Progress:

Competence in initiative and entrepreneurship

Which language area do you need to improve? Prioritise the following language areas for you to improve. Use this scale:

1	2	3	4	5
more important				less important

	Term 1	Term 2	Term 3
Reading			
Speaking			
Listening			
Writing			
Language (Grammar / Vocabulary)			

Choose strategies to improve the language area that is most important to you. Tick (✓) the strategies you want to use. You can also add ideas of your own.

Reading	
I will read the text two or three times to help me understand it.	☐
I will read the questions carefully, so I can find the answers in the text.	☐
I will try to guess unknown words.	☐
I will use the title, headings and pictures in the text to help me understand.	☐
	☐
Speaking	
I will try to speak to my teacher in English.	☐
I will try to speak only English in speaking activities in class.	☐
I will practise speaking English outside class once a week with my friends.	☐
	☐
Listening	
I will read the questions carefully and guess the answers before I listen.	☐
I will listen to the whole text and try to understand as much as I can.	☐
I will listen to songs in English and follow the words.	☐
	☐
Writing	
I will write a list of useful words and expressions before I start.	☐
I will write a draft and correct it before I write a neat version.	☐
I will use the Writing Guide for help.	☐
	☐
Language (Grammar / Vocabulary)	
I will read the Grammar Appendix.	☐
I will try to memorise the vocabulary list in the Language Builder for each unit of my book.	☐
I will practise and learn the vocabulary for dictation.	☐
	☐

Over the year, check if your strategies are working. If not, try something else!
Are my strategies working?

Term 1 - ☺ 😐 ☹	Term 2 - ☺ 😐 ☹	Term 3 - ☺ 😐 ☹

Self-Evaluation:

Competences in linguistic communication and initiative and entrepreneurship

Unit 1

I can ...	Need to practise	OK	Great
name five school subjects and five school items.			
name ten activities.			
use the Present Simple and Present Continuous correctly.			
use *There is / There are*, articles and quantifiers and *How many / How much* correctly.			
describe a picture.			
use linking words.			

Tell your partner three activities you do.

Unit 2

I can ...	Need to practise	OK	Great
name ten verbs.			
name ten life events.			
use the Past Simple correctly.			
use *used to* correctly.			
discuss biographies.			
use connectors of sequence correctly.			

Tell your partner three things you did yesterday.

Unit 3

I can ...	Need to practise	OK	Great
name ten adjectives.			
name ten words connected to geography.			
use comparison of adjectives correctly.			
use *(not) as … as, too …* and *(not) … enough* correctly.			
plan a holiday.			
organise my information in paragraphs.			

Tell your partner about one geographical feature in the north of your country, one in the south, one in the west and one in the east.

Unit 4

I can ...	Need to practise	OK	Great
name ten words connected to the weather.			
name ten family words.			
ask subject and object questions correctly.			
use adverbs of manner correctly.			
ask and answer questions in a personal interview.			
use correct word order (adverbs of frequency and time expressions).			

Ask your partner three personal questions.

Unit 5

I can ...	Need to practise	OK	Great
name ten crime words.			
name ten words connected to people and crime.			
use the Past Continuous and Past Simple correctly.			
ask and answer questions for an investigation of a crime.			
use narrative linkers correctly.			

Write three sentences from a narrative using different narrative linkers.

Unit 6

I can ...	Need to practise	OK	Great
name ten types of transport.			
name ten verbs connected to the environment.			
use the future tenses correctly.			
use the First Conditional and Second Conditional correctly.			
discuss plans.			
use connectors of result correctly.			

Tell your partner about your plans for the weekend and your predictions for them.

Unit 7

I can ...	Need to practise	OK	Great
name ten experiences.			
name ten adjectives.			
use the Present Perfect Simple correctly.			
use *for* and *since* correctly.			
talk about experiences.			
use correct word order (adjectives, adverbs of manner and adverbs of degree).			

Tell your partner about two experiences you've had and two experiences you haven't had.

Unit 8

I can ...	Need to practise	OK	Great
name ten nutrition words.			
name ten words and phrases connected to fitness.			
use modals correctly.			
give advice.			
use prepositions correctly.			

Tell your partner about something you couldn't do when you were younger and can do now and something you have to do this week.

Unit 9

I can ...	Need to practise	OK	Great
name ten fashion words.			
name ten adjectives.			
use Reported Speech correctly.			
Use gerunds and infinitives correctly.			
talk about buying a gift.			
use correct adjective order.			

Tell your partner about three of your favourite fashion items.

New English in Use

ESO 2

LANGUAGE BUILDER

New English in Use

ESO 2

Language Builder

New English in Use ESO 2 Language Builder facilita el repaso y consolida el vocabulario y las expresiones útiles aprendidas en el ***Student's Book***.

El ***Language Builder*** ofrece los siguientes contenidos en cada unidad:

- Listas de palabras y expresiones para ayudarte a preparar tu propio glosario de consulta rápida. Esta herramienta de referencia te servirá de ayuda cuando repases para los exámenes o prepares actividades de expresión oral.
- Actividades divertidas que suponen un reto y te ayudarán a repasar el vocabulario aprendido en la unidad.

El ***Language Builder*** de ***New English in Use*** te ayuda a mejorar el vocabulario y a desarrollar competencias lingüísticas productivas de una forma divertida.

¡Diviértete!

Contents

Language Builder

Getting Started

1 Write the words in your language.

Adjectives

adventurous	curly	honest	shy
athletic	dark	light	small
beautiful	fat	long	straight
brave	funny	medium height	strong
clever	generous	old	weak
creative	good-looking	round	young

The house

armchair	curtains	kitchen	rug
bathroom	desk	lamp	shelf
bedroom	duvet	mirror	shower
cooker	fridge	pillow	toilet
cupboard			

Animals

ant	crocodile	horse	snake
bat	dolphin	lion	spider
butterfly	elephant	lizard	tiger
chicken	frog	mosquito	whale
cow	giraffe	shark	wolf

Places around town

amusement park	chemist's	hospital	post office
arcade	church	library	restaurant
bank	cinema	museum	sports centre
bar	department store	police station	sweet shop
café			

Sport

basketball	football	scuba diving	swimming pool
bowling	goggles	skiing	tennis
catch	golf	surfing	throw
climb	karate	swimming	volleyball
cycling	rollerblading	swimming cap	weightlifting
dancing	running		

2 Write the expressions in your language.

Greetings and Introductions

Are you new here?

This is my friend (*Adam*).

Is this (*06-321789*)?

Can I please speak to (*Mark*)?

Hi, welcome to our school.

Sorry, (*he*) isn't here.

Thanks, my name's (*Jack*).

Nice to meet you.

Yes, it is. Who's calling?

Yes, I'm from (*Oxford*).

Hi, I'm (*Valerie*).

Hello, (*Mrs Devon*). This is (*Ronny*).

Call again later, (*Ronny*).

Classroom language

Listen carefully.

Can you explain this to me, please?

Where is your homework?

I'm sorry I'm late.

Can you spell this word?

Can I borrow a (*ruler*), please?

Who knows the answer to this question?

When is the (*English*) exam?

What page are we on?

3 All the words in the puzzle have got double letters. Read the clues and find the words.

1. three adjectives
2. three household items
3. two animals
4. two sports
5. one place: post ...
6. two rooms

f	g	a	s	b	u	t	t	e	r	f	l	y
u	i	b	m	b	a	t	h	r	o	o	m	i
n	r	e	a	c	o	o	k	e	r	t	z	s
n	a	d	l	t	m	i	t	e	n	n	i	s
y	f	r	l	a	s	t	a	e	t	u	z	y
h	f	o	g	l	r	o	p	i	l	l	o	w
s	e	o	i	l	o	f	f	i	c	e	a	p
n	o	m	d	m	i	r	r	o	r	z	m	t
s	k	i	i	n	g	i	l	h	a	t	r	i

4 Circle the correct answer.

1. **Beautiful** is to **ugly** as ... .
   a *creative* is to *clever*
   b *old* is to *young*
   c *light* is to *long*
2. **Swimming** is to **swimming cap** as ... .
   a *cycling* is to *helmet*
   b *swimming pool* is to *goggles*
   c *basketball* is to *throw*
3. **Kitchen** is to **fridge** as ... .
   a *sports centre* is to *karate*
   b *museum* is to *cinema*
   c *bedroom* is to *lamp*
4. **Young** is to **lion** as ... .
   a *shark* is to *dolphin*
   b *shower* is to *toilet*
   c *big* is to *department store*

Language Builder 1

Write the words and expressions in your language.

School

art
atlas
calculator
compass
computer technology
dictionary
drama
English
flash drive
French
geography
globe
glue
history
laptop
literature
maths
microscope
music
paintbrush
paints
science
scissors
sport
stapler
tablet
textbook

Activities

build models
check e-mails
do experiments
do judo
go horse-riding
learn a new language
learn competitive diving
paint pictures
perform in a band
play the piano
repair computers
send text messages
take a nap
take photos

Describing a picture

There are (*two girls in white clothes*).
The (*policeman*) looks (*very tired*).
There's a (*robot*) and a (*band*) in the picture.
I can see (*two girls*) and they're (*building a model*).
In this picture, (*a woman*) is (*wearing a pink dress*).
The (*students*) are (*looking into their microscopes*).

Everyday English: Talking About Activities

Do you enjoy (*performing in the band*)?
What do you think of the (*science lessons*)?
What's your favourite (*activity*)?
Do you prefer learning (*French*) or (*German*)?
Do you want to learn (*competitive diving*)?
I don't like (*sport*) and I can't (*swim*).
I love (*painting pictures*).
I like them both. I'm good at (*languages*).
I don't mind (*doing experiments*), but I prefer (*building models*).
I really like (*performing in concerts*), but I hate (*playing the piano at home*).

2 **Find 11 activities. Use each word at least once.**

do | paint | a | learn | judo | competitive diving
text messages | take | check | experiments | e-mails
computers | nap | new language | photos
models | build | pictures | repair | send

1 ……………………
2 ……………………
3 ……………………
4 ……………………
5 ……………………
6 ……………………
7 ……………………
8 ……………………
9 ……………………
10 ……………………
11 ……………………

3 **Circle the correct answers for each clue. Then complete the sentence below with the remaining word.**

1. two items you use in maths lessons
2. two items you use to put two pieces of paper together
3. two activities you can do in a music lesson
4. two different books
5. two sports activities
6. two types of computers
7. three school subjects

do judo | laptop | flash drive | glue | stapler | French | play the piano | perform in a band | atlas | literature | dictionary | tablet | compass | calculator | go horse-riding | history

Many students save their homework on a …………………… .

4 **Solve the code and write the sentences in your notebook. Circle the sentence which is not correct.**

a	b	c	d	e	f	g	h	i	j	k	l	m	n	o	p	q	r	s	t	u	v	w	x	y	z
n		p		r		t		v		x		z		b		d		f		h		j		l	

1. Fghqragf fbzrgvzrf hfr cnvagf va neg yrffbaf.
2 Lbh hfr n tybor va trbtencul yrffbaf.
3. Lbh pna phg unve jvgu fpvffbef.
4. N zvpebfpbcr znxrf ovt guvatf ybbx fznyy.
5. Fghqragf hfr n grkgobbx va zbfg fpubby fhowrpgf.

Language Builder 2

1 **Write the words and expressions in your language.**

Verbs

attach
bite
borrow
cross
demonstrate
develop
fight
freeze
improve
light
prevent
pull
reach
save
steal
survive
volunteer

Life events

belong to
(be) born
die
fall in love
get a job
get divorced
get married
go to university
graduate from
grow up
have a child
join
move to
receive awards

Discussing biographies

When was (*he*) born?
Where was (*he*) born?
What did (*he*) do?
Why was (*he*) famous?
When did (*he*) get married?
Did (*he*) have children?
When did (*he*) die?
Where did (*he*) die?

Everyday English: Making Recommendations

It was boring.
The characters were great.
I really recommend it!
It was very interesting.
It was too long.
The plot was very exciting.
The characters weren't at all realistic.
I like (*adventure books*) and I love (*biographies*).
Can you recommend a book for me to read?
That sounds interesting.
Who are the main characters?
Then you must read (*Crocodile Hunter*).
I think it's an amazing book.
What types of books do you like?
What's it about?

2

Copy the words with the same colour into your notebook. Then put them in the correct order to write sentences about Eva's life events.

award	she	she
in	had	an
got	divorced	love
child	received	a
Eva	she	she
got	fell	married

Look at the pictures. Which sentence hasn't got a match?

....

3

Order the blocks of letters to complete the sentences about Tom's life.

1 [AIN] [TOM] [IN] [S B] [ORN] [WA] [SP]

Tom was born in Spain.

2 [W U] [N T] [GRE] [HE] [OLE] [P I] [DO]

....

3 [ED] [MAD] [HE] [MOV] [RID] [TO]

....

4 [T T] [HE] [ERS] [O U] [ITY] [NIV] [WEN]

....

5 [OB] [E G] [THE] [A J] [N H] [OT]

....

4

Find 14 verbs in the puzzle.

b	o	r	r	o	w	y	z	u	s	v
f	p	o	d	f	c	r	o	s	s	o
r	r	s	e	i	r	e	a	c	h	l
e	e	t	v	g	b	o	c	k	e	u
e	v	e	e	h	i	b	t	i	m	n
z	e	a	l	t	l	a	a	g	f	t
e	n	l	o	a	t	t	a	c	h	e
p	t	o	p	s	i	e	t	s	r	e
l	i	g	h	t	h	a	z	a	l	r
q	u	a	i	m	p	r	o	v	e	g
u	s	s	u	r	v	i	v	e	d	i

Which verbs are negative?

....

....

5

Follow the lines to make five newspaper headlines.

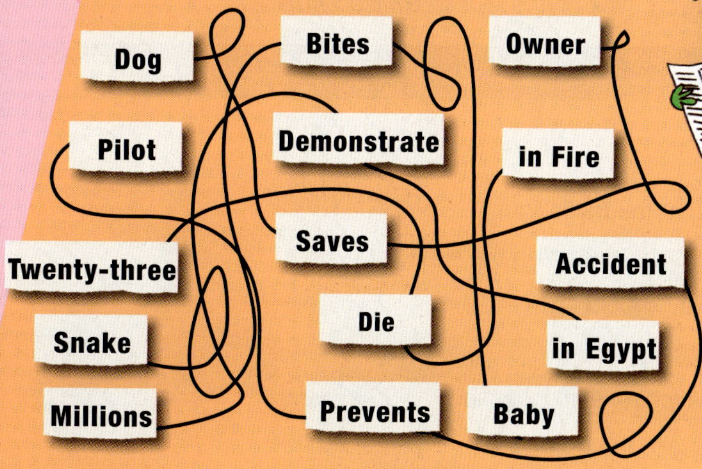

1 ....

2 ....

3 ....

4 ....

5 ....

Language Builder 3

1 **Write the words and expressions in your language.**

Adjectives

calm
dull
elegant
extraordinary
frightening
ideal
isolated
lively
peaceful
pleasant
relaxing
rough
safe
terrible
wonderful

Geography

canyon
cliff
coast
coral reef
east
field
glacier
ground
harbour
north
rainforest
scenery
south
stream
swamp
west

Planning a holiday

What kind of holiday do you want?
Where do you want to go?
When do you want to go?
How long do you want to be away?
What do you want to do there?
What do you think of (*the Alps in Switzerland*)?

Everyday English: Giving Directions

Turn (*left*) at the traffic light.
Take the (*second exit*) on the right.
Which way should I go?
Go straight.
There's a (*petrol station*) in about (*500 metres*).
Should I take the (*A21*)?
Stay on the (*M25*).
Which exit do we need?
Is this the fastest way?
We must get petrol.
Don't turn.

2 **Which letters are missing from the alphabet? Put them in the correct order to make adjectives.**

1 w n j u g t z i d s f p x b k o e y r h v q ....
2 x h w q j b v f c p n g u k z m r y ....
3 v q s h b k w n r g z c x o f p y j t m u ....
4 o j y t c w k b z f v q u d h p m s ....
5 s k n y d f x t j a w c m e i l q z b v p ....
6 r i k q m w b z p v g u y c n j h l d x o t ....
7 t b j z g x p i a k v c m y q h s ....

3 **Complete the puzzle with adjectives according to the clues below. Then unscramble the letters in the green squares to complete the sentence.**

Across →
1. quiet and calm
5. unusual
7. boring
8. nice

Down ↓
2. the opposite of *casual*
3. full of energy
4. scary
6. very bad

The beautiful .... in the north of Italy makes it a very popular holiday destination.

4 **Find words in the boxes to match the pictures.**

1

t	s	r
m	c	a
p	g	o

2

r	l	c
k	i	f
n	f	e

3

r	e	i
b	l	c
g	a	f

4

n	o	d
c	y	n
g	a	i

5

d	s	h
w	a	o
l	m	p

6

c	g	e
r	n	d
o	u	t

5 **Solve the code to read the definitions. Then match the words below to the definitions.**

a	b	c	d	e	f	g	h	i	j	k	l	m	n	o	p	q	r	s	t	u	v	w	x	y	z
52		48		44			38				30					20						8			

east • coral reef • stream • field • south • rainforest • harbour

1 50 24 52 14 16 16 14 52 4 38 44 18 44. ....
2 10 44 40 44 14 52 50 30 44 16 40 18 24 8 38 44 18 44. ....
3 14 18 24 22 36 48 52 30 42 36 16 38 30 36 10 44 38 44 18 44. ....
4 52 16 28 52 30 30 18 36 10 44 18. ....
5 14 38 44 24 22 22 24 16 36 14 44 24 42 26 24 18 14 38. ....
6 14 38 44 24 22 22 24 16 36 14 44 24 42 8 44 16 14. ....
7 36 14 ’16 40 24 14 28 52 26 4 14 18 44 44 16. ....

Language Builder 4

Write the words and expressions in your language.

The weather

cloudy
cold
cool
dry
foggy
hot
lightning
rain
snow
stormy
sunny
thunder
warm
wet
windy

The family

aunt
cousin
daughter
granddaughter
grandfather
grandmother
grandson
husband
nephew
niece
parents
son
uncle
wife

A personal interview

How many (*brothers and sisters*) have you got?
What are your favourite (*school subjects*)?
What (*after-school activities*) do you do?
How often do you (*do sport*)?
Where does (*your mother / father*) work?
What's the weather like where you live?

Everyday English: Describing Homes

Do you live in a house or a flat?
What's your address?
What floor do you live on?
Have you got (*a garden*)?
How many rooms have you got?

2 **Find two weather words in each cloud. Use all the letters.**

3 **Put the letters with the same colour in order to find nine weather words. Then use the words to complete the weather report.**

o	t	a	c	l	n	n	y
d	u	m	i	r	y	u	o
m	o	r	w	s	h	a	w
r	i	o	d	d	o	c	s
n	n	t	y	y	l	y	r

Well, I'm sure you all felt that it was really 1. ______ and 2. ______ today. The temperature reached a high of 35°! However, I've got good news for tomorrow. It will still be 3. ______ and 4. ______ , but not as hot. Temperatures will reach 30°.
Thursday will be 5. ______ and 6. ______ with temperatures dropping to 18°. For those of you planning weekend activities, we're expecting 7. ______ weather. It will be extremely 8. ______ and there'll be quite a lot of 9. ______ .
That's all for today's weather.

4 **Complete the puzzle. Then write the letters from the circles in the correct order to find out how many brothers and sisters Josh has got.**

Across
3 My sister's daughter is my ..... .
5 My mum's sister is my ..... .
6 My mum's father is my ..... .
7 My brother's son is my ..... .

Down
1 My mum's mother is my ..... .
2 My dad's brother is my ..... .
4 My aunt's children are my ..... .

Josh has got .... brothers and sisters.

5 **Lara has brought her boyfriend, Leo, to a family dinner. Read the introductions and complete the family tree with the correct names.**

Language Builder 5

1 Write the words and expressions in your language.

Crime

arrest
court
criminal
evidence
fingerprints
gun
hijack
investigate
knife
murder
police officer
prison
robbery
weapon

People and crime

burglar
detective
expert
forensic scientist
forger
judge
jury
lawyer
prisoner
security guard
suspect
thief
victim
witness

Investigating a crime

What were you doing on (*Main Street*) at (*11.00*) last night?
What happened?
What did you do?
Can you describe the (*man*)?
What was (*he*) wearing?
Can you give us any more information?

Everyday English: Following Rules

Can I (*eat my sandwich*) here?
No, I'm afraid you can't.
Is (*smoking*) allowed here?
No, it's prohibited. Look at the sign.
Excuse me, is it alright if I (*play football*) here?
No, it isn't permitted.
Is it possible to (*turn left*) here?
Absolutely not! It's against the law!

2 Follow the true sentences to reach the end.

START

1. Every person has got different fingerprints.
2. A criminal usually helps people.
3. A police officer fights crime.
4. If there is a murder, somebody dies.
5. A forensic scientist works in a post office.
6. You can find a jury in court.
7. A paintbrush is a weapon.
8. A victim steals things from other people.
9. An art expert knows a lot about art.

END

3 Complete the puzzle with the missing words. Then find the hidden word to complete the sentences.

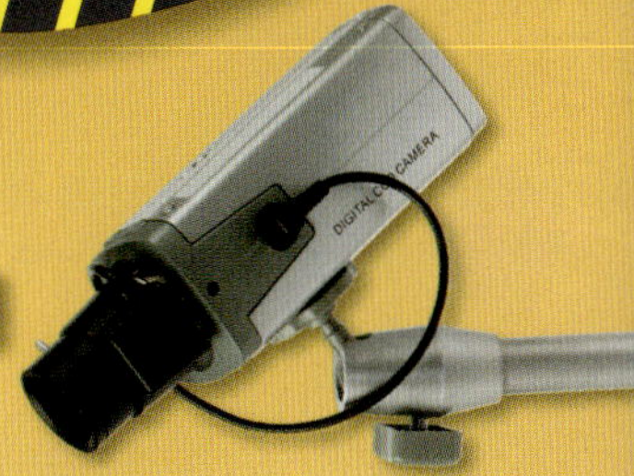

- The ... checked people's bags at the airport.
- The detective didn't find any ... of a murder.
- There was a ... at the bank last night.
- The ... stole my mobile phone from my bag.
- The ... asked the expert questions in court.
- The police officer ... the murder.
- The ... saw a man kill the victim.
- A ...works in a court.

The detective department of the London Police is called .... Yard.
1 2 3 4 5 6 7 8

4 Follow the crime words in the maze to find the name of a famous mystery writer.

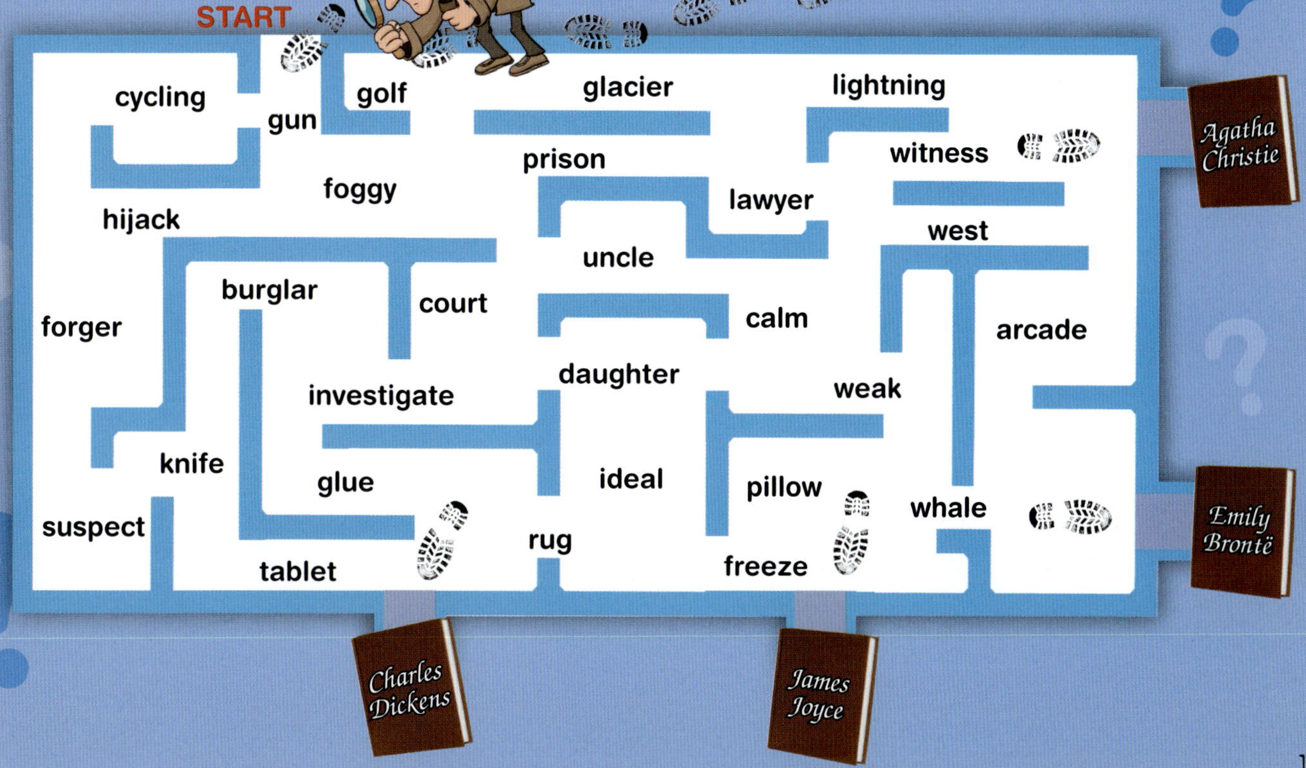

Language Builder 6

Write the words and expressions in your language.

Transport

aeroplane
cruise ship
ferry
helicopter
jeep
lorry
minivan
motorbike
motorboat
scooter
tram
underground
yacht

Verbs

clean up
damage
destroy
harm
pick up
plant
protect
recycle
reuse
throw out
unplug
waste

Talking about plans

Where are you going?
What are you going to do?
Who is doing the project with you?
Do you think it'll be difficult?
Will it really help?

Everyday English: Getting Information

Excuse me, when does the flight to (*Moscow*) leave?
Let's see. That's flight number (*YL233*). It leaves at (*6.50*).
Which gate does it leave from?
That's in (*terminal 1*).
Sorry to bother you, but is the flight to (*Cape Town*) on time?
Passengers can board at gate (*43a*). Have a good flight!
Excuse me, is flight (*BM948*) leaving from gate (*32b*) or (*32c*)?
It's leaving from gate (*32c*).
Oh, but I'm afraid the flight is delayed / cancelled.
Keep an eye on the information board.

2 Look at the picture. Correct the word in colour in each sentence.

1. The man is driving a white **jeep**. ....
2. The woman wearing a green shirt is getting on a **cruise ship**. ....
3. The **ferry** is leaving the harbour. ....
4. The woman wearing the yellow helmet is riding a **scooter**. ....
5. There is a **helicopter** next to the church. ....
6. A boy is getting on the **aeroplane**. ....
7. The police officer is getting on the **bus**. ....

3 Unscramble the letters to make verbs. Then write them in the crossword.

Across →

2 osdyter
6 aagdem

Down ↓

1 yecrlce
3 sreeu
4 rhma
5 twsea

4 Use the letters to complete the verbs. Use each letter once.

p p p	c c	u u u
l l l	e e	n n
t t t t	r r	o o

1 ..... i ..... k ..... p
2 c .... a ..... u .....
3 ..... h .... w o ....
4 .... an .....
5 p .... t ....
6 u ..... p .... g

5 Use the verbs from Exercises 3 and 4 to complete the signs.

Language Builder 7

1 Write the words and expressions in your language.

Experiences

break a record	go abroad	take lessons in self-defence
fail the test	go on a cruise	take part in a carnival
feed a wild animal	perform in a circus	tell lies
forget things	put out a fire	walk a tightrope
get lost	row a boat	

Adjectives

angry	ridiculous	unique
exhausted	risky	unpleasant
frightened	rude	upset
nasty	silly	worried
proud	surprised	

Talking about experiences

I'd love to try that, wouldn't you?
But why would I do such a risky thing?
That's not my idea of fun.
My parents would be really worried.
I'd be too frightened.
It sounds like a ridiculous idea to me.
What a silly thing to do.
I've always wanted to do that, haven't you?

Everyday English: Doing a Survey

How much TV do you watch each week?
When do you usually watch TV?
What is your favourite type of TV programme?
Do you eat in front of the TV?
Have you ever fallen asleep in front of the TV?
Does your family watch the news together?

2 **Find ten experiences in the puzzle. Use each word at least once.**

lessons wild abroad animal take part
a cruise carnival walk self-defence boat
feed perform tightrope on row put out
circus record fire go in take break

1 ....
2 ....
3 ....
4 ....
5 ....
6 ....
7 ....
8 ....
9 ....
10 ....

3 **Follow the lines and unscramble the words to find out what each person did wrong.**

oldt a ile

goftor sihgnt

dfalie a sett

tog solt

Now match each person to what he / she said.

I didn't tell the truth. ....

I don't know where I am. ....

I got a very low mark. ....

I didn't remember to buy butter and cheese. ....

4 **Find 14 adjectives in the puzzle.**

m	r	i	z	t	f	i	m	r	u	d	e
i	i	o	s	u	r	p	r	i	s	e	d
s	s	u	i	l	i	n	k	d	v	e	e
n	k	n	l	i	g	o	r	i	e	l	x
a	y	i	l	m	h	w	a	c	i	l	h
s	v	q	y	a	t	r	n	u	w	e	a
t	e	u	p	s	e	t	g	l	n	h	u
y	u	e	a	m	n	p	r	o	u	d	s
w	o	r	r	i	e	d	y	u	a	h	t
s	e	s	r	m	d	o	r	s	e	t	e
p	u	n	p	l	e	a	s	a	n	t	d

5 **Order the blocks of letters to learn about Dean's experiences.**

1 BRO | HE | KE | REC | ORD | A
....

2 TIG | WAL | HE | KED | HTR | A | OPE
....

3 LED | ST | TE | FAI | HE | A
....

4 T L | HE | GO | OST
....

Now complete the sentences about Dean's experiences with adjectives from Exercise 4.

1. He felt ....
2. It was ....
3. He felt very ....
4. It was an .... experience.

Language Builder 8

1 Write the words and expressions in your language.

Nutrition

balanced diet	fat	nutrition	snack
caffeine	healthy lifestyle	processed food	sugar
calories	junk food	protein	unhealthy
carbohydrates	liquid	salt	vitamins

Fitness

bone	gain weight	lose weight
dietician	get fit	muscle
exercise	gym	team
fitness trainer	heart	track
fresh air	injury	

Giving advice

What should I do?

The best thing for you to do is (*join a gym*).

I think you need to (*get up earlier*).

Maybe you should (*walk or ride a bicycle*).

I think it's a good idea to (*see your doctor*).

Why don't you (*try fresh fruit and cheese instead of processed food*)?

You can either (*see a dietician*) or (*speak to a fitness trainer at the gym*).

Everyday English: Sharing Information

Did the (*LA Clippers*) win the game?

Who played against the (*Clippers*)?

Where did they play?

Who scored the most points?

What was the final score?

Did you see the (*Euroleague championship match last night*)?

Did the (*Russian team*) win?

2 Which word DOESN'T go with the word in red?

1. silly, strong, weak — **muscles**
2. gain, exercise, lose — **weight**
3. healthy, unusual, upset — **lifestyle**
4. fresh, rude, cold — **air**
5. worried, balanced, unhealthy — **diet**
6. gym, animal, fitness — **trainer**
7. cycling, swimming, running — **track**

3 Answer true or false and follow the arrows. Collect the letters next to each true sentence and unscramble them to complete the sentence.

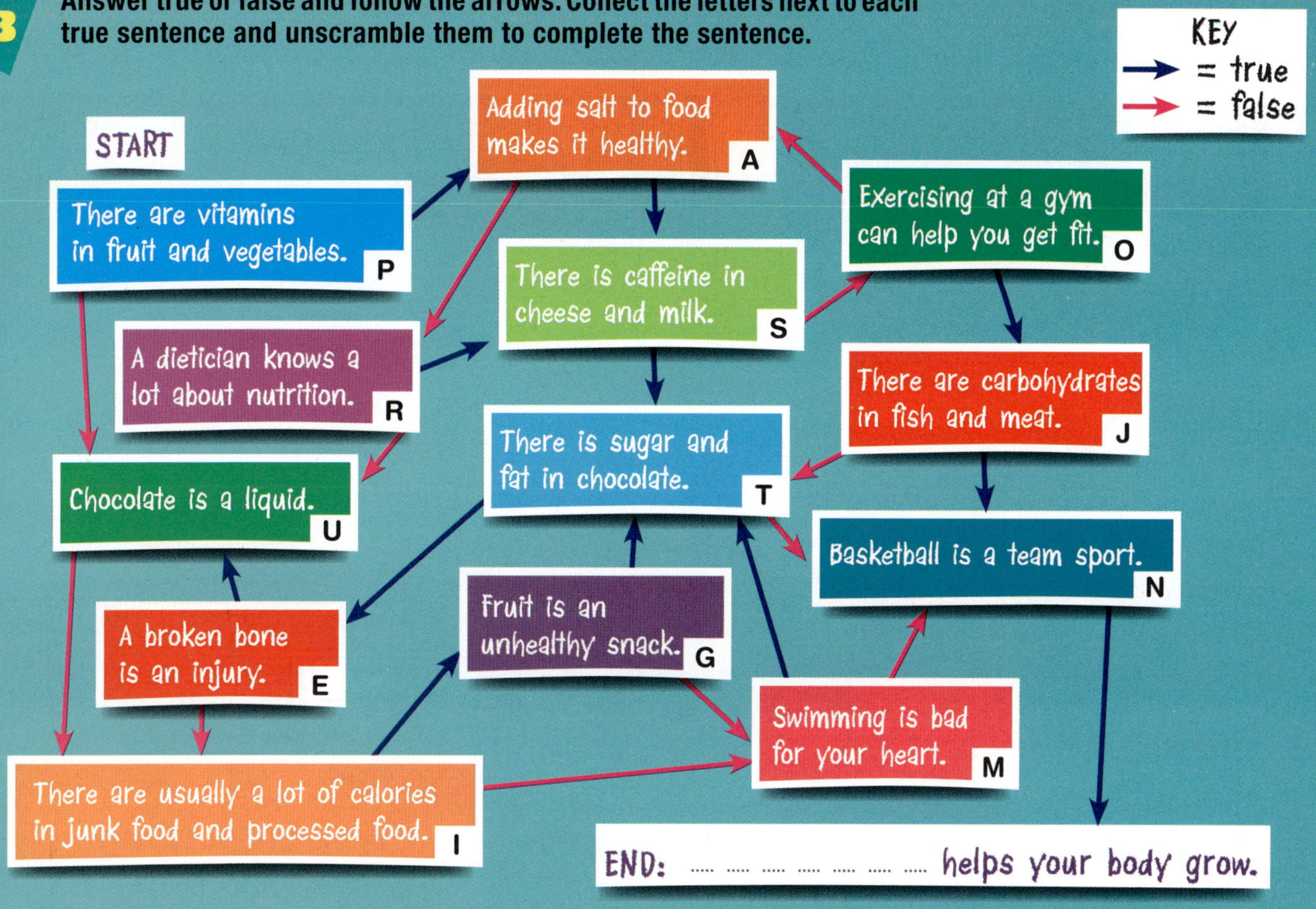

4 Solve the code to complete the sentences. Then write the correct name next to each picture.

a	b	c	d	e	g	h	i	k	l	n	o	p	r	s	t	u	y
1	2	4	7	11	16			37		56	67			106			154

1. Pippa enjoys 106 56 1 4 37 106 with a lot of 106 137 16 1 92 in them.
2. Jacob eats food with a lot of 4 1 92 2 67 22 154 7 92 1 121 11 106.
3. Erin eats a 2 1 46 1 56 4 11 7 7 29 11 121 and doesn't eat 79 92 67 4 11 106 106 11 7 food.

a ....

b ....

c ....

Language Builder 9

1 Write the words and expressions in your language.

Fashion

belt	make-up	ring
bracelet	nail varnish	sunglasses
earrings	necklace	tights
handbag	phone case	wallet
hoodie	purse	watch

Adjectives

casual	fashionable	practical
cheap	formal	pretty
colourful	lovely	second-hand
comfortable	modern	sophisticated
cool	old-fashioned	trendy
expensive	plain	

Buying a gift

Does that sound like a good idea?	What a great idea!
How much do you want to spend?	I don't think so.
Let's get (*them*)!	What do you want to buy for (*Mum*)?
Let's buy (*it*)!	These are very (*pretty*).
It's quite (*expensive*).	What do you think of (*this watch*)?
How about getting this (*ring*)?	That looks (*cool*).

Everyday English: Going Shopping

Can I help you?	Have you got my size?
Have you got any (*red tights*)?	Which colour do you prefer?
Are there any (*trendy belts*)?	How much are the (*handbags*)?
What size are you?	Who is it for?

2 Use the letters to make 10 adjectives to describe clothes. Use each letter once.

s s s s s	c c c
e e e e e e e	o o o o o o o o
a a a a a a a a	r r
n n n n n n	i i i i i i i
f f	d d d d

1 ..... l ..... -..... a ..... h .... d
2 m .... n
3 c .... u l
4 c ..... l ..... u .... ul
5 pr .... t ..... c l
6 f .... h .... abl .....
7 s .... d - h ....
8 exp .... v .....
9 pl ....
10 s ..... ph .... t .... t ....

3 Circle the adjective that can't describe the word in white.

1. 

sophisticated casual cool

2. 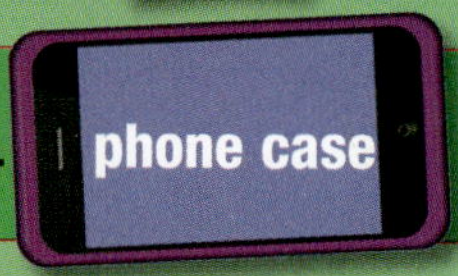

trendy cheap comfortable

3. 

cheap second-hand lovely

4. 

formal pretty unusual

4 Follow the labyrinth to find eight fashion items and write them below.

start →	m	e	finish
k	a	s	r
e	u	p	u
r	p	s	t
i	n	g	h
w	g	i	t
a	l	g	s
e	l	n	i
t	s	r	r
n	u	a	e
g	l	c	h
s	a	t	a
s	e	s	w

make up, ...

5 Look at the two pictures of Sharon. Find seven differences and write sentences about them in your notebook.